Prentice-Hall
Contemporary Topics in Accounting Series
ALFRED RAPPAPORT, SERIES EDITOR

BEDFORD, *Extensions in Accounting Disclosure*

DYCKMAN, DOWNES, and MAGEE, *Efficient Capital Markets and Accounting: A Critical Analysis*

HOPWOOD, *Accounting and Human Behaviour*

JAEDICKE and SPROUSE, *Accounting Flows: Income, Funds, and Cash*

KELLER and PETERSON, *The Uniformity-Flexibility Issue in Accounting*

LEV, *Financial Statement Analysis: A New Approach*

PALMER, *Analytical Foundations of Planning, Programming, Budgeting Systems*

REVSINE, *Replacement Cost Accounting*

SHANK, *Accounting for Intercorporate Investments*

WAGNER, *Auditing and the Computer*

ZEFF and SEIDLER, *A Critical Analysis of the Accounting Principles Board*

ACCOUNTING
AND
HUMAN BEHAVIOUR

First published in Great Britain 1974 by Accountancy Age Books, Haymarket Publishing Limited, Craven House, 34 Fouberts Place, London W1A 2HG. Copyright Haymarket Publishing Limited.

ACCOUNTING AND HUMAN BEHAVIOUR

ANTHONY HOPWOOD

Oxford Centre for Management Studies

PRENTICE-HALL, INC., ENGLEWOOD CLIFFS, NEW JERSEY

Library of Congress Cataloging in Publication Data

HOPWOOD, ANTHONY G
    Accounting and human behavior.

    (Prentice-Hall contemporary topics in accounting series)
    Includes bibliographical references and index.
    1. Accounting—Social aspects. 2. Budget in business. I. Title.
HF5657.H65 1976   657'.01'9   76-20577
ISBN   0-13-002063-X
ISBN   0-13-002055-9 pbk.

FIRST AMERICAN EDITION PUBLISHED 1976 BY PRENTICE-HALL, INC.,
ENGLEWOOD CLIFFS, NEW JERSEY

PRINTED IN THE UNITED STATES OF AMERICA

10   9   8   7   6   5   4   3   2   1

Prentice-Hall International, Inc., LONDON
Prentice-Hall of Australia Pty. Limited, SYDNEY
Prentice-Hall of Canada, Ltd., TORONTO
Prentice-Hall of India Private Limited, NEW DELHI
Prentice-Hall of Japan, Inc., TOKYO
Prentice-Hall of Southeast Asia Pte. Ltd., SINGAPORE

Contents

vii

Foreword

Accounting, broadly conceived as the measurement and communication of economic information relevant to decision makers, has undergone dramatic changes during the past decade. Recent advances in quantitative methods, the behavioral sciences, and information technology are influencing current thinking in financial as well as managerial accounting. Leasing, pension plans, the use of convertible securities and warrants in mergers and acquisitions, inflation, and corporate diversification are but a few of the challenging problems facing the accountant.

These developments and the very pervasiveness of accounting activity make it difficult for teachers, students, public accountants, and financial executives to gain convenient access to current thinking on key topics in the field. Journal articles, while current, must often of necessity give only cursory treatment or present a single point of view. Many of the important developments in the field have not crystallized to a point where they can be easily incorporated into textbooks. Further, because textbooks must necessarily limit the space devoted to any one topic, key topics often do not get the attention they properly deserve.

The Contemporary Topics series attempts to fill this gap by covering significant contemporary developments in accounting through brief, but self-contained, studies. These independent studies provide the reader with up-to-date coverage of key topics. For the practitioner, the series offers a succinct overview of developments in research and practice in areas of special interest to him. The series enables the teacher to design courses with maximum flexibility and to expose his students to authoritative analysis of controversial problems.

ALFRED RAPPAPORT

ix

Preface

I have noted, in the prefaces to other books in this series, the shortage of books which discuss modern developments in accounting and finance for British readers.

Several books have been written which describe techniques for planning financial activities and controlling their implementation; and, indeed, such books provide evidence of the rapidly expanding sophistication of available techniques. However, readers who have experience of financial planning and control must have thought that the books generally fail to capture the practical essence of the activities. The books have often neglected to mention that company employees have personal goals which may conflict with the commonly assumed concern for shareholder well-being; neglected to discuss the hard bargaining for shares of a budget between section heads with different vested interests; neglected to consider the strife which may be caused by an inflexible control system, based on accounting data. The procedures have often been presented as technical mechanics, neglecting their dependence on human behaviour—which is usually far from mechanical.

It seems important to question the implications of behavioural considerations for the design of systems for planning and control. Accountants have turned to a study of this question only recently—and it is easy to understand why. It is an area in which measurements and predictions are particularly difficult. However, it is also an area which holds the promise of progress of dramatic practical importance. The behavioural study of accounting has not yet reached the stage at which firm general conclusions can be supported by scientific evidence; but important conclusions are available and Anthony Hopwood explains them in this survey of the modern state of the subject.

Accounting analysis for decision purposes has recently become recognised as a scientific subject, as other books in the *Accountancy Age* series have explained. It involved the building and validation of models which relate assumed objectives to decision variables. Some commentators discuss the 'scientific approach' and the 'behavioural approach' as if they were competing alternatives. As Anthony Hopwood makes clear, this dichotomy is unfortunate; there is no room for two cultures in accounting. A scientific model; and behavioural models must meet the scientific test of efficient predictions before they can be useful. We require an integration of the two lines of development; and this book is therefore particularly useful as a complement to others in the series dealing with the quantitative analysis of accounting problems.

Anthony Hopwood is well qualified to write about the behavioural aspects of accounting; indeed, he is one of the leading specialists in the area in Britain. He has an excellent academic record in both Britain and the United States and he has conducted successful investigations of accounting systems in companies in both countries. His writing is illuminated by many illustrations drawn from this experience of practical studies; and he has tested this experience in lecturing to groups of managers on post-experience courses.

Department of Accounting and Business Finance   Bryan Carsberg
University of Manchester

Introduction

Despite the mass of technical procedures and detailed financial reports, accounting is fundamentally concerned with managerial action in human organisations. It is therefore encouraging that the accountant's task is increasingly being viewed in terms of the contribution which he can make to the overall management of the enterprise rather than in terms of the mere procedures by which he tries to achieve his own more limited financial objectives. People are now interested in the means by which the accountant contributes to the long-term direction of the enterprise. How, it is being asked, does accounting, as one form of information processing, relate to the wider management of information flows within the enterprise? And how do the procedures of management accounting fit in with changing views on organising and managing? After a period when perhaps too much attention has been devoted to the techniques of accounting in isolation from their organisational context, people are now quite rightly beginning to ask some more fundamental questions about the role which accounting plays in the management of today's complex and rapidly changing enterprise.

An important aspect of the changing view of accounting is that increasing attention is being given to its human and social dimensions. Both accountants and managers are now explicitly recognising that it is impossible to deal adequately with accounting problems without also considering the motivations, values and behaviours of the human members of the enterprise. For however sophisticated the procedures of management accounting may be, and they are continually getting more sophisticated, their fundamental rationale always remains behavioural in nature. The accountant contributes to the success of an enterprise primarily by the way in which he influences the behaviour of other people and, at least in theory, his procedures should be designed to stimulate managers and employees to behave in a manner which is likely to contribute to the effectiveness of the enterprise as a whole.

As a consequence, the social settings within which management accounting procedures operate can exert a profound influence on their relevance and organisational impact. However, having thus implied that social and human factors are vital aspects of the design and operation of any accounting system, it should not be thought that there is anything new about this claim. Accountants have never operated in a behavioural vacuum. The human aspects of accounting are as old as accounting itself. Accountants have always had to make some working assumptions about the way in which people are motivated, how they interpret and use accounting reports, and how their systems fit in with the realities of power and influence in the enterprise. Indeed, the general esteem in which the accountant is held suggests that many members of the profession have been particularly skilled in making appropriate assumptions.

However, while it is consoling to point to the large number of accountants who might be sensitive to the human implications of their activities, it is known that many management accounting systems still face innumerable human difficulties. Sometimes their very acceptance and use are problematic. In other cases, managers are known to deliberately manipulate accounting reports. Some informed commentators have even suggested that accounting systems, if used inappropriately, encourage a certain rigidity of approach which concentrates on the financial aspects of performance to the detriment of other equally important factors and on the immediate consequences of actions rather than on their more long-term implications. And of equal importance, even where such difficulties are not evident, one seriously wonders how many accounting systems achieve their real organisational potential.

Of course, it is always easier to make such generalisations than to justify them. However, the concerns which they reflect are important enough, and together with a changing social consciousness, they have stimulated a much more active interest in both the human difficulties and potentials of accounting. More than ever before, accountants and managers are aware of not only the problems, but also the importance of gaining practical improvements. It is increasingly being realised that the potential of the accountant's role as adviser, decision maker and communicator of information can be enriched by using the significant recent developments in the social and behavioural sciences. Some enterprises are actually undertaking practical experiments in the area, and at a more fundamental level, the amount of research into the underlying issues has grown rapidly in the last few years. So whilst the problems are not new, the interest which is being shown in them is.

Since this book is a reflection of a developing interest in the human and social aspects of accounting it can only aim to give a tentative view of our emerging understandings. However, within these constraints, and with the occasional help of some more speculative leaps into the unknown, it seeks to illustrate the vital importance of considering the relationship between accounting and human behaviour. More than anything else, it aims to show why attempts to deal with accounting matters in isolation from their human context must of necessity run into difficulty.

Consideration is given to the particular problems of budgeting, investment appraisal and the means for gaining control over costs. The use of accounting information in decision making and the evaluation of managerial performance are also discussed, and some attention is given to the dilemmas which face accountants in designing accounting systems in highly uncertain situations.

I would like to think that the book provides a number of useful perspectives for diagnosing important accounting problems and moving towards their solution. However, at this early stage, I must warn the reader who is looking for easy solutions that he will be disappointed. It is indeed unfortunate that the expectations of so many managers, and one might regretfully add, fellow academics, have been raised by the exhortations of the prophets of behavioural wonders who have offered panaceas to the distraught, and packaged remedies to the gullible. They have much to *account* for! I hope, however, that many people now realise that regardless of the ethical questions which such approaches inevitably raise, they savagely misuse the value of the social and behavioural sciences. For rather than offering instant illumination and speedy solutions, most social scientists have aimed to help their fellow citizens to intelligently understand, appraise and improve their own conditions. If I can contribute to this end by illustrating the practical relevance which a human and social perspective gives to accounting problems I will be content.

I would like to acknowledge my indebtedness to the many colleagues and friends who have stimulated my interest in the behavioural and social aspects of accounting. At the University of Chicago, Nick Dopuch and David Green played a vital role, and Dick Hoffman, more than anyone else, was a constant source of encouragement, criticism and support. I owe a lot to him and I trust that he will not be disappointed by the present endeavour. Subsequently I was fortunate to be able to discuss my ideas with Tom Lupton and his colleagues at the Manchester Business School. Finally, I owe a particular debt to Bryan Carsberg. Not only did he suggest the need for this volume and then, as editor, patiently await its completion, but he also had sufficient confidence in the importance of the human and social aspects of accounting to allow me to test out some of my ideas on the students in the Department of Accounting and Business Finance at the University of Manchester.

I am also grateful to the authors who have given me permission to quote from their own works. Particular mention should be made of Professor C Argyris, Professor R A Brealey, Professor P Brown, Professor J R Galbraith, Professor P R Lawrence, Professor J G March, Mr J Morgan, Professor R Roll, Mr A M Tinker and Mr R L Woodruff. Many of these people not only willingly agreed to their material being used in the present volume but also expressed their interest in the overall objectives of the book.

Beryl Young worked wonders in so speedily turning the original manuscript into a publishable typescript and Joy Edland provided further assistance.

My wife, Caryl, has yet again had to endure the deprivations of an author's wife. Her patience has been remarkable and her loving support has helped to maintain my enthusiasm and determination.

ACCOUNTING
AND
HUMAN BEHAVIOUR

CHAPTER ONE

Why Consider the Behavioural Aspects of Accounting?

Accounting information is designed to serve as the basis for many important decisions both within and outside the enterprise. It is designed to assist in planning, coordinating and controlling complex and interrelated activities and to motivate people at all levels in the enterprise to make and implement those decisions which will further organisational purposes. Not surprisingly, the accounting procedures which are used to satisfy these and many other important organisational functions have become highly technical in nature. Economics is increasingly being used to provide a sound basis for selecting information which is relevant for decision making, mathematical skills now contribute to our potential for rigorously analysing complex financial problems, and advances in computer technology means that information is quickly available. But however sophisticated accounting procedures have become, the information which they provide is never an end in itself. The technical sophistications must never prevent us from recognising that the purposes which accounting serves are organisational rather than technical in nature, and that the effectiveness of any accounting procedure depends ultimately upon how it influences the behaviour of people in the enterprise.

1.1 *Accounting is About People*

With such a basic behavioural rationale, human and social factors are

1

clearly amongst the most important aspects of the design and operation of any accounting system. There is nothing new about such a viewpoint: accountants have never operated in a behavioural vacuum. Just try to imagine designing and operating an accounting system on technical expertise alone. What type of information would you provide and to whom? How would you design information for control purposes without considering how it would fit in with the other means of influencing behaviour in organisational settings? How would you provide information to motivate superior performance without having some understanding of human needs and aspirations? And how would you manage the processes of standard setting, budgeting and planning, all of which are essentially social in nature? The task is obviously an impossible one.

Accountants always have to make some working assumptions about the way in which people are motivated, how they interpret and use accounting information, and how their accounting systems fit in with the realities of power and influence in organisations.[1] If accountants are concerned about the wider organisational effectiveness of their procedures, they must also continually monitor the appropriateness of their assumptions against what they see to be the realities of organisational life.

In this way, through experience and practical insight, many managers and accountants have gained a greater understanding of the human aspects of their task. It has to be recognised, however, that many accounting systems still face innumerable human difficulties: even their very acceptance and use are sometimes problematic. Managers sometimes respond to accounting systems by deliberately manipulating the reported information. Accounts are 'fiddled' and decisions are made in the light of their reported results rather than their wider contribution to organisational effectiveness. Some of the present procedures can also result in undesirable restrictions on managerial initiative. The procedures can even become ends in themselves rather than mere technical means to wider organisational ends. Paradoxically, budgeting and planning procedures, for instance, can apparently result in a rigid concern for the immediate to the detriment of their avowed future.

One could go on to list many more problem areas. Even if the situation is not as bad as it could be, it is certainly not as good as it should be. Experience alone is not a sufficient guide for many accountants and managers for although these problems are frequently observed, widely discussed and occur in most, if not all, organisations, their solutions have in many cases remained far from obvious.

We must also recognise that not all accountants would be willing to follow the logic of our arguments. Accounting, to some, is about accounting! The pessimists in our midst, for instance, would argue that many of the unfortunate behavioural reactions to accounting systems are a necessary consequence of what accountants are trying to do. 'You just have to take the pros with the cons', they would say, 'and the problems, well, they're someone else's responsibility'. To be fair, the view contains some grains of truth. The accountant's knowledge is partial, his time is limited, and in today's complex organisations, it is simply unrealistic to expect all aspects of organisational life to mesh closely without tensions and strains. As a guide to action, however, this view represents too ready a compromise, and as an approach, might it not even border on the irresponsible?

Our technocratic colleagues, on the other hand, would argue that many of the problems stem from imperfect accounting systems. 'Let us improve them,' they would say, 'and things will be better.' Certainly, it is frequently possible to improve most accounting systems and work should be devoted to this end. Even some of the more behaviourally inclined members of the profession have been swayed by the apparent logic of the technical approach and proposals have been made to include human assets in accounting reports. But it must also be realised that beyond some point the search for technical perfection is doomed to failure. With real limits on the capabilities of accounting techniques in the foreseeable future, the problem is really one of gaining the most effective use of imperfect but nevertheless valuable procedures and this is both a behavioural and a technical problem. A single-minded focus on the technical issues alone can too easily result in a diversion of effort from the identification of the other important aspects of the problem.

Although my portrayals of both the pessimistic and technocratic responses are undoubtedly oversimplified, the approaches which they represent are not, unfortunately, uncommon. Many commentators on accounting matters have chosen to emphasise, in one form or another, the internal logics inherent in the operation of accounting systems. Whether they are satisfied with the status quo or whether they are continually searching for technical improvements, the essential organisational functions of accounting are often relegated to a relatively minor position. To such people, accounting *is* accounting. Yet so many of the problems which face accountants today emerge when accounting information is used as a means of influencing or controlling behaviour or when the information is designed to stimulate better performance or when it is seen as contributing to the decision making process. In order to understand these problems it is necessary to recognise the full variety of forces – human and social, as well as technical and economic – which influence the accountant's activities. It requires great social as well as technical sophistication.

It is at this point that an acknowledgement of the valuable insights which can be gained from the behavioural and social sciences can begin to pay dividends. Many of the theories of psychology, sociology, political science and organisation are undoubtedly tentative: in many vital areas their findings are even conflicting. Yet in spite of this they offer the potential for unravelling at least some of the processes which relate accounting systems to wider patterns of human behaviour. By systematically analysing the relationships between accounting systems, other forms of control, and human attitudes and decisions, the social and behavioural sciences can focus our attention not only on the underlying conflicts and contradictions which characterise so many accounting problems, but also on the undoubted organisational and social potential of accounting itself. For accounting is only one of the many human responses to the problems of organising and controlling complex activities. Its functions are complementary to those of other vital processes of influence in organisational and social settings, and its impact depends on the interconnections between a whole series of personal and social strategies for control. Before having any effect, accounting information has to influence individual motivations. It has to be communicated and interpreted in a social context and its final effectiveness often depends upon how it relates to the organisation's division of labour and structuring of individual responsibilities.

As is illustrated in Figure 1.1, the accounting function in an enterprise both influences and is influenced by the attitudes and needs of individual managers and employees, the often subtle processes of group influence and control, and the means for structuring and controlling complex and purposive human organisations. In addition, as a social artifact, accounting is shaped by the prevailing pressures in the wider

Figure 1.1 The social context of accounting

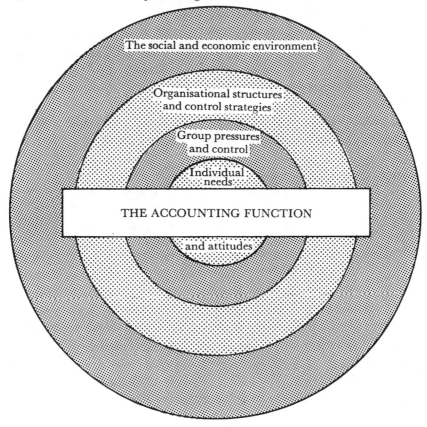

social and economic environment. Much of accounting as we know it today reflects the capitalist ethos, but as social and political pressures change, so we can also expect the forms and philosophies of accounting to change. The auditor's role in society is already being questioned, increasing demands are being made for the wider distribution of accounting information to such groups as employees and their trade unions,[2] and we are also witnessing the emergence of a significant debate on the means of conducting an audit of the social and environmental impacts of today's powerful business enterprises.[3]

1.2. *Accounting in Action*

'If you expect to get any kind of a price, you got to outwit that son-of-a-bitch! You got to use your noodle while you're working, and think your work out ahead as you go along! You got to add in movements you know you ain't going to make when you're running the job. Remember, if you don't screw them, they're going to screw you!'[4]

With these words an experienced worker advised a relatively new man on the job on the ways of dealing with the person responsible for setting their work standards. The sentiments expressed are a far cry from the detailed technical instructions on how to set operating and financial standards that are contained in accounting, industrial engineering and work study textbooks. While these texts discuss in great detail technical problems of estimating performance, such as deciding on the number of observations and the method of recording the information, they then proceed with apparent ease to discuss in the most clinical manner the role which the standards subsequently play in costing, budgeting and the operation of incentive payment schemes. They do play a crucial role in these activities in many organisations, but it must be remembered that the setting of standards and budgets is not a precise, purely technical discipline. Technical expertise is required, but it must be used within the context of what is often an intensely political bargaining process which draws on the personal resources of all parties involved and taps the deepest motives and attitudes.

'Remember those bastards are out to screw you, and that's all they got to think about. They'll stay up half the night figuring out how to beat you out of a dime. They figure you're going to try to fool them, so they make allowances for that. They set [rates] low enough to allow for what you do. It's up to you to figure out how to fool them more than they allow for . . . . Always keep in mind the fact that you can't make money if you run the job the way it's timed. They time jobs just to give you the base rate if you kill yourself trying to make it, no more. You've got to get the job timed below the speeds . . . you can use later. Whenever a piece is timed at maximum speeds. . . , there's no hope! You have as much chance as a snowball in hell![5]

All persons concerned with setting standards are striving to gain some measure of personal control over factors which are important in their organisational lives. While aiming to increase the efficiency of operations, accountants and industrial engineers are also concerned with demonstrating their technical skills and superior status. And they do not want to be seen as losing the battle! Managers and employees are trying to achieve a greater degree of control over both organisational resources and their own rewards and earnings. Their colleagues want to avoid a show of superior performance and earning power. Each party enters the situation with different needs, experiences and expectations, and these give personal meanings to the standards and subsequent budgets: they are not neutral.

Accountants and other members of the management team searching for means of understanding and improving standard setting and budgeting must therefore see the process in its entirety and respond to it as a complex human and technical problem rather than one standing in technical isolation.

Similar considerations are also relevant for longer-term planning. Here again, although accountants and other specialists have devoted an enormous amount of effort to finding appropriate ways of appraising the profitability of new investment projects, we find that comparatively little consideration has been given to the equally important social and political factors which determine the nature of the projects to be evaluated. Most large companies have now adopted many of the technical planning and investment appraisal procedures which have been developed. However, although the logic of such procedures is usually appealing, it is still important to understand how the technical perspectives and the social and political aspects of organisational life interact. How, in other words, do the procedures operate in practice?

We will return to this important question in a later chapter, but at this stage it is illuminating to consider briefly some findings on the way in which capital expenditure proposals were handled in one large company.[6] The process started with engineers' requests for expenditures. These were considered by the divisional manager at a regular meeting and the manager had the right to approve, cancel or postpone any proposal. He, of course, would also add any proposals of his own. Once the go-ahead had been given by the divisional manager an application for expenditure and detailed estimates were drawn up. These included the usual financial

Figure 1.2 A formal authorisation system

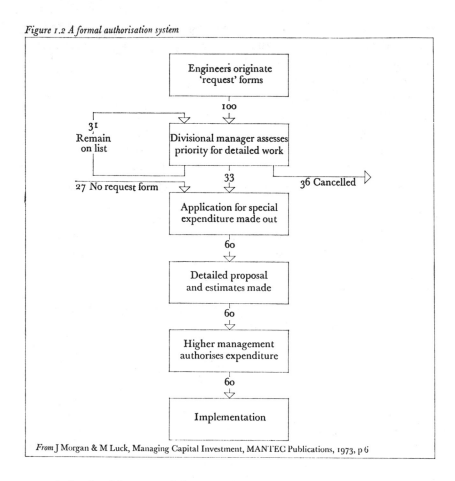

From J Morgan & M Luck, Managing Capital Investment, MANTEC Publications, 1973, p 6

appraisals. At this stage of the review process the project was considered by a higher management committee, and if their approval was received, the project was duly implemented.

Procedures of this type obviously vary from company to company, and even from division to division within a company, but in broad outline, they are fairly typical. But how did the procedures influence the selection of capital projects? This was the question considered by Luck and Morgan in their investigation, and the results of their analysis of the history of 100 engineers' proposals are shown in Figure 1.2.

Perhaps surprisingly, the detailed appraisal procedures which are the heart of the accountant's contribution to the review process apparently had no effect. Once a proposal had reached the stage of a formal application, it was assured of ultimate implementation. Sixty-six proposals were submitted by the divisional manager and all sixty-six were implemented. This observation was paralleled in another company which the same researchers investigated.

In fact, it was more than likely that the senior managers and the financial appraisal procedures did have some influence, but they were more likely to have influenced whether the engineers and divisional managers submitted proposals for approval, than whether their proposals were formally rejected. Faced with the necessity of making a choice from among a seemingly endless array of possibilities, managers, like the divisional manager in this company, tend to recommend proposals which are likely to be acceptable in a political sense, gain higher management approval and enhance their own position in the enterprise. Knowing the criteria for selection, proposals which have little chance of meeting them are not even submitted and those at the margin are often associated with intense lobbying.

Decision makers are human: it is difficult for them to divorce their own fate from that of the organisation and therefore both personal and organisational factors enter into the decision process. Projects are formulated and proposed in such away as to increase a manager's autonomy and sphere of influence. They are informally evaluated in terms of his understanding of the organisational rules of the game. Even potentially profitable projects, quite acceptable within the bounds of the financial criteria in use, can be withheld if their real benefits are not immediately reflected in the indices of performance which influence the recognition and rewards which the manager receives.

Obviously one study does not constitute a truth. The findings do however, emphasise the important fact that the final effect of accounting procedures is determined by both technical and social factors. We are all aware of the enormous literature on the technicalities of capital investment appraisal because the technical factors are easy to isolate and receive much attention. Yet by the time a project gets to the stage of formal evaluation, it has a history, and commitments and interests are marshalled behind it. In the enterprise in action, technical and social factors have no separate existence. Although the social and human factors may sometimes be less obvious to some of us, they are just as important as the technical factors in the inherently uncertain context within which all accounting procedures operate.

Even at the narrowly technical level, however, we need to recognise that accounting procedures are themselves human responses to organisational problems. Their ultimate logic must always be organisational rather than technical in nature, and as such, their construction and operation reflects the prevailing philosophies and perspectives of organising.

Again it is useful to refer to a specific example, and to illustrate the wider organisational assumptions of accounting we consider the endeavours of one company that was experiencing tremendous difficulties in coordinating a complex set of highly interrelated activities. Managers in different departments were actively competing against each other and the decisions in each department were often made on very partial bases which failed to consider all the important ramifications for the company as a whole. Parochialism and its attendant conflicts were rife, and senior managers were well aware of the high costs for the performance of the company, but they were unaware of any easy or obvious solutions. They therefore established two task force groups to investigate particular aspects of the problem. One group was formed to study the organisational problems and to recommend appropriate changes in organisational structures and responsibilities. The other group was asked to investigate the information needs of the company and to recommend new accounting procedures. Both groups duly reported and, with minor amendments, their recommendations were adopted.

The organisation group recognised the need to restructure the organisation so that the managers of interdependent activities would be obliged to liaise with each other and to jointly plan and coordinate their activities. One of the most important of their many recommendations concerned the appointment of a number of managers who would be primarily concerned with integrating the decision process. Rather than working within the existing departments and upwards through the management hierarchy, these persons would be concerned with working horizontally across the established departmental boundaries to assemble information and to champion the progress of individual projects and product groups. The task force realised that the creation of such positions did not necessarily establish their legitimacy in the organisation, particularly when the existing departmental heads had reigned supreme for so long. New organisational forms could not be spontaneously appended to their well established predecessors. They also realised that successful implementation depended upon the sustained efforts of skilled and committed individuals rather than upon the formal declarations of top management. So they recommended that the persons who served in the integrating roles should be acknowledged experts in the production technology of the enterprise, and that they should also possess the social skills which would enable them to remove at least some of the personal impediments to information sharing and joint decision making.

Just as the organisation group found it necessary to deal with information, so the information group found it necessary to deal with organisational considerations. More specifically, the information group wanted to clarify the existing patterns of departmental responsibilities. Much of the present confusion was, in their view, due to the fact that many managers could not be held responsible for all the consequences of their own actions. Given the size and complexity of the company, they thought that it was necessary to establish some degree of individual accountability and this required a regular reporting system which would isolate the impact of individual managers. With this as a base, they thought that it would be possible to motivate the individual managers to achieve specific objectives which were in the interests of the company as a whole and for which they could be held personally responsible. Accordingly, they recommended a comprehensive structure of performance centres and complementary sets of objectives and regular performance reports. Since many of the current difficulties involved the financial aspects of performance, the group gave a lot of attention to the means by which prices could be assigned to the many goods and services which were transferred between departments.

In their own terms, both sets of proposals looked eminently reasonable to the senior managers and both were in due course implemented but as soon as this had been done the problems of coordination became even more difficult. Although the two sets of proposals had seemed compatible in procedural terms, their underlying philosophies and perspectives were very different.

The organisation group had attempted to deal with the problems of coordination by defining certain managerial roles in terms of wider organisational responsibilities. The integrating managers were required to persuade the powerful departmental managers to view their own individual concerns within the context of the overall needs of the company. But in trying to achieve this, they could only call on their expert knowledge and social skills: they had no formal authority and no special sources of information. It was a difficult task at the best of times, but it had been made considerably more difficult as a result of the reports developed along the lines proposed by the information group. For the new reports provided even more detailed and comprehensive information on the activities within each department whilst doing very little to highlight the troublesome interdepartmental flows and they were now quite explicitly departmental performance reports.

At the crucial lower levels of the company, the objectives, budgets and information flows became increasingly oriented towards the separate departments. Even if any manager had originally experienced some doubt about his loyalties, he could now really start to see himself as being abstracted from, rather than integrated within, his wider organisational setting. He could see this quite clearly set out for him in black and white on regular reports. As this occurred, the conflicts intensified and it became all the more difficult to gain the appropriate degree of coordination.

The experiences of this company – a real one I might add just in case any of you were beginning to have any doubts – quite dramatically illustrate that accounting systems do reflect quite important assumptions about the organisation and its members. The doctrines of individual responsibility and accountability which provided the basis for the accounting recommendations, and which are so dominant in accounting thought, were based on quite definite assumptions about the management of the organisational task and both individual and group motives and behaviour. Whether these are appropriate or not depends on the specific circumstances under consideration, but one really does wonder how often assumptions of this type are explicitly recognised and questioned.

The company's difficulties serve to emphasise that the effectiveness of accounting procedures, viewed in organisational rather than accounting terms, depends on their relationship to the other organisational and personal means which are used to influence behaviour within the organisation. In this instance, there was a severe imbalance in the information flows and the accounting reports reinforced a pattern of organisational relationships which was in conflict with another quite explicit means for gaining coordinated action. Other integrating devices could also have been used, but all such approaches require detailed, regular and relevant flows of information. Accounting must therefore be viewed as merely a part of a wider whole, and tremendous care must be given to achieving some measure of congruity between all the flows of information, formal and informal, and the wider patterns of organisational relationships. If they follow different courses of action or incorporate different philosophies of control and influence, conflicts are bound to occur. When this happens, because of the very visibility which they were designed to create, it is not uncommon for the perspectives and assumptions incorporated into the formal information systems, whether appropriate or not, to have the dominant influence on managerial decisions and behaviour.

1.3 *The Behavioural Aspects of Accounting*
While an increasing number of people have given some acknowledgment to the behavioural and social aspects of accounting in recent years, there has been a tendency to view them as mere trimmings on the top of a rather substantial accounting ediface. The behavioural perspective, according to this view, may well serve to make accounting systems more palatable and acceptable to the mass of managers and employees and this is of course important. It may also serve to eliminate certain troublesome problems which interrupt the free flow of accounting ideas and actions and this is also of some value. Viewed in this way, however, behavioural and social considerations do not go so far as radically altering the recipe for the accounting task. Accountants in both the industrial and academic communities can, according to this rather popular view, proceed to develop their own perspectives and approaches so long as some occasional insights are drawn from our understanding of human behaviour in organisations.

However, we have just seen how some of the vital ingredients of most management accounting systems – the basic operating standards – reflect both technical understanding and personal motives and needs. We have considered how the impact of such important accounting procedures as the mechanisms for the financial appraisal of investment projects is conditioned by the multitude of other influences on the decision process.

And finally, we have discussed why accounting systems, as only one of the numerous human responses to the problems of controlling complex organisational tasks, must of necessity be considered from an organisational rather than from an accounting perspective.

Our brief look at accounting in action suggests that there is a much wider and more meaningful vision for the role of the behavioural and social aspects of accounting than many of our colleagues have so far acknowledged. If we recognise that accounting systems operate in human organisations, that they serve human purposes and that they ultimately have behavioural objectives, then their behavioural and social aspects can never be realistically considered as mere trimmings on the underlying technical structure. Viewed in this way, accounting is about human behaviour, and its social and behavioural aspects are just as much an indispensable part of the whole as the more traditional technical aspects.

Accordingly, in order to perform his task in the most effective manner, the accountant requires an understanding of human motivation, decision behaviour and the factors which influence the social climate which forms the context in which his systems operate. In designing just one part of an organisation's strategy for control, he also needs to be aware of current ideas on designing organisations which can function effectively in dynamic and uncertain business environments.

However, the technical aspects of accounting have undoubtedly received the most consideration to date and the resulting imbalance in our knowledge unfortunately means that our understanding of the behavioural and social aspects does not rise to meet the breadth of this wider vision. While both practical experimentation and more basic research are slowly but surely moving towards correcting the imbalance, the development of a coherent and well established behavioural view of the accountant's task still remains a rather distant dream. Certainly you should not expect to discover it in the pages which lie ahead. But we have gained many valuable insights into the role which behavioural and social considerations play in the design and operation of management accounting systems and in the following chapters we will consider these in more detail.

1.4 *References*
1. Caplan has attempted to unravel some of the more significant behavioural

assumptions implicit in traditional management accounting systems and to contrast them with insights derived from recent studies of actual patterns of behaviour in complex organisations. See:

CAPLAN, E H, 'Behavioural Assumptions of Management Accounting'. *The Accounting Review*, vol. 41, no 3, July 1966, pp 496–509

CAPLAN, E H, 'Behavioural Assumptions of Management Accounting—Report of a Field Study', *The Accounting Review*, vol 43, no 2, April 1968, pp 342–527

2. COMMISSION ON INDUSTRIAL RELATIONS, Disclosure of Information, Report no 31, HMSO, 1972

FOLEY, B J and MAUNDERS, K T, 'The CIR Report on Disclosure of Information: A Critique', *Industrial Relations Journal*, vol 4, no 3, Autumn 1973, pp 4–11

3. BAUER, R A and FENN, D H, *The Corporate Social Audit*, Russell Sage Foundation, 1972,

'The Case for a Social Audit', *Social Audit*, vol 1, no 1, Summer 1973

4. WHYTE, W F, *Money and Motivation*, Harper and Row, 1955, p 15

Similar episodes can be found in numerous other reports, including:

DALTON, M, *Men Who Manage*, John Wiley and Sons, 1959

LUPTON, T, *On the Shop Floor*, Pergamon Press, 1963

ROY, D, 'Making–Out: A Counter-System of Workers' Control of Work Situation and Relationships', in: BURNS, T (ed), *Industrial Man*, Penguin, 1969, pp 359–79

5. WHYTE, W F, *Money and Motivation*, Harper and Row, 1955, p 15–16

6. MORGAN, J R and LUCK, G M, *Managing Capital Investment: The 'Total Investment' System*, Mantec Publications, 1973

CHAPTER TWO

Control

in

Organisations

Have you wondered how today's mammoth enterprises are held together as purposeful organisations? They employ vast numbers of people, each with their own separate needs, interests and loyalties. They use ever more sophisticated technologies and engage in an increasingly diverse array of activities. Complexity and uncertainty are, as a consequence, inherent conditions of organisational life. However, despite the apparently insurmountable difficulties, individual members of enterprises manage to work together in a more or less coherent and purposeful manner. Of course, tension and conflict occur at all levels of the enterprise, but compared with the potential for strife and disorder, a surprising degree of order and co-ordination nevertheless emerge.

The complex processes by which the overall control and direction of enterprises is achieved have attracted the attention of numerous specialists. Cyberneticians have attempted to represent whole enterprises as controlled systems. Engineers have concentrated on the more mechanical aspects of control, although the understanding which they have gained has stimulated others to investigate the control of the more troublesome man-machine interface. Accountants, operational researchers and other management specialists have also developed their own views on the problems of control. Sociologists and psychologists have concentrated on control as a social and personal phenomenon. Yet despite these efforts, our understanding of the overall processes of control in complex enterprises remains inadequate. Actions, in this area at least, still speak much louder than words.

The gaps in our knowledge partly result from the fact that a lot more attention has been devoted to the design and development of *controls* on behaviour than to understanding the nature of *control* itself. Statisticians, for instance, have considered quality and inventory controls, management experts have suggested patterns of personal responsibility and authority which might contribute to control, and accountants have designed information and reporting systems for control purposes. Nearly all these efforts have concentrated on devising controls which are intended to contribute to the ultimate control of the enterprise but these have often been considered in isolation from the concept of purposeful control as an end in itself.

It is, however, increasingly being realised that the distinction between controls and control is a crucial one.[1] In many cases, for example, managers have actually achieved less overall control over the behaviour of the other members of their enterprises as a result of using the ever increasing number of individual controls. Subordinate members of their enterprises have used all their ingenuity to find ways of satisfying or even beating the controls, resulting in both intended and unintended consequences. The paradox often goes further. After recognising the reduction in real control, many managers have quite naturally become even more concerned with regaining it. In order to do so they have called upon yet further controls with the result that the desired degree of control has become ever more distant.

2.1 *Do Controls Always Lead to Control?*

The means by which organisational controls influence the behaviour of managers and employees have been investigated by many students of human behaviour. However, in our discussion we focus on the studies of three eminent sociologists who have been concerned with isolating both the unanticipated effects of the controls as well as their desired and hence anticipated outcomes.[2]

Merton was one of the pioneering investigators of the means by which senior managers seek to control the behaviour of their colleagues and subordinates as enterprises grow in size and complexity.[3] In these circumstances, he noted how tempting it is for managers to equate personal control with the control of the organisation. Merton sought to emphasise, however, that the origins of the desire for control are often rather personal in nature, and although they are quickly translated into organisational terms, he described how the personal rationale nevertheless finds its reflection in a concern with gaining regular and predictable, rather than necessarily effective, behaviours.

Organisational controls such as job descriptions, operating manuals and budgets are introduced and the control exercised by senior management takes the form of ensuring that the procedural outlines are followed. With the controls making at least some consequences of behaviour more visible, management by exception is then the name of the game. However, since senior managers are concerned with predictability and hence certainty, rather than effectiveness, Merton proceeded to note how easily they can start to regard the organisational rules of the game as being more significant than the efforts of the subordinate managers who are actually playing the game. Official positions start to attain greater significance than the characteristics of the individual holders of the positions, and as a result, relationships become increasingly more formal. But if subordinate managers are only evaluated on the basis of their conformity to organisational rules, why should they worry about anything else? The rules accordingly become accepted as valuable in their own right rather than as merely a means to a wider end. As this occurs, however, it is in the managers' interests to find the easiest rather than the most effective means for satisfying them. They therefore start to adopt the simplest forms of decision making, the clarity of which do much to remove the uncertainties inherent in their own tasks.

Managerial behaviour becomes increasingly rigid and defensive. As a result, the organisation's ability to respond to both its own internal problems and the needs of its customers is impaired. As the consequences of this start to appear, Merton suggested that the logic of the situation is such that the nature of the problem is more likely to be intensified than eliminated. With the subordinate managers feeling under pressure to defend their own actions, they place even greater value on following the rules of the game. As the problems are recognised by senior managers, they also feel an even greater need to control the situation. The existing rules therefore become even more significant to both parties and yet further controls may be introduced. Without care this dilemma can develop into a vicious cycle.

Delegation of authority is another means of controlling large and complex enterprises. In contrast to the above approach, delegation is designed to place the locus of decision making nearer to both internal management problems and the enterprise's external clients and customers. Selznick,[4] together with numerous other students of behaviour in organisations, has noted how these advantages, real though they may be, are often gained at the expense of fragmented loyalties within the organisation. Managers in different departments have different experiences and training, and with time develop their own departmental identities and philosophies. They become more committed to their own department than to the enterprise of which it is a part, and as a result their decisions are increasingly based on departmental rather than organisational needs. Such parochialism can, however, not only engender interdepartmental conflict but also, by making co-ordination more difficult, impair organisational performance. Yet, after studying the dilemmas faced by one enterprise, Selznick rather pessimistically reported that senior managers responded to the problem by delegating even further authority! For some reason they did not appear to learn from their own experiences.

Like Merton, Alvin Gouldner was concerned with the extent to which managers use general and impersonal rules to control the behaviour of subordinate members of the enterprise.[5] In his opinion, such rules help to legitimise the role of senior mangement by reducing the extent to which they must use overt power for control purposes. However, although the rules usually succeed in guiding the behaviour of subordinates, they very often do so by specifying the minimum rather than effective standards of performance. For in complex and uncertain enterprises it is always much easier to state in advance what constitutes a minimum acceptable standard of performance. Desirable behaviour, on the other hand, requires an adaptation to circumstances which cannot be anticipated and a degree of vision which often extends beyond what is readily quantifiable.

However, in situations where subordinates do not really accept the conceptions of organisational purposes formulated by senior managers, the specification of a minimum acceptable standard can easily result in a lower level of organisational performance. As senior managers quite naturally see this as a failure, they will be tempted to supervise the other members of the enterprise much more closely. If this makes the differences in power more overt than before, subordinates may start to feel threatened and may respond to the pressure which they believe is being exerted upon them by feeling even less identification with senior management's statements of the purposes of the enterprise. Yet again, as with the findings of both Merton and Selznick, the dynamics of the situation can easily result in a vicious cycle of controls and countercontrols, and if this occurs, the overall level of organisational control can fall.

2.2 *The Patterns of Organisational Control*
Whilst the findings of Merton, Selznick and Gouldner certainly have their differences, they all illustrate the widespread effects which controls can have on behaviour within the enterprise and all three writers noted that the effects can be both anticipated and unanticipated by senior management. Moreover, they all suggested that the unanticipated effects can be due not only to the fact that the controls are resisted by subordinate members of the enterprise, but also, and perhaps more surprisingly, because the individual controls are followed too closely.

The difficulties emerge because the control of complex and uncertain enterprises can never be achieved by the use of administrative controls alone. Rules and patterns of organisational relationships are necessary means to a wider end, but even their intended impact depends upon how they activate the social pressures and personal desires for control which exist within the managers and employees. If the rules are to be followed, they must be reinforced, accepted and acted upon. They must, either directly or indirectly, become the rules of the managers and employees rather than the rules of the enterprise. Ultimately they must work as individual and social controls rather than as impersonal administrative devices.

There are many ways by which senior managers can seek to achieve the acceptance of these rules. Where aims are shared, this acceptance will readily emerge from the needs of the members themselves but where the purposes of the enterprise are in dispute, senior managers will have to exercise their power by making the receipt of the valued resources which they control contingent upon personal conformity to the rules of the enterprise. Some organisations can still rely on coercive means to achieve this end; others more commonly use such material rewards as wages and

Figure 2.1: The pattern of organisational control

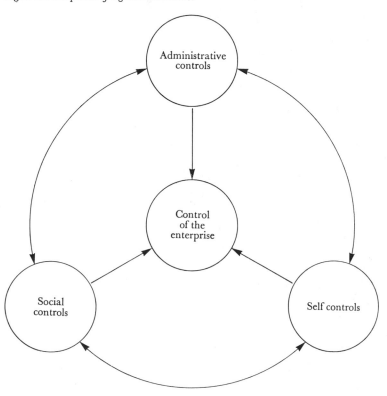

salaries, fringe benefits and commissions. The conferring of social recognition, prestige and esteem also have an important role to play. However,
the value and hence desirability of these rewards is determined by the
needs of individual managers and employees, and even if they are valued,
the need for some of them can also be satisfied by other colleagues within
the enterprise and by family and community ties outside. As illustrated
in Figure 2.1, the administrative controls coexist with equally important
social and personal pressures. The final impact of senior managements'
attempts to influence managerial and employee behaviours can never
therefore, be precisely determined in advance, but must always be seen
as an uncertain outcome of a dynamic interplay between the administrative, social and personal pressures which are simultaneously com-

peting for influence and control. Hence, in many cases, the outcomes are just as likely to be unanticipated by senior managers as they are to be anticipated.

In addition, administrative controls must of necessity remain almost naïvely simple compared to the complexity of the tasks which they are designed to control. Simplicity is often a virtue, since it makes understanding and use easier, but it also results in partiality, if not error. So if the individual administrative controls are to achieve their desired ends, the many gaps, inadequacies and errors must be complemented and supplemented by the more subtle forms of control which can be exercised by thoughtful members of the enterprise. Most senior managers would acknowledge that this is the case. However, in large enterprises where personal desires for self control become confused with the need to regulate the performance of· the enterprise, and where control has to transcend several hierarchical levels, the impersonal controls may easily be associated with social pressures which emphasise the rules and procedures to the detriment of their wider organisational purpose. If this happens the inevitable partiality and error of the controls can exert an effect just as profound, though unintended, as the consequences which senior managers intended to achieve.

Hence, it is important for anyone who is concerned with understanding either the overall control of the enterprise or the detailed effects of such controls as budgets, standards and hierarchical patterns of relationships to appreciate the operation of the full variety of forces for influence and control, whether they are administrative, social or personal. For the accountant, such an appreciation is vital.

2.3 *Administrative Controls*

Most large enterprises use formal rules and standard procedures to regulate the behaviour of subordinate managers and employees. Additional rules are given verbally or learned through experience. By reducing the need for the managers and employees to personally search for desirable courses of action, the rules and organisational procedures increase the probability that organisational requirements will dominate individual needs. With the range of alternative behaviours accordingly constrained, the overall predictability of their actions is also likely to be considerably increased.

For many areas of activity within an enterprise, however, the uncertainty of events is such that predetermined rules can only be specified with the utmost difficulty, if at all. When the managers and employees are allowed to use their own discretion in these areas, the formal administrative controls focus on the consequences of their behaviour rather than on the behaviour itself. Plans, budgets and standards are used to provide subordinate managers and employees with a means of judging the organisational context and significance of their own actions, and to provide their superiors with a means of evaluating performance on the basis of objective standards rather than subjective impressions or personal idiosyncrasies. These, together with the use of formal rewards and sanctions, then enable senior managers to reinforce actions which are seen as being in line with their conception of the enterprise's purposes and punish actions which are seen as contrary.

Organisation manuals also prescribe the division of activities which is thought to promote the optimal use of the expertise and resources available to the enterprise. Closely associated patterns of authority serve to delineate the areas of expected performance so that subordinate managers and employees know which decisions they can take without approval and which decisions require authorisation. In addition, the formal patterns of organisational relationships are designed to provide subordinates with the means of knowing when an instruction or rule is authoritative and whom to consult when exceptions occur which are not covered by the rules.

Accountants are, of course, closely involved with the operation of many of the most significant formal administrative controls. Their standards, budgets and plans are often the most important guides to performance. In addition, the structure of accounting reports must of necessity be fairly closely related to the patterns of authority and responsibility within the enterprise.

Formal administrative controls are designed to structure the process of decision making in large and complex enterprises. By specifying preferences and limiting alternatives, they enable some of the uncertainty to be removed from the minds of subordinate managers and employees. By being so closely related to the structure of power within the enterprise, they also try to ensure that subordinates' individual goals are subservient to the interests of more senior managers. However, no formal controls can ever completely achieve these aims, and in dynamic situations where the enterprise's environment and possibly its power structure is changing, the gap is all the greater. Accordingly, senior managers also use a series of equally important but frequently less obtrusive forms of administrative controls. In so doing, they often attach much greater significance to controlling the basic values and information premises which surround the decision making process than to controlling either the decisions themselves or their immediate consequences.

Recruitment policies represent an important means of such control. By hiring professionals, for instance, enterprises can often acquire the services of persons who have values and experiences which are consistent with senior management's needs. While such persons are considered to be flexible and adaptive in approach, in practice they often require fewer formal controls to regulate their behaviour because the training of many professional groups instils expectations and commitments which are appropriate for the management of large enterprises. Similarly, for non-professional managers and employees, careful recruitment on the basis of attitudes, aptitudes, education and previous experience can, in many cultures, provide a workforce which, even if it does not readily share and practise the preferences and aims of the senior management group, is certainly less likely to actively work against them.

Training within the enterprise and experience on the job are further means of control. Training is, of course, frequently concerned with conveying the technical rules and skills which are thought to contribute to efficient performance. In addition, in many enterprises, it is also used to inculcate the social values and organisational life styles and ideologies which can shape the premises which managers and employees use in decision making. And more generally, through its control of a wide variety of standards, rewards and sanctions, both formal and informal, senior management can do much to influence the vital levels of expectation and satisfaction.

The channels of communication within the enterprise can also be influenced by senior managers. The formal patterns of organisational relationships and the regular performance reports are naturally very important in this respect but there are innumerable ways of supplementing the more formal outlines. Specific organisational vocabularies and even the underlining of items on existing reports can indicate quite subtle shifts in priorities and areas for concern. The use of notices, reports and internal memoranda also come to mind. These are, however, only specific examples of the many means by which information can be controlled within enterprises. Channels of communication can be narrowed or widened, some persons can even be bypassed, and through the provision of such resources as computers, market researchers, attendance at outside meetings and corporate libraries, senior management can have an influence on the range of courses of action which are considered.

At this stage, administrative controls begin to take on many of the subtleties which we associate with more social means of control. But the broad view of the form which administrative controls can and do take, especially of the manner in which senior management attempts to influence the premises which underlie the decision making process, is essential for understanding the operation of today's complex control systems. Indeed, without such a view, it is easy to concentrate almost exclusively on the more mechanical outlines, and in so doing, draw quite erroneous conclusions. Many people have, for example, done just this in reporting on the patterns of hierarchical relationships which have been developed by many enterprises in the present century. At a procedural level, it is tempting to discuss these developments in terms of decentralisation of power and authority. With organisational forms such as investment centres, profit centres, and cost centres, which are so familiar to accountants, many decisions are indeed made at much lower levels in the enterprise than might conceivably be the case. But such decentralisation, if this is what we want to call it, usually takes place within the context of a very controlled organisational environment. Although the control of senior management may well have been shifted to give more consideration to the organisational context within which action occurs and the premises underlying the decision making process, it is nevertheless still very real in its impact.

2.4 *Social Controls*

However, there are dangers inherent in any approach which emphasises elements of the administrative structure of the enterprise, unobstructive though some of them may be, at the expense of the prevailing social perspectives and the patterns of social interactions. For despite the availability of similar administrative controls, managers may choose to use them in different ways, and in so doing, elicit different responses. For example, even though two managers who are responsible for two similarly troublesome groups of employees can both legitimately use the same administrative controls, we are likely to find that they do so with very different results. One manager may be able to maintain order and improve performance, whilst the other manager's attempts to do precisely the same are reduced to chaos. We might observe that the first manager, although apparently successful, has no need to use the sanctions which are at his disposal. Given his approach to management, rewards tend to be more important than sanctions, and even where he finds it necessary to employ sanctions, the threat of doing so is often sufficient to remind his subordinates of the prevailing structure of power in the enterprise. The other manager, in contrast, may resort to sanctions out of sheer desperation. As a result his subordinates may get increasingly defensive, and if this happens, his attempts to control the situation may well lead to even further chaos.

No doubt you could cite many similar comparisons which you have witnessed on the shop floor, in the office or even in the school-room. Such examples point to the fact that effective control is a much more complex and subtle process than the limitation of behaviour by either administrative devices or the use of personal power. Control, in whatever direction, is not only achieved by formal means but also by pressures exerted by individuals over one another. For in any situation, the controllers and the potentially controlled have a social relationship with one another. The motivations, expectations and personal relationships of all the members of the enterprise therefore exert a significant effect on the outcome of the control process. The personalities of the managers and subordinates, their approach to their job and the subordinates' acceptance of the ligitimacy of managerial roles are also important influences.

It should hardly be surprising that in recent years a number of influential writers have not only emphasised that the task of management can never be merely a technical one, but have also outlined the nature of the social relationships which they see as contributing to the effective control of the enterprise. The ideas of such writers as McGregor, Blake and Mouton, Likert and others are accordingly now widely known and accepted by many practising managers. In so far as their philosophies and recommendations are concerned with helping managers to improve the performance of the enterprise, even if at the same time satisfying more basic human needs, it is appropriate to discuss them within the context of social controls.

In *The Human Side of Enterprise*, McGregor made a sharp distinction between two patterns of social relationships which can exist within an enterprise.[6] With the first pattern, which McGregor referred to as Theory X, efficiency is seen as resulting from the pursuit of clear objectives set by senior management. These objectives are reflected in tight impersonal managerial controls over the performance of individual subordinates and are reinforced by the use of punitive sanctions, usually of a financial nature. McGregor thought however, that such an approach to management was more likely to result in vicious rounds of controls and counter-controls than in superior performance. The contrasting pattern of relationships, which McGregor called Theory Y, was in his view likely to result in both effective organisational performance and the personal satisfaction and development of the managers and employees. Under this alternative view, subordinate managers and employees are given tasks which utilise their talents and catch their enthusiasms, and not only are they allowed to participate in establishing their work objectives, but they are also encouraged to develop the wider organisational environment within which they are working.

Blake and Mouton also suggest that the solution to the problem of creating organisational environments which are conducive to high performance and human satisfaction lies in the pattern of social relationships which prevail within the enterprise, or in what some people have called the style of management.[7] They classify management style on the basis of two dimensions, namely concern for people and concern for the task, and then suggest that a style which combines a very high concern for people with a very high concern for the task is optimal in that it leads to both good economic and human results.

Whilst McGregor and Blake and Mouton are overtly popularising a particular managerial ideology, Rensis Likert's conclusions, although very similar in orientation, are based on much more extensive and systematic research.[8] As a result of studying behaviour in organisations for many years, Likert evolved a four-fold classification of managerial attitudes, beliefs and behaviours:

System 1 : An exploitive and authoritative style of management

System 2 : A benevolent but authoritative style of management

System 3 : A consultative style of management

System 4 : A participative and group orientated style of management

To Likert, System 4 is undoubtedly the preferred approach to managing the social environment of the enterprise, and compared with the generalities of the McGregor and Blake and Mouton recommendations, as Likert describes it, it is a much more precisely defined style of management.

Many other writers have produced very similar recommendations on how to manage the social environment of the enterprise and most of them have sought to stress that their concerns are not based on pure human benevolence but on sound economic reasoning.[9] Of course, in recommending approaches to management which stress individual development, equality and participation, these views have appealed to emerging social values and political ideologies, and they have often appealed despite the fact that so often they are based on comparatively little empirical evidence. Likert is unusual in this respect. He and his colleagues have attempted to assemble an impressive amount of evidence. Much of it supports his views, but even so, unlike many of his fellow writers in the area, he is quite prepared to recognise that the precise impact of any style of management depends upon many other factors which constrain behaviour within the enterprise. He admits, for instance, that such factors as the size of the enterprise and the nature of its technology and product and labour markets can influence the effects of a System 4 approach.

The partiality of many of the rapidly growing number of recommendations on the social aspects of management cannot be sufficiently emphasised and if you proceed to read further on this topic, I would advise you to do so with great care. A healthy measure of scepticism is often in order. At the same time, however, it must also be admitted that these writers have done much to encourage a vital and important concern with the relationship between organisational performance and the more subtle mechanisms of social influence and control.

Social control is not only exercised by senior managers over subordinate members of the enterprise. The very essence of social control is that it is exercised by individuals at all levels of the enterprise over one another. Indeed the means which small groups within the enterprise use to regulate the performance of their own members and to bring them into line when they deviate from group norms are often much more effective controls on behaviour than almost any of the control procedures which can be used by senior managers. For within the small group, it is often possible, if anyone so desires, to police and regulate the most minute aspects of behaviour.

Social controls emerge from the shared values and the mutual commitments of members of a group to one another, whether on the shop floor or in the executive office. Often within the framework of the controls initiated by senior management, group norms develop about levels of work performance, standards of mutual help and the sharing of valued resources. Informal guidelines about relationships with other groups may be adopted,[10] ceilings may be placed on productivity[11] and attempts may be made to smooth earnings.[12] At first, when any member of the group deviates from these norms, he may be rather jokingly reminded of their existence. But if it is an important norm to the group, the reminders can become much more strongly worded, and if this still fails to achieve a change in behaviour, the deviant member may even be ostracised.

Although such social controls are potentially very important influences on behaviour, their form and strength, and the direction which they take, can vary from enterprise to enterprise, and even from one group within an enterprise to the next. After numerous studies, social scientists have now recognised that patterns of group behaviour and pressure are influenced by the technological and administrative arrangements which define the organisational roles and relationships, the product and labour markets which define their environmental context, and the personal characteristics, values and beliefs of the group members which determine how the other pressures are seen and responded to. As these factors vary, so do the patterns of group norms and behaviours.

In an electrical engineering workshop, for instance, Lupton found that there was a well developed system of social sanctions which was designed to regulate the earnings and work amongst the men employed on the assembly work.[13] However, in a garment workshop which employed women on assembly work, he found that although there was a great deal of sociability, as a result of both personal and external factors, the social pressures had not been directed towards controlling either output or earnings.

Whether concerned with the mutual influences which characterise relationships at all levels of an enterprise or the managerial strategies which are necessary for creating a social environment which is conducive to personal involvement and commitment, the complexities inherent in social forms of control prevent any easy prediction of the effects of particular control strategies. Despite this difficulty, the theories and findings on all the forms of social controls provide important insights into the means by which large groupings of individuals can be guided to work together as a purposeful entity.

2.5 *Self Controls*

Ultimately, all forms of control must be expressed through the actions of individual managers and employees. As the design of many strategies for control reflects, the administrative and social controls have either directly or indirectly to be internalised by the members of the enterprise and operate as personal controls over attitudes and behaviours. It is for this reason that many administrative controls attempt to elicit personal needs for material well-being and social acknowledgement. This is also why many of the recent more management oriented theories of the social control of the enterprise have stressed the need to promote personal satisfaction and development. For if the needs and desires of the individual members of the enterprise are in conflict with the requirements of either senior managers or other members of the group, the individuals are more than likely to feel under considerable pressure and anxiety, and the final impact of the external controls may be small indeed. For the novice, however, the study of the mechanisms of self control is exceedingly complex. Philosophers, psychiatrists and psychologists have now debated their different views for many centuries and fundamental issues ares still subject to a great deal of conflict. This is the area where the views of Sigmund Freud can still be juxtaposed with those of his early followers such as Adler, Jung and Rank. The views on human needs and motivations of the whole psychoanalytic school still contrast radically with those of the behaviouralists, the neurophysiologists, the existentialists and the management pragmatists.[14]

In a short monograph it is impossible to deal with the full richness of the arguments in this area, important though they may be. Rather than even trying to summarise the state of the debate, which would be an incredibly difficult task, we will focus on only a few of the many scholars who have contributed to our growing awareness of the real complexity of human motives and needs. In order to provide a further focus to our discussions, we will tend to review the ideas of some people who have perhaps done more to popularise the thoughts and theories of others rather than themselves contribute to the ongoing debate at a more fundamental level.

As conceived by the influential American psychologist, Abraham Maslow, men and women are wanting animals with a hierarchy of needs.[15] As each need is satisfied, so it ceases to operate as an active influence on behaviour and our demands proceed to rise through the scale of needs. At the bottom of the hierarchy are the physiological needs for food, security and shelter, which in organisational terms, are capable of being satisfied by more material rewards. Since Maslow did not choose to emphasise the way in which advertising and social gregariousness might even create a hierarchy of material needs, he conceived of a point of satisfaction beyond which the higher social needs for group membership, acceptance and belonging exert the dominant influence on behaviour. Then, if these are in turn satisfied, the need for self-expression and the use and development of one's own abilities ultimately become dominant.

Building upon Maslow's more personal framework, Douglas McGregor, whose views on different styles of management we have already considered, saw modern industrial society as satisfying all of our lower order needs.[16] In those seemingly distant days when American sociologists and economists were heralding the end of ideological debates and the birth of the affluent society,[17] before some commentators had rediscovered poverty in our midst, McGregor saw industrial man and woman as having all the food, shelter and security that they needed. He also saw many social needs as being satisfied. Hence, in McGregor's mind, industrial man and woman now have a hunger for self-expression and personal creativity, and these are what today's large enterprises should be providing if they want to retain a motivated and involved group of managers and employees.

At about the same time, Herzberg, another popular management psycholgist, reached very similar conclusions by a somewhat different route.[18] Being concerned with establishing the causes of general satisfaction and dissatisfaction on the job, the starting point for his enquiry was to ask managers and employees what things in their jobs made them feel good and bad. He found that it was necessary to distinguish between factors which contributed to satisfaction and those which contributed to dissatisfaction. For although the dissatisfying factors could constrain performance if they were not up to standard, unlike the satisfying factors, they did not positively motivate superior performance.

People complained about their earnings, the working conditions and the people they worked with and for. However, the factors which resulted in feelings of satisfaction were of five main types. The first referred to occasions when people had been able to complete a task which represented a personal achievement of which they could be proud. The second included occasions when their performance had been recognised, praised and complimented. The third occurred when a special amount of trust or responsibility had been vested in them. Occasions when they had been promoted or moved to face new challenges provided the fourth type and lastly, there were occasions when the tasks were intrinsically interesting. So according to Herzberg and his colleagues, people are really interested in opportunities for recognition, achievement, responsibility and intrinsic interest. He would then argue that if large enterprises could provide for these through job enrichment instead of engaging people on minor repetitive tasks, many of the problems of motivation would be solved.

The views of Maslow, McGregor, Herzberg and similar writers must be acknowledged to contain many important grains of truth. Indeed many managers are now successfully putting their theories into practice. But it must be recognised that the views of these writers often reflect a rather single-minded managerial perspective and I hope that by now you are beginning to question the universalistic claims which are inherent in their views on motivation. Far too many of these writers hardly provide for the possibility that different people, and groups of people, might be interested in different things, let alone for the possibility that the needs of individuals vary with their circumstances. Yet some evidence from the British car industry suggests that these are real and significant possibilities.

Goldthorpe and his colleagues studied the Vauxhall car assembly workers at Luton.[19] Almost more than any other task in the labour market, this job epitomises the dehumanisation of work through assembly line mechanisation. Yet the car workers had sought their jobs voluntarily and they had often given up jobs which offered more interest, status, responsibility and opportunities to use their skills and abilities. Equally, whilst working on the car assembly lines they were aware of alternative jobs with greater intrinsic rewards which they could do and get. But they stayed on the lines. The reason why they had sought the job, given up more interesting and possibly satisfying work to take it, and had stayed when they could find more intrinsically rewarding jobs, was because they attached a very high priority to money. They sought high earnings from their jobs and they defined their place of work as primarily a source of income. Accordingly, they were prepared to endure the hardships, pressures and the repetitiveness of the assembly line for a high salary. They were prepared to give a very high rating of satisfaction with the job and their employer if the job and their employer gave them what they wanted – money.

The social experiences and circumstances of the car workers were such that they saw work as a means to an end rather than an end in itself. They did not necessarily want to be encouraged and praised by their supervisors. They were quite content so long as they were left alone. Nor did they necessarily want the acceptance and approval of workmates, and they certainly did not want to fraternise with them outside work. They had, in other words, an instrumental orientation to work.

Unlike McGregor and Herzberg, Goldthorpe and his colleagues studied the behaviour as well as the attitudes of managers and employees thinking that if you want to know what motivates behaviour, it is wise to look at social experiences, social situations and how people actually behave. They found that in today's consumer oriented society, there are sufficient desires to keep Maslow's lower order material needs as fully operative influences on behaviour within the enterprise.

At this stage, it would be tempting to think that the apparent discrepancies between the views of those who have emphasised the influence of social and personal needs and those who have stressed the continuing power of material needs could be reconciled in terms of the operative position on the hierarchy of needs. But recent research suggests that such an approach assumes far too simple a view of the structure of human needs.[20] It is, of course, true that some managers and employees consistently attach a higher priority to the intrinsic interest of the job, or alternatively, to financial earnings, but the majority of people seek both intrinsic and material rewards from their work, although with differing priorities in different situations and contexts. Any understanding of the control which individuals exert over their own behaviour must therefore be based on a knowledge of the needs which are elicited in specific situations by both the individuals themselves and the other constraints and controls on their behaviour.

2.6 *Control in Organisations*

Although we have dealt with administrative, social and self controls separately, it should be obvious that in an organisational setting, they can never be considered independently of one another. For if one type of control is working at counter-purposes with another, the potential power of each is considerably reduced and their joint outcome can often be problematic. The administrative controls in an enterprise may, for instance, be designed to reward productivity increases, but they may have little effect if the employees have developed their own social controls which place restrictions on productivity improvements. Or alternatively, the most sophisticated budgetary system may be of little practical consequence if it fails to elicit the achievement motivations of a significant number of managers and employees. If, on the other hand, all three types of control are working in the same direction, the total amount of control being exercised may be very considerable. When senior management's plans for superior sales performance are consistent with the norms which the sales managers have set amongst themselves, and if all the individual managers are seeking to actualise their own talents and abilities, then the total effort devoted to improving sales should be very high indeed. In these circumstances, where the social and self controls are compatible with the administrative controls, the total amount of control may be both high and relatively unobtrusive.

The synergistic nature of control in organisations has been recognised by Arnold Tannenbaum.[21] Whilst studying the control of many different types of organisations, including business enterprises, trade unions and voluntary associations, he devised a means of monitoring the patterns of organisational control. He asked people at different levels in an organisation to say how much influence they exercised over their organisations' activities. Then, by putting all these reports together, he was able to construct a graph showing not only the relative hierarchical differences in perceived influence but also the total amount of control at work.

As a result of these studies, Tannenbaum found that the total amount of control exercised in organisations can expand and contract. He noted that many attempts to redistribute influence within organisations not only changed the relative pattern of control over different hierarchical levels, which was perhaps the primary intention, but also changed the total amount of control at work. Since control always depends upon a reciprocal relationship, properly conducted programmes to decentralise influence over decision making have the potential of increasing the absolute amount of influence exercised by lower members of the organisation whilst at the same time maintaining or even increasing the influence of the more senior managers. If the latter possibility occurs the organisation's overall performance may be enhanced. For Tannenbaum found that in many circumstances, organisational effectiveness bore a much closer relationship to the total amount of control at work than to the pattern of its internal distribution.

However, even though control can be expanded in this manner, practical barriers still prevent the easy utilisation of this powerful property. For one thing, it is simply unrealistic to presume that the motivations and self controls of individual managers and employees can be readily marshalled behind the administrative controls designed by more senior managers. Conflicts and differences in fundamental needs and objectives have to be recognised as basic features of organisational life in democratic societies. Whilst much can be done to reduce the level of discord and strife, different social experiences, values and expectations will always place some real constraints on how far cooperative endeavours can proceed.

In addition, our knowledge of the means for integrating the different approaches to control remains far from adequate. In some circumstances, in order to be effective, the pressures created by many administrative means of control need to be associated with more personal and social forms of control. In other circumstances, especially where the complexity and uncertainty of the task make many of the traditional forms of administrative controls less useful guides to action, the necessary element of clarity and predictability may have to be provided through the actions of individual managers and employees.

Because of the possibility of interrelationships between the different forms of control, effective control strategies need to reflect a view of the enterprise which includes its administrative, social and personal aspects. To date, however, there has been a frequent tendency to consider each aspect in isolation from the others. Administrative controls have been considered in administrative terms, social controls in social terms and self controls in personal terms. Given the complexities of organisational life, the reasons for the prevailing partiality are perhaps obvious enough. Recently, however, a number of people in the academic and industrial communities have recognised the urgent need for a wider vision. As yet, practical actions are undoubtedly more advanced than our theoretical understanding, although this is an area where we can anticipate significant developments in the years to come.

In the meantime, all who are concerned with the management of complex enterprises need at least to understand the wider nature of organisational control. For accountants, no less than for other management experts, this is particularly important. Whilst their procedures can readily be viewed as necessary and rather neutral mechanisms for administrative control, they must also be recognised as means for propagating the views of a particular but powerful group of people within the enterprise. Whatever their ultimate role, the final effect of plans, budgets and financial performance measurements depends upon how they influence, and in turn, are influenced by the social and self controls of individual managers and employees.

2.7 *References*

1. See, for instance, the discussion in:
   DRUCKER, P, 'Controls, Control and Management', in : BONINI, C P, JAEDICKE, R K, and WAGNER, H M, *Management Controls: New Directions in Basic Research*, John Wiley and Sons, 1964, pp 286–96
2. A useful summary of the theories and perspectives of the three men is given in: MARCH, J G and SIMON H A, *Organizations*, John Wiley and Sons, 1958, pp 36–47
   Much of the present discussion is based on March and Simon's review

3. MERTON, R K, *Social Theory and Social Structure*, The Free Press, 1957, pp 195–206
4. SELZNICK, P, *TVA and the Grass Roots*, University of California Press, 1953
5. GOULDNER, A W, *Patterns of Industrial Bureaucracy*, The Free Press, 1953
6. MCGREGOR, D, *The Human Side of Enterprise*, McGraw-Hill, 1960
7. BLAKE, R R and MOUTON, J S, *The Managerial Grid*, Gulf Publishers, 1961
8. LIKERT, R, *New Patterns of Management*, McGraw-Hill, 1961, and; *The Human Organization*, McGraw-Hill, 1967
9. See, for instance:

   ARGYRIS, C, *Integrating the Individual and the Organization*, John Wiley and Sons, 1964

   FIEDLER, F E, *A Theory of Leadership Effectiveness*, McGraw-Hill, 1967

   REDDIN, W J, *Managerial Effectiveness*, McGraw-Hill, 1970

   STOGDILL, R M and COONS, A E, *Leader Behaviour: Its Description and Measurement*, Ohio State University, 1956
10. DALTON, M, *Men Who Manage*, John Wiley and Sons, 1959
11. ROETHLISBERGER, F J, and DIXON, W J, *Management and the Worker*, Harvard University Press, 1939

    WHYTE, W F, *Money and Motivation*, Harper and Row, 1955
12. LUPTON, T, *On The Shop Floor*, Pergamon Press, 1963
13. LUPTON, T, *On The Shop Floor*, Pergamon Press, 1963
14. A useful introduction to motivation in organisations is provided in:

    KATZ, D, 'The Motivational Basis of Organisational Behaviour', *Behavioural Science*, vol 9, no 2, March 1964, pp 131–46

    Many of the important articles on the subject are collected in:

    VROOM, V H, and DECI, E L, (eds) *Management and Motivation*, Penguin Books, 1970

    For the reader who wants to pursue the topic in greater detail, Vroom gives a useful synthesis of the relationship between motivational factors and work performance, and Cofer and Appley provide a very comprehensive summary of all aspects of the work which has been done on human motivation. See:

    VROOM, V H, *Work and Motivation*, John Wiley and Sons, 1964

    COFER, C N, and APPLEY, M. H, *Motivation: Theory and Research*, John Wiley and Sons, 1964
15. MASLOW, A H, *Motivation and Personality*, McGraw-Hill, 1960
16. MCGREGOR, D, *The Human Side of Enterprise*, McGraw-Hill, 1960
17. See, for instance:

    BELL, D, *The End of Ideology*, Collier-Macmillan, 1960

    GALBRAITH, J K, *The Affluent Society*, Hamish Hamilton, 1958
18. HERZBERG, F, MAUSNER, B and SYNDERMAN, B B, *The Motivation To Work*, John Wiley and Sons, 1959
19. GOLDTHORPE, J H, LOCKWOOD, D, BECHHOFER, F and PLATT, J, *The Affluent Worker: Industrial Attitudes and Behaviour*, Cambridge University Press, 1970
20. DANIEL, W W, *Beyond the Wage—Work Bargain*, PEP, 1970
21. TANNENBAUM, A S, *Control in Organizations*, McGraw-Hill, 1965

CHAPTER THREE

Some Issues
in Budgeting

Budgeting now occupies a central position in the design and operation of most management accounting systems. Almost regardless of the type of organisation, the nature of its problems and the other means for influencing behaviour, the preparation of a quantitative statement of expectations regarding the allocation of the organisation's resources tends to be seen as an essential, indeed indispensable, feature of the battery of administrative controls. Nevertheless, despite its wide acceptance, budgeting remains one of the most intriguing and perplexing of management accounting procedures. With many fundamental questions remaining unsolved, it provides an ideal focus for considering some of the social and human factors which influence the operation of accounting systems in complex organisations.[1]

Even a casual acquaintance with the budgetary process in only a few organisations will soon instil in you an awareness of a whole series of rather basic difficulties. How, you might ask, are budgets actually formulated? Who influences them and how? Then you might notice that budgets serve a variety of purposes, ranging from the obvious planning of essential supplies, funds and facilities, through the coordination of interrelated activities and the consequent delegation of managerial authority, to the motivation of both managers and employees. In that case, might not the purposes themselves conflict, and if so, with what consequences? Furthermore, perhaps more implicitly than explicitly, budgetary procedures are often used as one means of resolving some of the disagreements and conflicts which are prevalent in organisational life. Yet we also know that budgets can themselves generate conflict and even frustration, and all too frequently, can seem to accentuate the internal competition for scarce organisational resources.

Finally, and perhaps more importantly, after looking at a few budgetary systems in operation you might gain the impression that budgets are least contentious and easiest to prepare, use and achieve, in precisely those circumstances where they may be of least value. For if the organisation is comparatively stable and unchanging, it really requires little effort to set down a budget which is likely to be achieved. But in such circumstances where management is so easy, the budget may be very pleasing from a technical point of view, but in what way will it help the management of the organisation? Doesn't it merely codify the existing situation? A budget is really needed when its foundations are complex, unstable and changing; when, in other words, intuition and previous experiences are no longer sufficient to fully comprehend the situation. Yet in such circumstances, where the structure and guidance which a budget can provide may be most necessary from a management point of view, not only do we possess fewer insights for directing its preparation and use, but the uncertainty inherent in the situation may also imply that the final budget is less likely to be achieved. Seen in such terms, which are not uncommon, one may indeed wonder why people are so concerned about meeting their budgets.

Considering the breadth of organisational involvement and the variety of purposes served by budgetary procedures, it is hardly surprising that many highly relevant questions remain unresolved. The problems are important ones, however, because although many of the technical procedures of budgeting are well developed, if not highly sophisticated, the nature of their relationship to human behaviour in organisations, despite providing the very basis for their organisational rationale, remains an area subject to a great deal of uncertainty and doubt. We deal with a number of these issues in the present chapter and the two subsequent chapters. In this chapter, budgeting is viewed as a goal setting process set in an organisational context where conflicts, power differentials and uncertainty cannot be avoided. Then, turning to the impact of the goals on action, we see that the relationship is far from simple, being mediated by human and social circumstances, and surrounding organisational events. Certainly, many of the classically simple views of the role of budgetary systems in managerial and employee performance evaluation need, as we discuss in Chapter 5, to be viewed with caution. Budgetary systems can and do influence behaviour and action, but not always in the anticipated or even desirable direction. An understanding of these problems requires, however, a much wider perspective than is contained in many prescriptive texts and a number of the recommended universal remedies, such as managerial participation and involvement, also need, as we discuss in Chapter 4, to be examined with care and insight. Budgeting represents an important means of influencing behaviour, but its organisational setting should serve to emphasise the relevance of the human motives, meanings, aspirations and expectations which impinge upon its operation.

3.1 Budgeting as a Multi-purpose Activity

One of the basic purposes served by any budgetary system is to encourage an active concern with the future. In the budgetary context, as distinct from that of more strategic planning approaches, the perspective may not be long, but within what is often a yearly horizon, its procedures serve to guide the development of the financial and wider organisational implications of possible future activities. By iteration and deliberation, the discipline and structure which are an essential part of the process can help to ensure that the resources which are likely to be available to the organisation, be they financial, physical or manpower, are allocated in an agreeable, if not rational manner.

In this sense, the budgetary process is really trying to organise and structure some vital elements of the wider organisational decision making process. By providing a framework within which subsequent delegation of authority may be allowed to take place, the budgetary process must also be recognised as a part of the wider process by which influence is distributed within the organisation. Initially, the budgetary structure might be seen as being directed towards economic and financial considerations alone. Certainly, the final statement often appears exclusively in such terms and the budget data are also used to arrive at a number of important economic decisions. They can, for instance, suggest the necessity for the organisation to raise additional finance, the time when it is required and the extent to which the organisation can repay loans, pay dividends or time investment expenditures. But budget estimates are also used in pricing and market analysis, and in the control of inventories, production scheduling and a whole series of other crucial decision areas. Although these certainly have a financial aspect within the integrated system which is the organisation, the financial aspects reflect and influence many other facets of organisational life.

The financial schema is regularly used as no more than a convenient – to some at least – and well tried means of modelling and representing a mass of interrelated organisational activities. The financial preoccupation certainly has its problems if people focus on the means of budgeting rather than on the underlying purposes, and changes can perhaps be expected in this area in the not too distant future, but it should be remembered that as a financial statement, the budget both summarises and influences the market, technological, human and financial environments of the organisation. It reflects a multitude of managerial and physical constraints inherent in the existing pattern of activities, and in so doing, it can permeate the whole fabric of organisational decision making. This multitude of organisational factors also influences the nature and relevance of the budgetary procedures and processes. Budgets vary from organisation to organisation: the planning of future capacity in the electricity supply industry, for instance, is a completely different task than planning for fashion boutiques. A new power station takes about eight years to design, commission and construct; a new shop on a short-term lease, perhaps only a matter of months. Not only are the durations of projection different, but these in turn influence the uncertainties to be coped with and the commitments and constraints incorporated into the ongoing budgetary process. Similar factors influence the more immediate planning of cash flows.

Behind the essential technical façade of the budgetary procedures, lies a prior and less formal bargaining process in which the managers compete for organisational resources. In practice, budget requests can vary from being a statement of a manager's anticipations to being one of his most optimistic aspirations. Since the amounts requested often have an important effect on the amounts received, and hence on the subsequent control over organisational resources, the requests are themselves strategies in a bargaining process in which the issues transcend the immediate future state of the organisational economy to include personal motives for status, recognition and advancement. The budgetary process at least attempts to provide a means for reconciling the conflicts between diverse components of the organisation so that they move in a coordinated and integrated manner towards managements' conception of the wider organisational purposes. However, while budgeting can provide a means for coordinating the decision behaviour of specialist but interlocking activities, reducing the amount of internal uncertainty and organising the complexity, coordination is itself one of the scarcest of organisational resources: it is rarely achieved by fiat alone. To get departments and specialist groups to work together requires the most complex of strategies and a sensitivity of approach. It is at such stages that we begin to see the budgetary process in all its richness, highly interrelated with the overall management task, and at times, an exercise in human political ingenuity.

Budgets also serve as communication devices by which it is possible to relay top management style and authority, and to establish a particular company ethos or organisational climate which it is believed will lead to superior performance throughout the organisation. One commentator's views on the situation in GEC are illustrative of this use:[2]

'Even the famous system of annual budgets and monthly operating reports should be kept in perspective. Budgets are not the key to the running of GEC . . . there is no system for detailed amendment of each company's budget. By and large budgets go through. But the dialogue, the exchange of views at the budget meeting, the searching investigation and sometimes blistering criticism which Weinstock and Kenneth Bond level at the assumptions behind each manager's budget, these are what count.'

Frequently, a new top management group will use the budgetary procedures, often installed or radically changed for the purpose, as a vehicle for conveying power and more wide ranging messages than the formal reports would superficially suggest. There are numerous examples, both industrial and governmental. For instance, on becoming the American Secretary of Defence with the Kennedy administration, McNamara installed the controversial 'Programme – Planning – Budgeting System' with such a view in mind. Whilst it was designed to serve a variety of purposes, not least amongst his concerns was the problem of exercising civilian control over the relatively independent military authorities. By viewing most important decisions as highly interdependent, cutting across the separate military prerogatives, the seemingly neutral and decision oriented budgeting system served his purpose admirably.

Budgets are also used to motivate the members of the organisation by serving as targets and mechanisms for gaining involvement and commitment. To this end, a budget provides a means for measuring accomplishment against goals and for comparing actual with planned outcomes. Budget reports are used to measure the performance of not only the organisational components as economic entities, but also of the managers responsible for their administration. They form an important part of the logic of superior evaluation and also of self-review and control. With a successful budgetary system, the communication of knowledge of results can reinforce or discourage previous behaviour, stimulating a learning and adaptive organisational atmosphere. Equally, it is possible for budgets to be seen as an end in themselves, rather than as a means to an end, motivating in the process, but not necessarily with desirable results. The borderline between the two approaches is thin and ambiguous, yet as we shall see, of great practical importance.

At the more individual level, the members of an organisation, both managerial and employee, are more likely to be effective and satisfied if they have a clear sense of purpose which enables them to comprehend better where they are going and whether they are getting there.[3] As one would expect, this consideration is all the more important when organisational relationships are complex and changing due to technological developments, growth and personnel changes. Budgets can certainly help in this regard. However, as the severe practical problems in the area show, it is all too easy to fail to distinguish between a concern for structure which serves as a basis for clarifying purpose and context, and a rigidity of structure which constrains both enquiry and action. The former can easily merge into the latter, yet if it does, the structuring can become an unbearable constraint on independent initiative and a consequent source of anxiety and tension.

The listing of purposes need not be comprehensive to illustrate that budgets in action can differ radically from mere predictive devices set in a behavioural vacuum. Perhaps more importantly, I hope that the listing and descriptions, brief though they have been, have already encouraged you to question whether the diverse purposes are necessarily congruous with one another. Can the need for realistic budgets for planning and coordination, and for meaningful feedback for comparison with actual accomplishments, conflict with the view of budgets as playing a significant role in motivating performance and as a means for ensuring an active organisational atmosphere? Viewed in this way, things are far from simple. In fact, it is the very mixture of purposes which results in so many practical problems and why it is so difficult to provide easy prescriptions for action and improvement.

3.2 *The Nature of Objectives in an Organisational Setting*

By setting down a detailed outline of a future course of action, budgets reflect, develop and institutionalise the objectives held by at least some members of the organisation. They reflect objectives because the budget only states the anticipated allocation of organisational resources in the immediate future. Current plans are moulded within the context of the wider and more long-term aspirations held by members of the organisation. Even the influence of past objectives tends to persist since not only does their reflection in prior actions impose psychological as well as economic constraints on new actions, but also the values which they represent often persist despite major organisational changes. However, budgets also develop the wider aims. Through the arguments and conflicts which are an inevitable part of setting any budget, the otherwise general and only partially articulated objectives are usually stated in more precise terms. The final statement however, often represents a shift in emphasis, if not a new orientation, since the demand for precision is quite capable of exposing conflicting aims and unrecognised constraints, and given some flexibility and a willingness to re-evaluate priorities, new forces emerge to create new opportunities and aspirations.

Yet although objectives are as fundamental to budgeting as they are to many other management activities and prescriptions for improvement, they remain one of the most elusive of concepts. In accounting literature, many discussions, both practical and academic, draw heavily on conventional economic thought in emphasising the presence of an agreed single organisational objective, or at least, a more or less integrated set of organisational objectives, usually expressed in financial terms and roughly ordered in some hierarchy of values. The objectives of profit or shareholder wealth maximisation, so readily attributed to both whole organisations as well as to their individual members, are well engrained in economic and financial thought. Even the recent modifications which are a feature of more managerial views of the enterprise still find it easy to specify equally simple alternatives.[4] For anyone who requires an understanding of the management process, both the earlier attributions and the subsequent modifications all too frequently beg the issue. For in what sense can organisations be said to have objectives, or to put it rather differently, how are the members of the organisation or outside parties able to perceive or attribute the objectives towards which organised behaviour is orientated? In fact, is not the use of the concept of organisational objective inadmissable in any sense other than either a very simple heuristic device or as a reflection of the presence of highly ambiguous and far from operational aims, since it implies that the powers of thought and action reside in social entities, the organisation or the enterprise, rather than in the people within the organisation?

On such grounds, some social scientists have objected to the use of the concept of organisational objective, finding that it adds little or nothing to the explanation of behaviour in organisations. Yet while recognising the simplicity, if not naïvety, of many traditional viewpoints, as accountants interested in budgetary and other procedures we still need to understand the broad factors which induce organised behaviour. Since we recognise a lot of behaviour as being anticipatory and purposive in nature, it is vital that we deepen our understanding of the nature of objectives in organisational settings.

Given the significance of the problem it is surprising how few investigations have been made of the nature of corporate objectives. However, one early study, although it raised more questions than it answered, can provide a useful starting point for our discussion. Dent asked 144 American chief executives to list the objectives held by top management in their companies.[5] The results of the exercise are summarised in Table 3.1. Unfortunately, the responses were taken at their face value with no probing for further meanings, and perhaps as a result, the declared aims may look too obvious and rather conventional to some of you. Certainly, the objectives appear to be far from independent of each

Table 3.1 Objectives of management

Objectives of management	Percentage of managers mentioning objective	
	As the objective first mentioned	Among the first three objectives mentioned
Make money or profit	36	52
Provide a good product or service	21	39
Growth	12	17
Organisational development	9	14
Employee welfare	5	39
Meet competition	5	13
Efficiency	4	12
Shareholder dividends	1	9
Community contribution	—	3
Miscellaneous	7	18

Adapted from: DENT, J K, 'Organisational Correlates of the Goals of Business Management', *Personnel Psychology*, vol 12, no 3, Autumn, 1959, pp 369.

other and their precise meanings are uncertain, although these factors do point to the difficulties which managers experience in trying to talk freely about their aims. Despite the numerous occasions when they might be mentioned in everyday life, objectives are rarely well articulated, and in the research context there is also the temptation to list intentions or stereotypes which reflect little more than cultural norms rather than the realities of organisational life.

Let us proceed with the analysis for the time being because by relating the objectives held by the managers to a series of indicators of organisational size, composition and behaviour, Dent provided some insights into the pressures influencing the stated aims. Conventional though they may be, the objectives which he elicited did not occur in isolation. The proportion of managers concerned with making money or profits, for instance, declined as the white collar component of employment increased. Dent found that managers in companies with a large white collar component tended to be more concerned with growth for its own sake, a finding which is consistent with some managerial theories of firm behaviour. He also found that in unionised companies the concern with employee welfare increased with total employment, whilst the opposite relationship held in the non-unionised companies. It is interesting to note that the stated corporate objectives in the employee welfare area were actually related to behaviour within the companies, a rare finding in the social sciences, although it is too optimistic to hope to distinguish between cause and effect on the available evidence. In those companies where the top managers endorsed employee welfare as an important objective, provision tended to be made for employee health services, as compared with only five per cent of the managers mentioning employee welfare in companies which made no provision.

There were many other similar findings, some more puzzling than others, but all of them suggesting the important point that the stated corporate objectives reflected much more than the personal aims of the chief executive or even the group of senior managers. Obviously some important organisational actions do emanate from the personal motives of such powerful people, but in many cases, the relationship is more indirect than many would have us believe. As the significance of unionisation serves to demonstrate, even senior managers are limited by the amount of influence they can exercise, the alliances they make and the means available to them to formulate their objectives. The final corporate objectives are moulded by the patterns of dependency within the internal dynamics of the organisation, and the nature of the external environment.

It is particularly important to consider the effects of the constraints and exchanges which characterise the relationship between the organisation and its environment. Action is not simply within the confines of the members of the organisation. Economic and social pressures impinging upon the society, the economy, the industry and the particular enterprise all constrain behaviour. Government actions, financiers' expectations and trade union strategies all narrow the freedom of movement. The particular technology and the means for organising add further constraints.[6] Of course, depending upon the type of organisation and its setting, and also upon the particular area of concern, some of these constraints are negotiable and the members of the organisation seek to arrive at an agreement on what they, either as individuals or as a group, will or will not do. Lobbies, alliances, and pressures, subtle or otherwise, all play a role. In this way, fragmented though it may be, an image of the organisation's role and purposes in the larger system is achieved which serves to legitimise and guide subsequent actions by providing a context in which specific objectives are developed and bargained over.

When a particular problem is recognised, possibly because a prior objective has not been fulfilled, some specific objective with reference to the problem will be formulated in a subsequent stage of the adaptation process.* Over time, a mass of these specific objectives, both major and minor, ever evolving, and not necessarily congruent with one another, interact and interlock to form an unstated representation of desired future states for the organisation. Although orientated towards the future, the mixture of expectation and aspiration which is reflected within them continuously relates current constraints to past experiences and future possibilities. The objectives are therefore not 'out there', separated from the organisational members' definitions of the situation, but are part of the organisation's ongoing management process, continuously moulded as a result of emerging opportunities and constraints, and feedback on the organisation's own performance.

Problems may, however, be differently perceived by different members of the organisation and the new objectives ultimately formulated may well represent particular interests and experiences. As a consequence, there is usually no well defined set of specific objectives in the organisation, in terms of which the members seek to resolve all their problems. 'Rather they represent', in the words of March and Simon, two influential theorists on the topic, 'the vaguely related, conflicting, contradictory and complementary interests of a coalition [of members] characterised by differently distributed power, continual bargaining and conflict'.[8]

Differential power is an important factor in this process, although its direct translation into the view that the primary orientation of any organisation can be obtained from the personal motives of the people currently in positions of authority is, as we have already discussed, far too simple. In most situations, power is distributed amongst the individuals and groups which control the use of crucial organisational resources, regardless of their position in the formal hierarchy.[9] In these circumstances, the objectives which emerge to influence behaviour, whilst

* It is tempting to presume that the formulation of objectives always precedes the activity of final choice. However, reality is rarely so simple. Although objectives are undoubtedly used in this manner, as most discussions assume, many decision makers also need to construct for themselves a rational argument to explain why a particular action has been chosen. Objectives, at a cognitive level, have an important role to play in this rationalisation process.[7]

Figure 3.1 Influences on individual objectives is an organisational setting

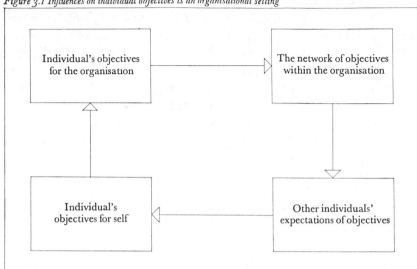

formulated and held by individuals and even groups, are determined by a dynamic process of exchange within the organisation, such as is character-ised in Figure 3.1. Within this process, certain individuals and groups, through their command of resources and position in relation to the means of social interaction and influence, can more readily shape the objectives held by other individuals and groups. The ability to determine the bases for organisational rewards, to design the flows of formal information and to select and train personnel can, for instance, provide the means for instilling, albeit imperfectly, a framework and ordering of values. Even so, the final outcome, is often a loosely integrated set of objectives, partially agreed, partially conflicting, and arrived at by a process of negotiation in which each group, powerful and otherwise, tries to main-tain as much room for manoeuvre as possible. The image of a tightly integrated structure of objectives is invariably a false one: a perfect mesh is an extremely rare occurrence, not an organisational steady state.

3.3 *Budgets and Objectives*
Budgeting is just one part of the continual process by which individual and group aims and aspirations evolve within organisations. In most

organisations it is, however, an important part of the process because budgeting is an institutionalised attempt to periodically confront at least some of the underlying conflicts and agreements which are an inevitable part of organisational life. Through bargaining and debate, the budgetary process constructs a temporary but nevertheless influential map of the emergent position in the form of a current operating plan and proposed allocation of organisational resources.

Aware of the organisational significance of the budget, managers enter the annual debate with an outline of the objectives which they want to satisfy. The translation of these objectives into operational budgetary strategies is then the next step, although when the underlying management task is either complex or uncertain, this can itself be a difficult endeavour. However, while undue complexity and uncertainty may reduce the managers' commitments to any single approach, and hence possibly reduce the potential for subsequent conflict between competing sectors of the organisation, the budgetary process requires that the managers select from the budgetary strategies which are in principle available to them, those which they will actually demand. Because it is often highly political in nature, this selection invariably draws on not only the objectives which have been formulated, but also on the managers' past experiences and their expectations regarding the later stages of the budgetary process.

Following the process as outlined in Figure 3.2, if the separate budget demands are compatible with each other, or if, as mentioned above, the managerial commitments are low, the final budget can be determined by a process of analysis and computation. However, arising as they do from separate individuals and groups within the organisation, there is a fair probability that at least some of the budgetary demands will be incompatible. In the budgetary context, however, compatibility does not necessitate a perfect mesh, but rather a degree of consistency within the confines of the available resources and time constraints. So if time is not a constraining factor, some seemingly conflicting demands can be attended to sequentially, and where the vital organisational resources, be they financial, physical or human, are not in limited supply, some potentially competing demands may be able to be satisfied simultaneously. If there are time pressures or limited resources, such as prevail in poor economic conditions, the potential for conflict is more likely to be

Figure 3.2 The budgetary process

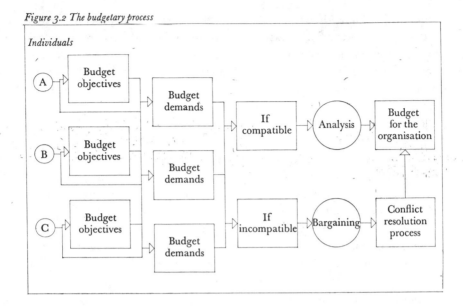

actualised and the final budget will have to be determined by a process of bargaining.

The popular managerial image of budgeting, so often phrased in terms of the bargaining strategies which are associated with the process, suggests that conflict and bargaining are, in some form or other, the organisational norms. However, although the outcome may be similar in different situations, many different organisational factors influence the potential incompatibility of budget demands and the means available for their resolution. The benevolence of the environment and the degree of uncertainty and complexity which characterise the management task have already been mentioned. In addition, the extent of budgetary conflict is heightened by differing individual or group objectives, reinforced, as they invariably are, by limited social interaction, different and even competing reward structures and reliance on different sources of information. In large organisations, the potential for conflict is all the greater where product schedules or the demands of the task call for either a dependence on the same scarce resources or coordinated action.

Where conflicting budget demands exist, the preparation of a final budget depends upon at least their partial resolution. At this stage of the budgetary process, differences in organisational power, although far from being dormant at earlier stages, have a particular role to play. However, as a factor influencing the output of the bargaining sessions, whether openly conducted in meetings or carried on in a more secretive manner, power depends on personal and social as well as organisational factors.

Individual differences in negotiating skills play an important role, but to be effective, power has also to be socially recognised by other members of the organisation. In practice, this depends upon a much broader social assessment which individuals make of each others' skills and performance, not just on economic or bargaining dimensions, but in terms of perceptiveness of people and political judgment. While at the organisational level, differential position and size of responsibility can contribute to personal power, it can also be achieved through the control of vital organisational resources. In times of financial stringency, for instance, the accountants and financial executives have a more important role to play; when technological problems loom large, the engineers and production managers can gain in influence. We also know that power once achieved can be manipulated. Organisational perogatives need not necessarily change in accordance with economic and technological demands for the powerful often have the ability to locate the sources of organisational uncertainty. Individuals and groups of people can, in other words, use their power to maintain either a fiction of uncertainty and consequent dependence by manipulating the flows of information, or alternatively, steer the organisation into areas where the uncertainty will be in their own personal interest.

In such a context rigorous analysis and precise economic appraisals can help to structure possible budget decisions, but they always need to be viewed in a much wider perspective, and often need to be recognised as bargaining strategies adopted by a particular group within the organisation. For managerial approaches to budgeting reflect the fact that it is only a part of a complex and highly political process by which organisational resources are allocated to uncertain future courses of action.

3.4 *Budgeting Strategies*[10]

Assembling a budget for a large organisation is a massive endeavour and the persons engaged in the process have, of necessity, to use strategies which reduce both the uncertainty and the burden of sheer calculation. As a result, as the following example illustrates, budgeting is usually viewed as an incremental activity, grounded on a firm historical base. Because of, rather than in spite of, the complexity of the task, it is an activity which is invariably characterised by the use of the simplest rules of thumb.

> *Accountant*: '. . . we couldn't get a meaningful standard against which to judge how much R & D the company should be supporting.'
> *Interviewer*: 'How did you decide on the R & D budget then?'
> *Accountant*: 'That's a good question! A times, I myself wondered how we did it. In general though, it turned out to be pretty mechanical really. We might say, "Let's hold it at last year's budget" or "at last year's plus a certain percentage of whatever new things the R & D people want" or it could be just a plain 10 per cent increase over last year's. Occasionally you get some bright guy who wants to work it out as a percentage of sales or some such thing, but where does that get you? Does it have any greater logic than the 10 per cent bit?'
> *Interviewer*: 'How do you arrive at these 10 per cent figures?'
> *Accountant*: 'Oh, to be honest, it's a bit of ad-hocery really. 10 per cent sounds right doesn't it? And to be fair to ourselves, you arrive at a figure that fits in with where you want to get to in the overall budget. But then the R & D people may say that this will interfere with the natural growth of some crucial projects, so we give them 12 per cent. It's playing around with numbers really. And trends as well. We look at the past record and project the 12 per cent out into the future. Pushing it to 1975 you might find a total figure of so many million pounds. Then, someone in the accounts department will say, "Let's try and reach that by 1978 rather than by 1975". So we cut the figure by the necessary percentage.'
> *Interviewer*: 'Then what?'
> *Accountant*: 'The recommendation goes to the Budget Review Committee. In this case, I told them that the R & D guys asked for, let us say, a 20 per cent increase over last year and that we, the accounts department that is, had allowed 9 per cent. Then you get comments like, "We have to put a stop to this escallation of R & D" or "Let's hold it to last year's level". But in this case, the R & D people had been chatting up the marketing guys and managed to convince them that they needed their new products. That wouldn't be difficult either because the R & D manager and the Marketing Director are personal friends. So we heard that 9 per cent wasn't realistic: "There has to be some increase." Someone else chipped in then. "Can't we give them 13 per cent and get a bit of rationalisation in exchange for it?" So we had to go back and figure that one out.'

The largest factor determining the size and content of any single year's budget is usually the previous year's budget.[11] In fact, because of previous commitments and constraints, and of the impact of changing external conditions, there is often very little room for flexibility in budgeting. This is not to deny that lobbying, exhortations and friendships have a role to play. They do, but the debate is usually centred on the changes in the budget from one year to the next. These may be small in total compared with the budget as a whole, but they represent the main areas which can be influenced. In this way, despite losing the opportunity for an overall appraisal of activities in relation to wider objectives, the magnitude of the task is brought within reasonable bounds.

An incremental approach reduces the burden of calculation and the breadth of debate, but these benefits are gained at the expense of focusing the remaining debate on the areas of particular uncertainty and controversy – changes. Is an increase justified? And what of the overspending on last year's budget? Does it represent inefficiency, non-recurring conditions or an inadequate budget? Should this year's budget be lower, the same or higher? Careful analysis can, of course, provide some assistance and the analytical procedures at our disposal are being continually developed, but since the basic problem involves the extrapolation of an uncertain past into an uncertain future, analysis alone cannot solve the problem. Besides the complexities of budgeting for individual activities, there is also the problem of making comparisons among different activities that have different values for different people. The competing claims of marketing, R & D, personnel, production and administration, for the limited organisational resources have all to be appraised and integrated into the final budget. Yet in many vital areas, we have still to develop useful means for arriving at a common denominator.

In practice, senior managers and accountants tackle the problem with the knowledge that difficult questions do not have to be solved once and for all on a year to year basis: the process is evolving. The budgeting cycle rarely precludes further action during the year when more detailed knowledge may become available, and although precedents are important in this context, it is still possible to adopt an idea in another year which was not considered in a previous year. Also within the annual review, the process is usually organised so that experience and insights accumulate as the budget moves from department to department and iterates between one level in the hierarchy and the next.

There still remains a need to radically simplify the complexity, so at times, personalities rather than activities may be appraised. Where activities and technologies are beyond the comprehension of the senior managers and accountants, the final budget decision may well depend on their impressions of the management of factors which, although relatively minor, are nevertheless within the bounds of their own experience. Many of the financial procedures are implicitly used to force the debate along more predictable lines. Budgetary decisions can also be made within the context of a predetermined amount of resources which are to be allocated. 'How much can we afford' then becomes more important than the objectives which can be attained and organisational norms develop to guide the priority to be given to individual requests.[12] There are a multitude of other similar simplifying strategies, but in the end, if all else fails, the 'big meat-axe' approach may be used and 'just arbitrarily, without logic, dictate a cut of x per cent across the board'.[13]

Such strategies are a response not only to the uncertainty and complexity which are inherent in the budgetary process, but also to the fact that managers' budget demands reflect both organisational necessities and individual ambitions. Intertwining the logics of both economics and politics, the demands are themselves strategies in an intensely serious game. The ability to estimate 'what will go' is a vital skill. Managers seek out and receive facts and opinions in order to arrive at an estimate of what they should ask for in the light of what they can expect to get and then, with due 'padding' made to allow for anticipated cuts, they seek to market their budgetary demands. As in the initial example, the support of other parties can be actively canvassed and demands packaged in the most appealing form. Tangible results can be given undue weight and complex activities described in either the simplest or the most complex of terms – but not the more understandable mean! Emphasis can be placed on the qualitative rather than measurable advantages, the forthcoming rather than current results, and the procedures rather than the outcome. Points can always be stretched a little, but never so far as can be tested. If some cuts are seen to be inevitable, essential or popular activities can be pruned first in the anticipation of their subsequent restoration. In times of real urgency it can be pleaded that even the smallest cut could damage the entire programme of activities. For new activities it is often beneficial to emphasise their relationship to the old, and in the early stages it is often best to make modest demands. Another argument is whether they can be shown to 'pay for themselves' or whether it is really a case of 'spending a bit now to save a lot later'.

Of course, there are dangers of overselling, but with experience managers learn to gauge how far they can go and which strategies are appropriate for different people. On both sides of budgeting, in asking and in granting, the process is usually characterised by a certain subtlety of approach. Nevertheless, the activity is a serious one and whatever strategies are used in a particular situation can have an important influence on the content of the final budget.

3.5 Budgets as Targets

Although the final budgets almost inevitably reflect a compromise between expected future performance and the outcome of a political bargaining process, once set, they are frequently used as a means for motivating individual managers and employees. In this sense, the budget becomes a target intended to induce an active and possibly pressured organisational atmosphere which it is believed will result in higher levels of performance within the organisation.

There is considerable evidence that budgets can indeed serve this role. A number of studies in organisations have shown that both productivity and satisfaction are greater when managers and employees set objectives and the notion is incorporated into the increasingly popular 'management-by-objective' schemes.[14] One field study of performance appraisal interviews conducted in The General Electric Corporation by Kay, French and Meyer found that the conscious setting of objectives resulted in superior performance. When managerial concerns for improvement were translated into specific objectives over sixty-five per cent of the aims were subsequently achieved, compared with only twenty-seven per cent when this was not done. The researchers concluded that:

> 'Appreciable improvements were realised only when specific objectives were established with time deadlines set and result measures agreed upon. Regardless of how much emphasis the manager gave to an improvement need in the appraisal discussion, if this did not get translated into a specific goal, very little performance improvement was achieved.'[15]

Experimental studies conducted in the laboratory have repeatedly provided support for such a conclusion. In a large series of highly controlled experiments, Locke and his colleagues found that the higher the level of intended achievement, the higher the level of performance.[16] In what was intended to be a simulation of the budgetary context, Stedry found that the formulation of an explicit target improved performance, although the precise effect was determined by how the budget influenced the personal levels of aspiration.[17]

Although these and other studies point to the motivational advantages of budgets, they fail to answer many important questions. How difficult ought the targets to be? Do all people respond in the same way to targets and does the nature of the task influence their effect on final performance? Although there might be a relationship between targets and performance, how does this come about? How, in other words, do individuals internalise the targets so that they influence their personal aspirations and hence performance? Moreover, if budgets are used as targets, how does this effect their use for other, possibly more decision oriented purposes? These are questions of fundamental importance and not too surprisingly, numerous people have investigated them with rigor and insight.[18] However, in this discussion we will use an approach which draws on the famous studies of achievement motivation conducted by McClelland.[19] In the budgetary context, the approach developed by Atkinson, one of McClelland's colleagues, has the advantage of emphasising the role played by both relatively general and stable individual differences in personality and more specific and transient features of the immediate task environment.[20]

Atkinson presumes that in any situation which presents a challenge, of which the budgetary situation is a particular instance, the overall achievement oriented tendency or motivation to act (T_A) is always determined by the outcome of a conflict between two opposing tendencies. First, there is a tendency to approach the task with interest and with the intent of performing well. Atkinson calls this the tendency or motivation to achieve success (T_S), and in the budgetary context, it is represented by a manager's intent to exceed his budget in a favourable direction. Second, there is a tendency to avoid undertaking the task in so far as it is expected to result in failure. This is called the tendency to avoid failure (T_{-F}), and in the budgetary context is represented by a manager's intent to avoid failing to achieve his budget. Both the tendency to achieve success and the tendency to avoid failure are always present, for in so far as there is a probability that action will lead to success, there is also a probability that action will lead to failure, and while success will result in satisfaction, failure will result in dissatisfaction and some anxiety, both of which are to be avoided. Therefore, the overall tendency to act in such a situation can be expressed in the following manner:

$$T_A = T_S + T_{-F}$$

The tendency to achieve success (T_S) is considered to be a multiplicative function of three factors, namely an inate motive or need to achieve success (M_S), the expectancy or subjective probability that success will result from a particular activity (P_S), and the incentive or reward value of succeeding (I_S).

$$T_S = M_S \times P_S \times I_S$$

While the motive to achieve success is regarded as a relatively stable dimension of general personality, both the subjective probability of success and the incentive value of success are seen as characteristics of the particular situation. In the budgetary context, for instance, the subjective probability of success equals a manager's expectancy of favourably beating his budget and the incentive value of success expresses the magnitude of personal and organisational rewards which he anticipates as a result.

Similarly, the tendency to avoid failure (T_{-F}) is considered to be a multiplicative function of an inate motive or need to avoid failure (M_{AF}), the expectancy of failure (P_F) and the incentive value of failure (I_F).

$$T_{-F} = M_{AF} \times P_F \times I_F$$

Again the motive to avoid failure is regarded as a relatively stable dimension of general personality, while both the subjective probability of failure and the incentive value of failure are seen as characteristics of the particular situation. The incentive value of failure is, of course, seen as negative. The overall tendency to act can therefore be expressed in the following manner:

$$\begin{aligned} T_A &= T_S + T_{-F} \\ &= (M_S \times P_S \times I_S) + (M_{AF} \times P_F \times I_F) \end{aligned}$$

Before proceeding to demonstrate the implications of the Atkinson approach to motivation, it is necessary to briefly consider the relationship between the environmental factors, namely between the probability of success and the incentive value of success, and between the probability of failure and the incentive value of failure. The attractiveness or incentive value of success is quite reasonably assumed to increase with the difficulty of the task. Success in accomplishing an extremely difficult task is generally very gratifying, while considerably less reward is associated with accomplishing a very easy task. Hence the incentive value of success is inversely related to the probability of success. By similar reasoning, the incentive value of failure, which is always negative, is assumed to be positively related to the probability of failure.

Values must then be attached to all the relevant factors. For demonstration purposes, however, we can make a number of assumptions. Simplifying the relationship between the probabilities of success and failure, and their incentive values, we assume that the incentive value of success is equal to $(1 - P_s)$ and that the incentive value of failure is equal to $(P_F - 1)$, or on the condition that $P_s + P_F = 1$, $- P_s$. Then by assigning arbitrary values of 2 to the achievement motive M_s and of 1 to the motive to avoid failure M_{AF}, the strengths of the two conflicting tendencies and that of the overall tendency to act can be calculated as in Table 3.2.

There is a considerable body of evidence to support the main tenets of the argument. Carefully controlled studies have been conducted by psychologists in their own laboratories and university environments, and support has also been derived from studies of occupational choice, hourly earnings, income from savings and the extent of planning ahead, performance in educational institutions, and even intergenerational occupational mobility.[21] Although there have not as yet been any studies specifically conducted in the budgetary context some of the available evidence on both budgeting and management-by-objectives is consistent with the broad approach. We will return to this after we have considered some of the implications for budgeting.

Just how tight or slack should a budget be set for motivational purposes? Let us assume that the budgets in Table 3.2 represent different budgets which could be set for the same managerial activity. On the one hand, budget A to which the manager assigns a very low subjective probability of success represents a very tight budget and on the other hand, budget I, with a very high subjective probability of success, represents a very slack budget. Given a dominant motive for achievement $(M_s > M_{AF})$, such as is represented in Table 3.2, there is always a positive motivation to meet the budget regardless of how tight or slack it is. This motivation is strongest, however, for the budget which is seen as being of intermediate difficulty, E, where uncertainty regarding the final outcome is greatest. Therefore, if an achievement oriented manager was asked to set his own budget, other things being equal, he would choose E where $P_s = 0.50$, for this is the point of maximum motivation. To the extent that such a manager had, like the manager portrayed in the table, any motive to avoid failure $(M_{AF} > 0)$, this means that he would voluntarily choose that budget which maximised his own anxiety about failure. If, on the other hand, a budget was to be imposed on this type of manager, he would exert the greatest effort in performing a task of intermediate difficulty where P_s equals 0.50. If presented with either a more difficult task or an easier task, the strength of overall motivation and hence the final performance would be lower.

Table 3.2 The Tendency to act in a challenging situation where $M_s > M_{AF}$

Task	Motivation to achieve				Motivation to avoid failure				Overall tendency to act
	M_s	$\times\ P_s$	$\times\ I_s$	$=\ T_s$	M_{AF}	$\times\ P_F$	$\times\ I_F$	$=\ I_F$	T_A
Budget A	2	0.10	0.90	0.18	1	0.90	−0.10	−0.09	0.09
Budget B	2	0.20	0.80	0.32	1	0.80	−0.20	−0.16	0.16
Budget C	2	0.30	0.70	0.42	1	0.70	−0.30	−0.21	0.21
Budget D	2	0.40	0.60	0.48	1	0.60	−0.40	−0.24	0.24
Budget E	2	0.50	0.50	0.50	1	0.50	−0.50	−0.25	0.25
Budget F	2	0.60	0.40	0.48	1	0.40	−0.60	−0.24	0.24
Budget G	2	0.70	0.30	0.42	1	0.30	−0.70	−0.21	0.21
Budget H	2	0.80	0.20	0.32	1	0.20	−0.80	−0.16	0.16
Budget I	2	0.90	0.10	0.18	1	0.10	−0.90	−0.09	0.09

The available research evidence on budgeting supports the bell shaped relationship between perceived budget difficulty and performance which is illustrated in Figure 3.3. It can also be seen from the figure that the effects of perceived budget difficulty on final performance are all the more important the greater is the relative strength of the motive to achieve. While for managers with a positive but low overall achievement orient-

*Figure 3.3 Relationship between degree of budget difficulty and performance
when the motive for achievement is greater than the motive to avoid failure*

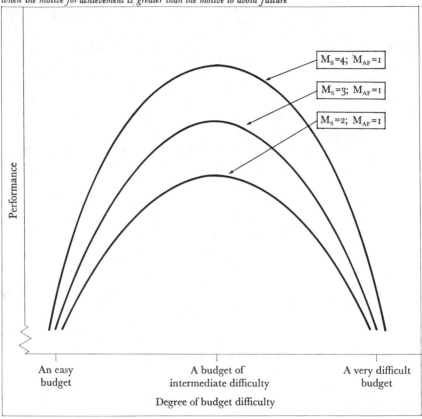

ation ($M_S = 2$; $M_{AF} = 1$) there is a bonus to be derived from budgets of
intermediate difficulty, the difference is not so great as for the managers
with a very high overall achievement orientation ($M_S = 4$; $M_{AF} = 1$).

In a field study conducted in five factories in the Netherlands,
Hofstede found that up to a certain degree of tightness, budgets became
stronger motivators as they became tighter, although thereafter motivation declined.[22] What is more, as in the Atkinson approach where the
relationship is stated in terms of the manager's own subjective impressions
of tightness rather than in terms of a more objective measure, the optimal
degree of tightness depended on both the situational determinants of the
objective degree of difficulty and the personality factors which influenced

how this was seen by the managers.[23] Similar findings were also reported by Stedry and Kay.[24] If objectively difficult budgets were perceived as challenging and within the bounds of reasonable possibility, they stimulated good performance, but if the managers saw the difficulty in terms of sheer impossibility, the final performance was very poor indeed.

Although the available evidence and the theory correspond, caution is required before too readily proceeding with action. For one thing, as we are concerned with subjective rather than objective probabilities, there is a suggestion that budgets need to be attuned to individual managers as much as they do to the situation. In addition, the budget resulting in the best performance is one that is unlikely to be achieved: there is only a fifty-fifty chance of meeting it. It is, in other words, a pulling budget, stated at a level higher than expected performance.

In practice, this problem presents a serious dilemma to management. A simple representation of the problem is shown in Figure 3.4. In the diagram it can be seen that while budgets which are best for motivational purposes need to be stated in terms of aspirations rather than expectations, the budgets which are so necessary for planning and decision purposes need to be stated in terms of the best available estimate of expected actual performance. So even though budgets are used for both purposes in many organisations, the types of budgets which are ideally necessary to achieve the separate ends are in conflict.

Where senior managers and accountants use a single budget and are reluctant to relinquish it as a motivational tool, which they often are, the problem gives rise to the 'bottom drawer phenomenon'. The main budget is designed to include some reflection of aspired performance levels, but the senior accountants keep another version in the bottom drawer of their desks which tries to make some allowance for the prevailing corporate optimism. Sometimes this merely takes the form of an overall 5 per cent or 10 per cent, but in other organisations, it is done on a departmental basis, with 5 per cent off Fred's budget and possibly 15 per cent off Joe's, depending on estimates of the aspirational element in each case. This is obviously done because senior management require a more realistic statement of expected performance for decision and planning purposes. One wonders how accurate the writer-downs are and how soon it is before they become more generally known in the organisation and in the latter case, what happens to motivation then?

Figure 3.4 The conflicting purposes of budgeting

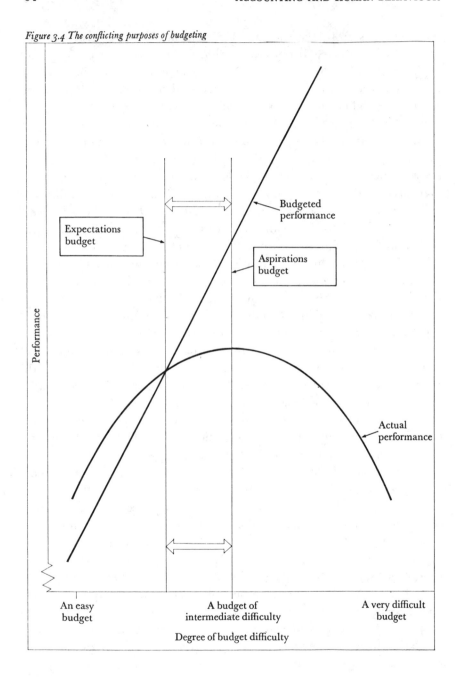

If vital decisions are based on the budget, would it not be preferable to concentrate on building up a more useful statement of expected performance? At least it should be realised that budgets are only one of many ways of motivating performance, but as a future oriented decision tool they are unique. Should their unique role be endangered because of an emphasis on their motivational potential?

Ideally there is a need for separate budgets for motivational and planning purposes. Of course, this suggestion has been made before,[25] and it is usually greeted by pleas of impracticality. There are difficulties in implementing the idea. It would require an enormous educational effort and a lot more careful attention would have to be given to budgeting itself. There are, however, benefits as well as costs and where the underlying problem is sufficiently important the overall benefits to be derived may justify the costs involved. Certainly a number of British companies are now making practical experiments in the area.

In one company, the managers are asked to formulate two budgets, one reflecting what they almost certainly expect to happen; in order to emphasise the inherent uncertainty of the process the wording used is 'with 90 per cent probability'. In the other budget they show what they would ideally like to happen; 'with 50 per cent probability' is the phrase used in this case. The company, as you may already have gathered, operates in a high technology area and employs a well educated work-force. Another company uses a similar approach, but in this case only the expectations budgets are known to other members of the organisation. The aspirations budgets are regarded as being personal to each manager and hence relatively unthreatening yardsticks for personal review and appraisal.* Although this latter approach may say more about the social climate prevailing in the company, a factor which we return to below and in Chapter 5, than the mere budgeting system, both experiments represent exciting approaches to what was seen as an important problem.

The practical problems do not stop at this stage. So far in our discussion we have presumed that the achievement oriented tendency

* The monthly report received by each manager contains six columns, namely expectations budget, actual results and variance, and the personal aspirations budget, actual results and variance. Columns 1 to 3, and column 5 are completed by the accountants. Columns 4 and 6 remain empty in anticipation of the manager entering his own figures.

(T_s) is stronger than the tendency to avoid failure (T_{-F}). But is this always the case? In some individual cases, due to differences in personality, the overall tendency to act may be dominated by the tendency to avoid failure. More generally, however, the relative strengths of the two tendencies can be influenced by the social situation, and in the budgetary context, this is a particularly important consideration.

Many people have documented the personal pressures which can result from budgets. In a famous early study, Argyris provided the following examples of how accountants saw budgets as a means of putting pressures on operating managers:

> 'The important thing for us to do is follow up. The supervisor's interest lags unless someone is *constantly checking up on him*. A little pressure. If you don't, the tendency is to lag. You can't blame supervisors. They are interested in their machines.
>
> I think that there is a need for more pressure. People need to be needled a bit. I think man is inherently lazy and if we could only increase the pressure . . . I think budgets would be more effective.'

But what type of pressure did they have in mind?

> 'As soon as we examine the budget results and see a fellow is slipping, we *immediately* call the factory manager and point out, "Look Joe, you're behind on your budget. What do you expect to do about it?"
>
> True, he may be batting his brains out already on the problem, but our phone call adds a little *more pressure* – er – well, you know, we let them know we're interested.'[26]

Maybe now that more managers have at least heard of modern theories of management the same language would not be used. Perhaps British managers would have phrased their feelings in a different manner but the sentiments themselves are not unfamiliar.

We discuss some of the personal and organisational implications of using budgets as a pressure device in greater detail in a later chapter. At this stage, however, we are more concerned with the direction of the pressure which is implied by such comments. You will, I am sure, have noticed the negative tone of the remarks. In practice, it is not unusual for senior managers and accountants to give a lot of attention to managers who have not met their budgets, while hardly acknowledging the desirable implications of favourably surpassing them. A small cost overrun is immediately queried, while a large saving may eventually be commented upon, if that is, it is not used as evidence for cutting next year's budget.

The use of budgets in this way implies an unbalanced reward structure. The negative incentive value of failure (I_F) exceeds the equivalent incentive value of success (I_s) at all levels of budget difficulty. In addition, since personal needs have to be elicited before influencing action, the management environment associated with this type of budgetary pressure can more readily elicit a stronger need to avoid failure (M_{AF}) than a need to succeed (M_s): while managers will certainly want to avoid falling short of their budget targets, they will be less concerned with actually beating them. Therefore on account of both personal and mangerial factors, it is possible in the budgetary context, for the tendency to avoid failure (T_{-F}) to dominate the tendency to achieve (T_s). What are the implications of this? To answer this question we must go back to Table 3.2. Looking at the columns concerned with the tendency to avoid failure, we see that this tendency is strongest when the budget is of intermediate difficulty. If this was the only motivation present our manager would feel impelled not to undertake the task because he expects it to lead to failure. However, man's motivational structure is never so simple. On the assumption that there are other motives for undertaking the task – material, personal and social – but that these are not related to the level of budget difficulty, we can conclude that the overall relationships between the perceived difficulty of the budget and the level of overall motivation, and hence performance, is of a U-shaped form such as that illustrated in Figure 3.5. When the desire to avoid failure is dominant, the overall motivation to perform is strongest for very low and very high levels of perceived difficulty where the need to avoid failure results in only small inhibitions, and weakest for budgets of intermediate difficulty where the need to avoid failure exerts its strongest impact. Yet in practice, those intermediate budgets may well be the ones which are associated with the overly negative use of budgets as pressure devices! Studies made of the operation of management-by-objectives schemes provide some support for this pattern of relationships.[27]

Budgets can be used as targets, but the numerous practical problems emphasise that this is far from being a simple mechanical activity for which commensense is a sufficient guide. Careful consideration needs to be given not only to the nature of the task but also to the

Figure 3.5 Relationship between degree of budget difficulty and performance when the motive for achievement is less than the motive to avoid failure

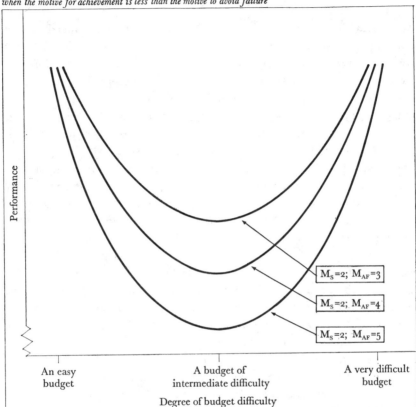

personalities and needs of the individual managers, the way in which budgets are used and the social climate which they create, and the other purposes served by the budgeting system. Such requirements make it into a much more demanding endeavour, but without due care, purposes can conflict and budgets which are intended to stimulate active performance can have the very opposite effect.*

* When used as targets, budgets are at least designed to stimulate managers' achievement needs and this has been recognised in the above discussion. However, success in the budgetary context can also satisfy other needs, such as those for social status and approval. The reader who is interested in considering the effects which such needs might have on the role of budgets should consult the studies by Atkinson and O'Connor, and Crocket.

3.6 *Conclusion*

Not all facets of budgeting have been investigated in this chapter. As yet little direct consideration has been given to the foundation which budgets provide for feedback and review. Nor have we explored the manner in which they are used to distribute uncertainty around the organisation and both of these are important. It should also be clear that there are many unsolved problems in budgeting. Although partial, the discussion has however tried to instil some awareness of the real complexity of the budgetary process and the need for a wider perspective.

Budgeting is concerned with human action, yet despite the significance of its behavioural, political and social dimensions, I am continually amazed by the dominant technical treatment which still pervades most discussions of the subject in management accounting textbooks. If the essential human nature of the process had no implications for the technical procedures, perhaps less would be lost, but this is not the case. Budgeting, and for that matter, all other management accounting procedures can never be viewed in technical isolation. Their effectiveness depends on merging technical and behavioural insights.

3.7 *References*

1. I do not propose to discuss the present state of budgetary procedures since there is no shortage of useful and comprehensive discussions. See, for instance:
   BEYER, R, *Profitability Accounting for Planning and Control*, Ronald Press, 1963
   KNIGHT, W D and WEINWURM, E H, *Managerial Budgeting*, MacMillan, 1964
   EDEY, H C, *Business Budgets and Accounts*, Hutchinson, 1966
   More recent developments in the governmental sector, particularly in the United States, are discussed in:
   SCHICK, A, *Budget Innovation in the States*, The Brookings Institution, 1971
   STEISS, A W, *Public Budgeting and Management*, Lexington Books, 1972
2. RICHARDSON, K, 'Weinstock's 1000 Days', *The Sunday Times*, July 18, 1971.
3. See, for instance:
   LYONS, T F, 'Role Clarity, Need for Clarity, Satisfaction, Tension and Withdrawal', *Organisational Behaviour and Human Performance*, vol 6 no 1, 1971 pp 99–110, and for a budgetary example:
   HOPWOOD, A G, 'An Empirical Study of the Role of Accounting Data in Performance Evaluation', *Empirical Research in Accounting: Selected Studies*, 1972
4. See, for instance:
   BAUMOL, W J, *Business Behaviour, Value and Growth*, revised edition, Harcourt Brace, 1967

LITNER, J, 'Optimum or Maximum Corporate Growth Under Uncertainty', in:
MARRIS, R, and WOOD, A, *The Corporate Economy: Growth, Competition and Innovative Power*, Macmillan, 1971
MARRIS, R, *The Economic Theory of 'Managerial Capitalism'*, Macmillan, 1964
Much of this literature is coherently surveyed in:
WILDSMITH, J R, *Managerial Theories of the Firm*, Martin Robertson, 1973

5. DENT, J K, 'Organizational Correlates of the Goals of Business Management', *Personnel Psychology*, vol 12, no 3, Autumn 1959, pp 365–94

6. See, for instance:
LIEBERSON, S and O'CONNOR, J F, 'Leadership and Organizational Performance: A Study of Large Corporations', *American Sociological Review*, vol 37, no 2, April 1972, pp 117–30

7. SOELBERG, P, 'Structure for Individiual Goals: Implications for Organizations Theory', in: FISK, G, (ed.), *The Psychology of Management Decision*, CWK Gleerup Publishers, 1967, pp 15–31

8. MARCH, J G and SIMON, H A, *Organizations*, John Wiley and Sons, 1958, Also see Simon's later discussion of the problem in:
SIMON, H A, 'On the Concept of Organizational Goal', *Administrative Science Quarterly*, vol 9, no 1, June 1964, pp 1–22

9. See, for instance:
CROZIER, M, *The Bureaucratic Phenomenon*, Tavistock, 1964
HICKSON, D J, HININGS, C R, LEE, D A, SCHNECK, R E and PENNINGS, J M, 'A Strategic Contingencies Theory of Intraorganizational Power', *Administrative Science Quarterly*, vol 16, no 2, June 1971, pp 216–29
MECHANIC, D, 'Sources of Power of Lower Participants in Complex Organizations', *Administrative Science Quarterly*, vol 7, pp 349–64

10. There have been remarkably few studies of the process of budgeting as distinct from the effects of budgets on managerial and employee behaviour. The available studies have also concentrated on budgeting in governmental agencies in the United States. The interested reader can consult:
WILDAVSKY, A, *The Politics of the Budgetary Process*, Little, Brown and Company, 1964
CRECINE, J P, 'Defense Budgeting: Organizational Adaptation to Environmental Constraints', in: BYRNE, R F *et al*, *Studies in Budgeting*, North-Holland, 1971, pp 210–61
PORTER, D O, *The Politics of Budgeting Federal Aid*, Sage Professional Papers in Administrative and Policy Studies, Sage Publications 1973
Short studies of the budgetary process in business organisations are reported in:
LOWE, E A and SHAW, R W, 'An Analysis of Managerial Biasing: Evidence from a Company's Budgeting Process', *The Journal of Management Studies*, vol 5, no 3, October 1968, pp 304–315
SCHIFF, M, and LEWIN, A. Y, 'The Impact of People on Budgets', *The Accounting Review*, vol 45, no 2, April 1970, pp 259–68

11. DAVIS, O A, DEMPSTER, M A H and WILDAVSKY, A, 'On the Process of Budgeting: An Empirical Study of Congressional Appropriations', *Papers on Nonmarket Decision Making*, vol 1, 1966, pp 63–132

    DAVIS, O A, DEMPSTER, M A H and WILDAVSKY, A, 'On the Process of Budgeting II: An Empirical Study of Congressional Appropriations', in: BYRNE, R F, *Studies in Budgeting*, North-Holland, 1971, pp 292–375

12. CRECINE, J P, *Governmental Problem Solving*, Rand-McNally, 1969

13. SCHWAN, C C, 'The Behavioural Aspects of Accounting Data for Performance Evaluations at Industrial Nucleonics', in: BURNS, T J, (ed), *The Behavioural Aspects of Accounting Data for Performance Evaluation*, College of Administrative Science, The Ohio State University, 1970, p 101

14. LIKERT, R, *The Human Organization*, McGraw-Hill, 1967

    MCGREGOR, D, *The Human Side of Enterprise*, McGraw-Hill, 1960

15. KAY E, FRENCH, J R P and MEYER, H, *A Study of the Performance Appraisal Interview*, Management Development and Employee Services, General Electric, 1962, p1

16. See the review in:

    LOCKE, E A, 'Toward a Theory of Task Motivation and Incentives', *Organizational Behaviour and Human Performance*, vol 3, no 2, October 1968, pp 157–89

17. STEDRY, A C, *Budget Control and Cost Behaviour*, Prentice-Hall, 1960

    STEDRY, A C, 'Aspiration Levels, Attitudes and Performance in a Goal-Oriented Situation', *Industrial Management Review*, vol 3, no 2, 1962, pp 60–76

18. See, for instance:

    LEWIN, K, DEMBO, T T, FESTINGER, L and SEARS, P S, 'Level of Aspiration', in: HUNT, J. M (ed), *Personality and the Behaviour Disorders*, Ronald Press, 1944, pp 333–78

    EDWARDS, W, 'The Theory of Decision Making', *Psychological Bulletin*, vol 51, 1954, pp 380–417.

    STARBUCK, W H, 'Level of Aspiration', *Psychological Review*, vol 70, no 1, 1963, pp 51–60

    VROOM, V H, *Work and Motivation*, John Wiley and Sons, 1964

19. MCCLELLAND, D C, *The Achieving Society*, Van Nostrand-Reinhold, 1961

20. ATKINSON, J W and FEATHER, N T, *A Theory of Achievement Motivation*, John Wiley and Sons, 1966, especially, pp 3–9, and 329–70

21. MAHONE, C H, 'Fear of Failure and Unrealistic Vocational Aspiration', *Journal of Abnormal and Social Psychology*, vol 60, March 1960, pp 253–61

    MORGAN, J N, 'The Achievement Motive and Economic Behaviour', *Economic Development and Cultural Change*, vol 12, 1964, pp 243–67

    O'CONNOR, P, ATKINSON, J W and HORNER, M, 'Motivational Implications of Ability Grouping in Schools', in: ATKINSON, J W, and FEATHER, N T, *A Theory of Achievement Motivation*, John Wiley and Sons, 1966, pp 231–48

    CROCKETT, H J, 'The Achievement Motive and Differential Occupational

Mobility in the United State's, *American Sociological Review*, vol 27, no 00, 1962, pp 191–204

22. HOFSTEDE, G H, *The Game of Budget Control*, Van Gorcum, 1967, pp 144–72

23. Atkinson anticipated a relationship between an individual's motive structure and his subjective estimates of the probability of success. Achievement oriented individuals were expected to give an upwardly biased estimate, and failure oriented individuals, a downwardly biased estimate. Hence the point of maximum achievement motivation for the former would be where the objective probability of success is somewhat lower than 0.50, and the maximum failure avoidance motivation for the latter, where the objective probability of success is somewhat higher than 0.50. See:
    ATKINSON, J W, 'Motivational Determinants of Risk-taking Behaviour', *Psychological Review*, vol 64, no 6, 1957, pp 359–72

24. STEDRY, A C and KAY, E, 'The Effects of Goal Difficulty on Performance: A Field Experiment', *Behavioural Science*, vol 11, no 6, November 1966, pp 459–70

25. STEDRY, A C, *Budget Control and Cost Behaviour*, Prentice-Hall, 1960

26. ARGYRIS, C, *The Impact of Budgets on People*, The School of Business and Public Administration, Cornell University, 1952, p 6

27. See:
    CARROLL, S J and TOSI, H L, *Management by Objectives: Applications and Research*, Macmillan, 1973
    KOLB, D A and BOYATZIS, R E, 'Goal-Setting and Self-Directed Behaviour Change', *Human Relations*, vol 23, no 5, October 1970, pp 439–57

CHAPTER FOUR

Participation
in
the Budgetary Process

The general debate on participation is one of the most significant and contentious debates of our time. The increasing number of people who are stressing the need for further participation are vitally concerned with the wider human welfare, valuing internally generated change over externally imposed change. Because they consider it desirable to reduce power differences between various levels in society, in organisations and even in small working groups, they place equal if not greater emphasis on human development and fulfillment than on productivity and more narrowly conceived criteria of organisational effectiveness. Many manage to unnecessarily exaggerate the causal relationship between the two as if not satisfied with the force of their own arguments. These arguments will, however, by emphasising the relationship between work in organisations and the society in which they operate, do much to shape our social consciousness and the nature of political debate in our more highly educated and personally sensitive society.

It is a big step from the consideration of such lofty arguments to an investigation of the role of participation in the budgetary process, although many of these more narrowly conceived arguments are equally polemical, even though their frame of reference is so very different. Increasingly, however, budgeting is being seen in much wider terms than a mere technique and procedure. It is being seen as part of a process which both influences, and in turn is influenced by, managerial and employee attitudes and behaviours. The need for the involvement, the commitment, and not least, the participation of the lower members of the organisation is viewed as a vital feature of these more modern approaches to budgeting. Indeed, there is a widespread belief, and belief is the appropriate term, that the participation of subordinates in setting their budgets is a panacea: a cure for all the many ills which have been associated with traditional budgetary systems.

Unfortunately, the arguments in favour of participation have been so varied and so vague that one might justifiably question what useful purposes such a concept is capable of serving. In ranging from an open process of group decision making to a process of consultation under the strict supervision of the more powerful, from a radical plan of action, through the soft and the sentimental to a scheming manipulative intent, it appears that participation can mean almost anything to anyone. In addition, the debate has often been carried on in terms of black versus white, with ideas converted into ideology and inquiry into dogma. We hear of participation versus hierarchical control, theory X versus theory Y, people versus organisation, democratic versus autocratic management, and so on. Until recently, there have been few systematic investigations of the subject and even fewer specifically concerned with participation in the budgetary process. Arguments are, however, rarely constrained by lack of evidence and even where evidence has been provided, the emotional and value overtones of many of the studies has often interfered with rational dialogue and the careful interpretation of the empirical findings. This is perhaps inevitable, and not necessarily undesirable when one considers the significance of the issue, although it is important to be aware of the distinction.

In this chapter we examine some of the available studies in an attempt to appraise the current state of knowledge. Few deal with the specifics of the budgetary process, although the findings of the more general studies are no less relevant in this particular context. The first section considers a body of literature which has emphasised the relationship between participation and the implementation of decisions, often interpreting the findings in terms of commitment, motivation and involvement. Later sections turn to other studies which although concerned with these issues have paid more attention to the impact which participation can have on the quality of decisions.

4.1 *Participation and the Implementation of Decisions*

It has long been recognised that many seemingly ideal solutions to organisational problems have been ineffective because they have been resisted by the people who have had to implement them.[1] Therefore it should not be surprising that many discussions of participation in decision making, as well as a lot of the managerial interest in the subject, have focused on the possibility that subordinate participation increases the probability that decisions will be effectively implemented.

Bass and Leavitt, in a series of experiments on planning, clearly demonstrated the importance of involving managers in planning and budgeting.[2] They devised a series of exercises in which groups of three managers developed a plan for themselves and then exchanged plans with another group. Each group therefore had two plans, one self developed and another created for them. Then moving to the implementation of the plans, half the groups operated their own plan first and half operated their own plan second. The results of the experiments showed that the managers were both more productive and more satisfied with their job and colleagues when operating their own plans. The managers experienced a great sense of accomplishment when they were implementing their own plans and they also had a greater commitment to making them work. They were trying, in other words, to make them become self fulfilling prophesies. In addition, after formulating the plans they had a greater understanding of their requirements and difficulties and as a result there were fewer communication problems and consequent errors in following instructions. In a changing environment, this could result in more rapid modifications and adjustments to the plans. Finally, when the managers were implementing their own plans, less time was wasted on competition between the planners and the doers.

Despite such apparent advantages, caution is required before too readily accepting and generalising the participative philosophy from the experimental context to the complexities of organisational life. One of the early studies of the phenomenon which usefully illustrates many of the problems, the inherent values and the state of the evidence, was conducted by Coch and French in an American pyjama manufacturing company.[3]

Four groups of workers who were of approximately equal efficiency before the study and who were just about to undergo comparable changes in their work methods were used in the experimental study. In one group,

Figure 4.1 The effect of participation on productivity

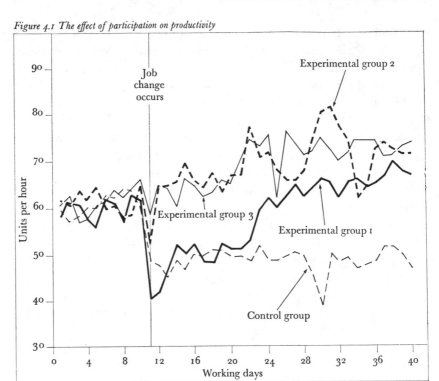

the change in work methods was introduced in the usual way. The jobs were redesigned by the production department, new rates were set and the workers were simply informed of the change. The other three groups were given an opportunity to participate in some aspects of the change. In one group, experimental group 1, the workers were permitted to influence the change through representatives. In the other two groups, experimental groups 2 and 3, each worker was allowed to directly participate in influencing the nature of the change. In comparison with a prechange standard of sixty units per hour, the productivity of the control group followed previous experience in the company, dropping to fifty units after the introduction of the change with little subsequent improvement. The results are shown in Figure 4.1. The productivity of the group who participated through their representatives, experimental group 1, also fell as soon as they started to work on the new job, but subsequently improved and stabilised at a little over the prechange level. The most favourable performance was achieved by the two groups, experimental groups 2 and 3, who had participated more directly in the change programme. These two groups quickly recovered their prechange level of productivity and thereafter continued to improve until they finally achieved a 14 per cent improvement over the original rate. In addition, to reinforce the impact of the participative programme, 17 per cent of the control group subsequently left their jobs while there was no turnover in any of the experimental groups.

There are many similar studies, but rather than describing them in detail, I will use this famous study by Coch and French as an example of the difficulties involved in generalising such results. First, one has to seriously question how much participation was allowed and the reasons for favouring the scheme. A clue is provided by the title of their study: 'Overcoming Resistance to Change'. There was, in fact, very little participation. The influence on the change was confined to relatively minor matters within a context which was already tightly specified by management. It is easy to think of the arguments in favour of participative approaches to management as always being directed towards a more equal distribution of power and influence in organisations. In fact, many of the traditional social science views either ignore or play down the patterns of dominance, power structures and the potential for conflict between different groups, and some times they perpetuate or even reinforce the very inequalities they pretend to overcome. In these latter situations, the procedures of participation are used to induce people to have the feeling of participation in situations which provide little freedom. In the Coch and French study, for instance, the problem was one of getting people to do what management wanted them to do. The solution was assumed to be known and only its implementation was problematic.

Even a small amount of influence might be viewed very favourably by subordinates if the previous approaches had been highly authoritarian, and there is some evidence that they were extremely so in the pyjama factory studied by Coch and French. Would such a slight amount of influence produce similar results in another less authoritarian organisation or with people who are a little less conservative or who have a greater tradition of working class militancy than the semi-rural workers who were the focus of this study? One also wonders whether the findings of such studies are even transferable to the same organisation on subsequent occasions, or for that matter, how long the improvements lasted. The answers to these and many other similar questions are in most cases still problematic, although by raising them, the nature of the argument starts to change. Rather than looking for general effects, we are starting to inquire into the nature of the underlying processes and the conditions which influence the outcomes of participative endeavours.

In another study which was designed to replicate the original French and Coch experiment in a different national setting, French and his associates did indeed find quite different results.[4] There was no difference in productivity between workers who did and those who did not participate in the design of the change programme, a finding which the authors attributed to the different cultural values prevailing in Norway. A more recent experiment by Fleishman raises further questions about the generality of the Coch and French findings.[5] He found that the productivity of workers who only had representative participation was identical, for the tasks which he was considering, to that of those who had direct participation. Finally, to further complicate the issue, Morse and Reimer compared the effects of two change programmes in a large clerical organisation.[6] One of the programmes involved increased participation in decision making by the clerks, while the other involved increased hierarchical control. The participation group had a higher level of morale and greater involvement in their job, but productivity significantly increased under both programmes with the greatest increase resulting from the hierarchically controlled programme.*

The reconciliation of such discrepant findings, and these are only a small sample of both viewpoints, is a far from an easy task. It is not

* You should realise, however, that the debate on participation is an area where values can often be more certain than empirical evidence. So much so, that you should always examine the findings of any study very carefully before accepting the conclusions. What a number of studies gain in persuasiveness, they loose in objectivity, especially when the authors have themselves been employed as consultants. Many authors, and their associates and fellow travellers, have a disconcerting habit of concluding despite their findings. For instance, two commentators on the rather equivocal Morse and Reimer study were able to state that 'the human resources of the [hierarchically controlled] divisions were being dissipated, and productivity would very likely begin to fall, although the experiment was not continued long enough to test this conclusion'. Such comments are not untypical in this area.

made any easier by the many meanings which have been attached to the idea of participation, the different motives which have been behind its introduction and the variety of settings in which the studies have been conducted. While it appears that an increase in participation in decision making can often improve morale, its effect on productivity is equivocal at the best, increasing it under some circumstances but possibly even decreasing it under other circumstances. The practical problem is in trying to identify which conditional factors determine the wider impact of a particular type of participative management programme. Here the emotionally charged nature of the debate has left its toll. Many researchers, like many of their managerial associates, have been concerned with the broad overall problem of either proving or disproving the general argument rather than specifying the conditions for various results. Like many interesting ideas, the believers feel that they are universally applicable.

4.2 *Some Factors Influencing the Impact of Participation in Decision Making*
In considering the conditional factors which influence the impact of participation we look at both the level of the individual manager and at the organisation, with the latter characterised in terms of both its technology and environment, and the patterns of internal social relationships.

At the individual level, we know that not all managers and employees are concerned with participating in either decisions which immediately affect their own personal interests or in the determination of wider organisational policies. Using measures of the extent to which workers felt that they participated in decisions related to their work, Vroom found that personality characteristics such as authoritarianism and the need for independence significantly affected the relationship between participation, and morale and effectiveness.[7] Highly authoritarian people with a low need for independence were unaffected by participative approaches. In a field study conducted in the Netherlands, Hofstede found similar results in the budgetary context.[8] Greater satisfaction might therefore be obtained when both superior and subordinate expectations are identical, with authoritarian supervisors in charge of subordinates with authoritarian expectations and more participative supervisors in charge of subordinates who are more appreciative of participative approaches.[9]

At the organisational level it is necessary to consider the effect which different work situations can have on the impact and scope of participative management programmes. In highly programmed, environmentally and technologically constrained areas, where speed and detailed control are essential for efficiency, participative approaches may have much less to offer from the point of view of the more economic aspects of organisational effectiveness, although perhaps no less from the point of view of morale. In contrast, in areas where flexibility, innovation and the capacity to deal with unanticipated problems are important, participation in decision making may offer a more immediate and more narrowly economic payoff than more authoritarian styles. Numerous studies support the notion that sophisticated and advanced technologies influence organisational behaviour in the direction of more participative approaches to management and it may well be that at least some of the advocates of participation have been stimulated by these developments.[10] The trend in such industries is for the nature of supervision to change, with managers doing less of their more traditional duties, acting more as facilitators and communication links for the work group, and liaising with interdependent units. There is at least the suggestion that participative change programmes are both facilitated and make a greater impact in this type of organisation because the changes are compatible with the requirements of the technology.[11] It could be that regardless of the social, political and educational pressures working towards more open styles of management, as technology continues to advance, the ideas of participative management will have more meaning and application.

Finally, it is not possible to consider the impact of a participative management programme without also considering the wider patterns of social relationship which help to shape people's expectations and beliefs. There is, for example, considerable evidence of definite national and cultural differences in both managerial preferences for, and the effectiveness of, different styles of management, participative and otherwise,[12] and it would be naïve to advocate, as many unfortunately do, one style of decision making as being optimal for all cultural groups. Within the organisation there are known to be problems in introducing a participative approach at only one level of management. In a study which involved several hundred managers and several thousand non-supervisory employees, Pelz found that the amount of influence which a manager felt he had with his own superior affected the response of his subordinates to his own approach to management.[13] When managers who had above average influence with their own superiors practised a more participative management style, their subordinates tended to react favourably. But when managers who had below average influence with their own superiors practised similar approaches to management, they usually failed to achieve any favourable reactions, and not infrequently, obtained an adverse reaction from their subordinates. Subordinates expect their superiors to at least be able to exercise similar influence upwards, for without this, not only is the rationale and purpose questionable, but the manager might not be able to meet his subordinates' expectations for supplies, working conditions, pay and promotions.

Furthermore, when a manager's behaviour changes radically so that it conflicts with his previous behaviour patterns and peoples conception of his personality, his behaviour is unlikely to have the effect he intends. Subordinates tend to view such changes with suspicion, looking for signs of their authenticity. An illustration of just how important this can be was provided by one of the few studies which has considered the effects of both the level of participation which subordinates usually have in setting their job objectives, financial and otherwise, and the increase in participation resulting from a change programme. French, Kay and Meyer found that the usual level of participation was positively related to mutual understanding, acceptance of job objectives, attitudes towards the appraisal system and occupational self-fulfillment, and that in general, an increase in participation resulted in better superior–subordinate relationships.[14] A full appreciation of the change in participation could only be obtained by looking at its relationship with the usual level. With a high usual level of participation, a further increase resulted in a favourable effect on subsequent job performance. However, if the subordinates had experienced a low usual level of participation, and especially if this was associated with a high degree of threat in the job appraisal sessions, the change programme had a strong negative effect on subsequent job performance.

Tantalisingly, the reasons are not so clear as the effects, although it would seem that the changes in management style were viewed in a relative sense, with the usual patterns of relationships serving as a benchmark. Apparently, an increase in participation which was in conflict with a manager's previous approach was seen as unauthentic, worthy of some suspicion and perhaps even threatening. This view was reinforced by a comparison of the subordinates' performance in relation to the job objectives which they established themselves and those imposed by their superiors. With a generally high usual level of participation, job performance was better on objectives which subordinates had set themselves, but with a low usual level of participation, performance was better on the job objectives which had been established and imposed by the superior.

Inauthentic participation can result in neither a reduction of resistance to change nor higher levels of efficiency, but rather the direct satisfaction of personal objectives. Within the budgetary context, while participation can at times result in higher motivation and commitment, it can also enable the setting of easier standards and more generous budgets if the wider patterns of social relationships are at variance with the idea of authentic participation. In the words of one manager who was under considerable pressure to meet his budget, regardless of circumstances:

> 'We had unrealistic production allowances in the budget last year, but I got them adjusted a bit. It's done by the industrial engineers and the accountants, but I have a bit to say in it. Some are too slack now, but they are very workable. There is never a perfect standard. The industrial engineers are back in the caveman era. Well, if there is going to be some imperfections, why not have them in my favour? We can modify them and we have done quite well. Why should I beat myself?'

Yet much of the existing literature, especially, one might add, in the accounting area, seems to encourage a variety of inauthentic participation 'How to get your people involved' is a frequent rallying cry, with little comment on how, or why, or involved in what. At best, it wrestles fairly effectively with questions of affect and involvement and there is no doubt that participation can be counterfeited and prior to its detection it may lead to higher morale.[15] However, if managers want to increase the quality of decisions or improve the transfer of information within the organisation or even to train their subordinates, then counterfeiting a variety of 'pseudo-participation' will not be of value. For the value of participation in these circumstances does not depend on producing a feeling of participation; it depends upon the activity of participation itself.

4.3 *Participation and the Quality of Decisions*

The amount of influence given to subordinates in the decision making process is capable of having an important effect on the nature of the decisions reached. A manager who makes a decision on his own may select a different course of action than if he consulted with his subordinates prior to making the decision, and both of these courses of action may differ from that which would result from a group decision. Possibly the most consistent evidence that decisions made jointly by a group of people do indeed differ qualitatively from individual decisions is provided by an extensive series of experiments on risk taking by individuals and by groups of people. Contrary to the popular stereotype of committee or group decisions being cautious and conservative, the results of these studies indicate that a group tends to select a riskier course of action than would have been chosen by the average member of the group.[16] The phenomenon is known as the 'risky-shift', and while at present there is some controversy over the underlying reasons, with explanations varying from diffusion of responsibility to the group eliciting values which favour risk, it is clear that under many circumstances groups select courses of action with higher payoffs and lower probabilities of success than the average individual.

While group decisions may be riskier than many individual decisions, what evidence is there that they are better decisions in an organisational sense? In order to answer this question it is necessary to consider research which has compared the solutions of groups and individuals to problems which have correct solutions, or on which reasonably objective judgments can be made concerning the relative quality of different solutions. Lorge and his associates have reviewed this literature in great detail and found a very frequent, although not unanimous, tendency for the average quality of decisions reached by groups to be greater than the average quality of decisions made by individuals.[17] The better results for groups were found to be due, in part, to the fact that a larger variety of information and problem solving capabilities were brought to bear on problem solving in groups, and in part from the fact that the individuals were interacting with one another during the problem solving process, commenting, appraising and jointly building up novel courses of action. Even so, these findings still do not justify the conclusion that the quality of decisions arrived at by groups is always preferable to that obtained by individual decision makers. The evidence suggests that the average quality of group decisions exceeds the average group member's own conclusions, but managers, at least, should be selected because they are considered to be above average. So yet again a reconciliation is required, and again this is achieved by focusing on the conditions for high quality decisions.

4.4 *Some Further Factors Influencing the Impact of Participation*

First of all, it is necessary to consider differences in access to relevant information. In the extreme situation where a manager possesses all the information necessary for the solution of a problem and knows how to use the information, encouraging subordinates to participate in making the decision is not likely to improve the immediate solution. At the other extreme, however, if the information necessary for the solution is widely dispersed among group members and no single person, including the senior manager, possesses more than a small amount, participation by subordinates is necessary to attain a high quality solution.

The importance of seeing participation as one part of a process by which information is communicated and exchanged within organisations was suggested by a study of the use of budgetary data in managerial performance evaluation.[18] We return to consider the findings of this study in greater detail in the next chapter, so at this stage, it is sufficient to say that one group of managers were being rigidly evaluated on the basis of how well they met their budget. Yet, as any accountant would expect, the budgetary system being used contained, like many others, a number of imperfections which were capable of systematically biasing the reported budget variances and thereby, the evaluations received by the managers. It was important to look at how these imperfections affected the managers being evaluated, in terms of the amount of tension and anxiety which they experienced on the job, and how participation in setting their budgets influenced the outcome.

Participation was found to exert a significant effect. With only minimal participation, the imperfections in the budgetary system served to heighten the tensions engendered by the rigid evaluative use of the budget reports but when the subordinate managers were allowed to participate in setting their budgets, many of the problems were 'thrashed out at the meetings'. As the supervisors became aware of them in this way, they apparently started to adjust their evaluative behaviour. For with participation, the imperfections in the system were either not related to tension or even, as less concern was rigidly given to the budgetary reports, negatively related.

Viewing participation as a mechanism for information exchange means that the degree of participation should vary, depending upon the circumstances, not only from decision to decision but also from organisation to organisation. There should, for instance, be a much greater need for participation when decision situations are heterogeneous and when managers have a greater variety of tasks. In particular, some degree of participation should offer greater advantages in situations of change and uncertainty where new information is continually needed, than in more stable situations where managers can rely to a much greater extent on the insights gained on from their own previous experiences. Lawrence and Lorsch, in what is perhaps one of the most significant studies of organisational behaviour undertaken in recent years, clearly demonstrated the effect that change and uncertainty have on participation.[19] In a comparative study undertaken in a variety of industrial contexts, they considered the forms of organisational arrangements which contributed to effective performance. Where the organisation had to cope with great uncertainty either in the market-place or in the technology underlying the product, as for instance in the packaged food and plastics industries, the organisational structures adopted by the successful firms were designed to facilitate the flow of information both horizontally and vertically. The result, as illustrated by the diagram of the distribution of influence over different hierarchical levels shown in Figure 4.2, is that the lower-level and middle-level managers who had the necessary technical insights seemed to have as much influence on decisions as their top-level superiors. In the more certain container industry, on the other hand, where the information required to make decisions was available to senior managers, the successful firms were more hierarchically organised. And as can be seen in the diagram, influence on decision making was more concentrated at senior management levels.

However, although the possession of relevant information and the ability to use it are important requirements for achieving high quality decisions, they are not sufficient. The quality of decisions also depends on the motivation to use the information in line with organisational require-

Figure 4.2 Distribution of influence in three high performing organisations

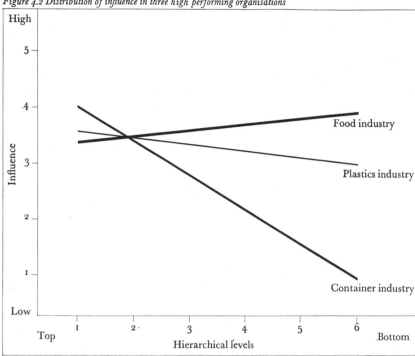

ments. For although participation may result in an exchange of information, its accuracy is known to be dependent upon the motives of the lower
level managers and their perceptions of the wider patterns of social
relationships in the organisation. For instance, in a field study conducted
in three major industrial companies, Read found that there was a significant negative relationship between a manager's desire for promotion and
the accuracy of his communications with his superior about major job
problems.[20] Ambitious subordinates withheld information that was
potentially threatening to their promotion prospects, reporting the good
news but failing to report the bad news. However, this effect was substantially dependent upon whether the subordinates trusted their
superiors. With a high degree of trust, the negative relationship was
significantly reduced.

    Furthermore, there are many situations in which the organisational
purposes, stated in terms of senior management objectives, are in conflict

with the desires and interests of individuals and groups at lower and middle levels of the organisation. For instance, the ideal decision from a senior management point of view may be to bring in an outsider rather than promote from inside, to tighten performance standards, eliminate jobs or close down a factory. If these really are the decisions which are required, further participation by the people involved may not improve their quality unless lower-level managers are able to present new inform-ation which either provides the basis for an even more appropriate solution or persuade the senior managers to change their objectives.

4.5 The Actual and the Desirable

The conditional perspective which we have outlined has tended so far to be normative in nature; that is, participation appears to be more desirable under some organisational and personal conditions than under others. The persuasiveness of the arguments would undoubtedly be increased if it was known that effective managers already adopted, at least in part, a conditional viewpoint, tending to vary their style of decision making with changes in circumstances.

Recent evidence suggests that managers do just this. In a study refreshingly different from other investigations in this area, Heller, rather than investigating the results of a contrived change in participation focused on the relationship between a series of situational factors and the extent to which subordinates were encouraged to participate in decision making.[21] Participation was not characterised in terms of an either-or dichotomy, or even the degree of overall influence, but rather as a con-tinuum of decision behaviours ranging from a manager making his own decisions without explanation or prior consultation at one end of the scale to complete delegation at the other end. Studying the behaviour of 260 senior managers in fifteen large and successful American companies, Heller found that the degree of participation used depended upon five broad circumstantial factors. First, participation was more likely to be used for decisions affecting lower levels of personnel rather than immediate subordinates and for decisions having greater importance for the sub-ordinate than for the company. An element of cautiousness was obviously present. Second, possibly because of the different requirements of their tasks, general managers and personnel managers tended to use more participative approaches than production and finance managers, with sales and purchasing executives lying in between. Third, because of the greater time which participative approaches often require they tended to be used less frequently as the number of subordinates increased. Fourth, probably because of the different nature of higher management jobs, the different capabilities of subordinates and the different values concerning appropriate levels of influence, there was a tendency for senior managers to allow greater subordinate participation. And fifth, when the senior managers had been on the job for a considerable period of time they tended to allow even greater participation. At more junior levels experience on the job had the reverse effect, possibly reflecting the important role which personal motives and aspirations can play in the process.

Although managers appear to vary their style of decision making according to circumstances, we also know that they are often reluctant to fully adjust to the situation. So, in consequence, the normative conditional perspective tends to suggest greater variations in decision behaviour than most managers voluntarily practise. This problem and its implications for effective organisational behaviour, has recently encouraged Vroom and Yetton to develop a way of helping managers to adapt their behaviour to the demands of the situation.[22] They suggest a framework for analysing both decision situations and the available approaches to decision making, participative and otherwise, and a means for suggesting the appropriate decision process for any problem. Undoubtedly, these are early days for such procedures, but progress is likely to come from the blend of descriptive study and normative analysis upon which this pioneering attempt is based.

4.6 *Participation and the Stage of the Problem Solving Process*

While we have been concerned with identifying the outline of a framework for viewing participation in a more conditional sense, the actual problem solving and decision process has still been seen as a whole. There is, however, some evidence which suggests that participative approaches may be most advantageous at particular stages of the process, while they may even be disadvantageous at other stages.

One study found that group decision-making procedures inhibited the generation of alternative solutions to problems. Taylor, Berry and Block[23] compared the performance, in terms of the number of alternative solutions generated for a series of problems in a fixed period of time, of twelve real four-man groups whose members interacted with one another, and twelve nominal four-man groups whose members worked completely separately. The results showed that for all the problems that they worked on, the nominal groups produced a greater number of different solutions and a larger number of high quality solutions. Replications of the experiment supported the view that group interaction, particularly when one member of the group has a higher status, is capable of inhibiting the creative phase of the problem solving process. On the other hand, a number of studies have found that group decision making may be advantageous in evaluating alternative courses of action.[24] The group discussion has the potential of serving as an error correcting mechanism, although whether the potential is realised may still be problematic for in a group reaching agreement or winning the argument are often confused with finding the right answer. Minority opinions can easily have little influence, despite their quality. Individuals can dominate group discussions through sheer talkativeness, persuasive ability, status, position, or even stubborn persistence, and since none of these factors have any necessary relationship to decision quality, influence patterns in groups can exert a significant affect on the final solution.

There is substantial evidence which suggests that the skills of the senior manager or group leader are crucial in this respect.[25] Rather than trying to evaluate at too early a stage, he must be sensitive to unexpressed feelings, receptive to ideas, assume responsibility for accurate communications and be able to restate an idea concisely and accurately. He must, if his influence is to be used to gain high quality solutions, serve as an integrator, concentrating on group process as well as the final outcome. Many senior managers do not, however, function in this way, and in many so-called participative situations, status and power differences are visible and their impact is very strong. This is one area, however, where the means for improvement are known; the problem lies in their implementation.

4.7 *Conclusion*

It is simply naïve to think that participative approaches are always more effective than more authoritarian styles of management or vice versa. The participation of managers and employees in the budgetary process, for instance, can do much to increase their acceptance of the budget, their subsequent involvement and commitment, and the quality of the budget as an aid to decision making, but it can also have the opposite effects. The critics as well as the advocates of participative management would therefore be wise to direct their energies towards identifying the situations in which a variety of decision making styles are effective, rather than towards universalistic claims for the applicability or otherwise of any single approach.

However, even within the more modest and more realistic conditional framework which has been presented in this chapter, the evidence on many important points is at best equivocal. To take an extreme view, while the authoritarian may well reject much of the evidence as unfounded, looking at the same studies, the sincere believer in greater openness in our large organisations, might claim that many are constrained by an overly restrictive vision of the human potential. While the findings certainly leave room for improvement, they do, in my view, offer the outline of a useful framework for anyone, be they accountant or not, who is concerned with increasing participation while at the same time still considering more traditional criteria of organisational effectiveness. At a pragmatic level, the question becomes what degree of participation is appropriate, by whom, in a given area in order to improve the acceptance and quality of decision making? Although apparently cautious, this approach may well be capable in our complex and rapidly changing environment, of directing us towards changes no less radical than many alternative suggestions.

Although our discussion has been at a general level, phrased in terms of a wider decision making process, there is no reason to expect that the peculiarities of the budgetary situation impose any restrictions on its applicability in this area, above and beyond those suggested by the conditional framework which has been emphasised. It should be realised, however, that what many people mean by participation in the budgetary process usually takes place within a context which is very tightly constrained by top management policies, a multitude of environmental and technological factors, and the nature of the budgetary system itself, including the previous history of budgeted and actual performance. So as a postscript, I would like to leave you to ponder on the possibility of a much wider vision.

Discussions of participation in the budgetary process have invariably focused on the determination of the current budget level. Most practising managers and accountants assume that designing and operating an accounting and budgeting system must be a specialised task and that the accountant is the specialist for the job. In many cases he is, but the manager, whether he is a production, marketing, purchasing or any other specialist, is also the expert in managing the tasks, searching for alternative courses of action, making the requisite decisions and appraising the sources of relevant information. In terms of organisational effectiveness, it may well be that the real advantages lie not, for instance, in the specialist production manager making whatever use he can of the budgetary system designed by the accounting specialist. Effectiveness comes neither from accounting expertise nor production expertise in isolation, but from a blend of the two. It comes from an understanding of the relevance of accounting information for production management and of the crucial interrelationship between the accounting system and the production system.

Viewed in these terms, the design of a budgetary system and many of the important aspects of system operation, including much more than the annual determination of the budget itself, may need to be seen as joint exercises. In the words of one manager who had identified the need for change in his budgetary system:

'Accounting is a bit like electricity. The average guy won't go and touch a shorted wire. He doesn't know enough about it. A lot of people don't know that much about accounting and they don't get into it. An accountant will win argument after argument. They're pleased with the system because we are paying more attention to it. I'll give them credit; I am, but I think that there has to be more responsibility. If I am going to give it my time and make my organisation pay more attention to it, there has to be more effective responsibility on the behalf of the accountant'.

It is a little too easy to point out that line managers cannot understand existing accounting and budgetary systems, so what hope is there for ever achieving this wider vision? Perhaps the question begs the issue. Perhaps the lack of understanding is related to the inadequate link between the two systems. Similar arguments on a lack of understanding are frequently used at the shop floor level in relation to the design of incentive payment systems. Yet no one would deny the extensive evidence that understand or not, employees are quite capable of manipulating such complex systems to serve their own interests. Shimmin has stressed the importance of making a distinction between a 'formal' understanding and a 'functional' understanding.[26] A person with a formal understanding comprehends the mechanics of the accounting system and is able to give an accurate description of the system. We would hope that all accountants have such an understanding. A person with a functional understanding of the accounting system knows from experience how his own behaviour and the ebbs and flows of the production process are related to the accounting reports. He might not be able to give a precise description of how or why, but he may be able to use the accounting system for his own advantage. Very often the functional understanding of an accounting system possessed by a manager is a rich source of information on the vital relationship between the production process and its characterisation in accounting terms, and a useful basis for system review and change.

In addition, one cannot be but impressed by the unofficial information systems designed by many managers when it is their own interest. Although they range from the simple to the complex and from serving as supplements to the official accounting system to serving as self interested warning devices and clues for possible manipulations, they illustrate the ability and the potential for a wider basis for participation. As the management task grows in complexity, the experience and views of line managers must be seen as a valuable and essential source of inspiration and ideas for the design of accounting and budgeting systems themselves, as well as for the periodic statement of forthcoming events.

4.8 *References*

1. See, for instance:
   CHURCHMAN, C W, 'Managerial Acceptance of Scientific Recommendations', *California Management Review*, vol 7, no 1, Fall 1964, pp 31–8
2. BASS, B M and LEAVITT, H J, 'Experiments in Planning and Operating', *Management Science*, vol 9, no 4, 1963, pp 574–85
   In a further study, similar results were found in six different national groups, see:
   BASS, B M, 'When Planning for Others', *The Journal of Applied Behavioural Science*, vol 6, no 2, 1970, pp 151–71

3. COCH, L and FRENCH, J R P, 'Overcoming Resistance to Change', *Human Relations*, vol 1, no 4, October 1948, pp 512–32

4. FRENCH, J R P, ISRAEL, J and Ås, D, 'An Experiment on Participation in a Norwegian Factory', *Human Relations*, vol 13, no 1, February 1960, pp 1–13

5. FLEISHMAN, E A, 'Attitude Versus Skill Factors in Work Group Productivity', *Personnel Psychology*, vol 18, no 3, 1965, pp 253–66

6. MORSE, N, and REIMER, E, 'The Experimental Change of a Major Organizational Variable', *Jornal of Abnormal and Social Psychology*, vol 52, 1956, pp 120–9

7. VROOM, V, *Some Personality Determinants of the Effects of Participation*, Prentice-Hall, 1960.

8. HOFSTEDE, G, *The Game of Budget Control*, Van Gorcum, 1967

9. See, for instance:

   FOA, V G, 'Relation of Workers' Expectations to Satisfaction With Supervisors', *Personnel Psychology*, vol 10, 1957, pp 161–8

   HAYTHORNE, W, *et al*, 'The Effects of Varying Combinations of Authoritarian and Equalitarian Leaders and Followers', *Journal of Abnormal and Social Psychology*, vol 53, no 2, 1956, pp 210–19

   It should be pointed out however, that these findings are not amenable to an unequivocal interpretation if you are prepared to extend your time horizon and social frame of reference. It has been said that the lack of effect merely reflects a repressed personality or psychological withdrawal from the job which are themselves the result of an alienating culture rather than any inherent limitation on the scope of programmes for more radical change.

10. See:

    BLAUNER, R, *Alienation and Freedom*, The University of Chicago Press, 1964

    MANN, F C and HOFFMAN, L R, *Automation and the Worker*, Henry Holt, 1960

    WALKER, C R, *Toward The Automatic Factory*, Yale University Press, 1957

11. TAYLOR J C, 'Some Effects of Technology in Organizational Change', *Human Relations*, vol 24, no 2, April 1971, pp105–23

12. See:

    HAIRE, M, GHISELLI, E E and PORTER, L W, *Managerial Thinking: An International Study*, John Wiley and Sons, 1966

    MOUTON, J and BLAKE, R, 'Issues in Transnational Organization Development', in: BASS, B M, COOPER, R C, and HAAS, J A, (eds), *Managing for Accomplishment*, Heath Lexington, 1970, pp 208–24

13. PELZ, D C, 'Influence: a Key to Effective Leadership in the First-Line Supervisor', *Personnel*, November 1952, pp 3–11

14. FRENCH, J R P, KAY, E and MEYER, H H, 'Participation and the Appraisal System', *Human Relations*, vol 19, no 1, February 1966, pp 3–20

15. HOFFMAN, L R and MAIER, N R F, 'Quality and Acceptance of Problem Solutions by Members of Homogeneous and Heterogeneous Groups', *Journal of Abnormal and Social Psychology*, vol 62, 1961, pp 401–7

16. Reviews of this literature appear in:
    BROWN, R, *Social Psychology*, The Free Press, 1965, Chapter 13
    DION, K L, BARON, R S and MILLER, N, 'Why Do Groups Make Riskier Decisions Than Individuals?', in: BERKOWITZ, L, (ed), *Advances in Experimental Psychology*, vol 5, Academic Press, 1970
    KOGAN, N and WALLACH, M A, 'Risk Taking as a Function of the Situation, the Person and the Group', in: MANDLER, G, *et al*, *New Directions in Psychology III*, Holt, Rinehart and Winston, 1967

17. LORGE, I, FOX, D, DAVITZ, J and BRENNER, M, 'A Survey of Studies Contrasting the Quality of Group Performance and Individual Performance: 1930–1957', *Psychology Bulletin*, vol 55, 1958, pp 337–72

18. HOPWOOD, A G, *An Accounting System and Managerial Behaviour*, Saxon House, 1973, pp 136–66

19. LAWRENCE, P R and LORSCH, J W, *Organization and Environment*, Graduate School of Business Administration, Harvard University, 1967

20. READ, W H, 'Upward Communication in Industrial Hierarchies', *Human Relations*, vol 15, no 1, February, 1962, pp 3–16

21. HELLER, F A, *Managerial Decision-Making: A Study of Leadership Styles and Power Sharing Among Senior Managers*, Tavistock, 1971

22. VROOM, V H and YETTON, P, *Leadership and Decision-Making*, University of Pittsburgh Press, 1973

23. TAYLOR, D W, BERRY, P C and BLOCK, C H, 'Does Group Participation When Using Brainstorming Facilitate or Inhibit Creative Thinking?', *Administrative Science Quarterly*, vol 3, no 1, June 1958, pp 23–47

24. HALL, E J, MOUTON, J S and BLAKE, R R, 'Group Problem Solving Effectiveness Under Conditions of Pooling vs Interaction', *Journal of Social Psychology*, vol 59, no 1, 1963, pp 147–57
    VROOM, V H, GRANT, L D and COTTON, T S, 'The Consequences of Social Interaction in Group Problem Solving', *Organizational Behaviour and Human Performance*, vol 4, 1, 1969, pp 77–95

25. MAIER, N R F, *Problem Solving Discussions and Conferences: Leadership Methods and Skills*, McGraw-Hill, 1963

26. SHIMMIN, S, 'Workers' Understanding of Incentive Payment Systems', *Occupational Psychology*, vol 32, no 2, April 1958, pp 106–110

CHAPTER FIVE

The Role
of Accounting Data
in the Evaluation
of Performance

One of the principal means by which senior managers attempt to motivate their managers and employees towards effective performance is by linking organisational rewards to the level of their performance. Naturally, many people have been concerned with such a relationship and in this chapter we have neither the time nor the space to provide a comprehensive discussion of all aspects of the problem. However, by focusing on some issues which are of concern to the accountant, a more limited perspective still enables us to consider questions of wider significance. The measures of performance used in specifying the rewards are often accounting measures. Budgets and plans, for instance, are used in this way, and even where the performance measures are somewhat wider in scope, managers and employees often see the accounting function as being responsible for them and adapt their attitudes and behaviour towards both the accountants and their systems accordingly. While this alone provides sufficient reason for the accountant to be interested in the problem, I believe, however, that a careful analysis of the nature of the more general relationship between performance and reward will enable the accountant to move from a purely defensive interest to a more positive and fruitful involvement.

5.1 *The Structure of Organisational Rewards and the Efficiency of Operations*
The relationship between the structure of organisational rewards and
organisational efficiency is a controversial topic with informed people
putting arguments for and against rather general approaches to the
problem, as well as particular schemes of reward or methods of performance appraisal. Although our knowledge of motivational principles has
advanced rapidly in the last few decades there have been relatively few
systematic investigations of the specifics of organisational reward structures
and perhaps even fewer applications of general psychological and sociological principles to actual situations. As a result, much of the debate
has been conducted at an almost philosophical level with peoples' values
tending to be more certain than their evidence. Recommendations for
practice often reflect general ideological concerns, homespun psychological theorising or personal introspection rather than the complexities
of behaviour in modern organisations.[1]

Such difficulties can be clearly seen in one of the most important
and influential set of views on how to motivate people to improve their
level of performance. Many recommend that organisational rewards and
punishments should be directly linked to the effectiveness of an individual's
performance. Behaviour which contributes to the attainment of organisational purposes, as interpreted by more senior managers, is rewarded,
while behaviour which either does not contribute or interferes with the
attainment of these purposes goes unrewarded or is even punished. The
accountant is usually very closely involved with measuring the level of
performance. Unfortunately it is often difficult to argue against the
general lines of thought inherent in such approaches because many of the
key concepts are amenable to a wide variety of interpretations. This is
certainly true of rewards which can include both monetary and social
incentives. Interestingly enough, it is also true of performance since this is
a concept whose meaning can vary from the precise specification of a
single output, through a multidimensional perspective with some dimensions being more objective than others, to a subjective evaluation of the
effort expended in performing a task.

However, in operational terms, such approaches usually attempt
to establish a series of clearly specified standards of performance, such
that when each is attained, the best interests of the organisation as a whole
are seen as being attained. A system of reporting is established to measure

Figure 5.1 The measurement-reward process

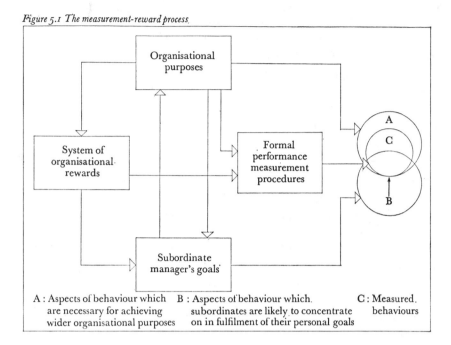

A : Aspects of behaviour which   B : Aspects of behaviour which.   C : Measured.
   are necessary for achieving   subordinates are likely to concentrate   behaviours
   wider organisational purposes   on in fulfilment of their personal goals

the actual performance of the employees and managers, and rewards and
punishments are then related to the actual level of performance assessed
in relation to the standard. The most obvious example of this approach
to motivation is the use of individual wage incentives for employees as
represented by payment by results schemes. Similar procedures are also
used as the managerial level, in the form of year-end bonuses, annual
salary reviews dependent on performance and stock option plans.

A simple representation of the approach is shown in Figure 5.1.
In the absence of any system for relating managerial or employee efforts
to organisational rewards, the aspects of behaviour which subordinates
are likely to concentrate on in fulfillment of their personal goals (B) do not
necessarily correspond with those which are necessary for achieving the
wider organisational purposes (A). Conflict is quite rightfully seen as a
prevalent condition of organisational life. It is assumed, however, that the
managerial and employee conceptions of significant behaviour can be
changed by relating the rewards which they receive from the organisation

to their performance on a series of dimensions abstracted from either senior management's or accountants' conceptions of the overall organisational purposes (C). In order to satisfy their personal needs for material prosperity, recognition and achievement, so the argument goes, managers and employees are likely to value the organisational behaviours upon which these have become, in part, contingent. As is shown by the arrow, subordinate conceptions of the organisational dimensions which have personal significance for them are likely to move towards at least those behaviours which are included in the measurement process (C). Actual behaviour is then presumed to change so as to include behaviours in C which formally existed only in A.

However, even in outline, the approach is hardly so simple. As is indicated in Figure 5.1, although there is unlikely to be complete agreement between managerial and employee goals, and organisational purposes, they are usually mutually dependent even in the absence of the measurement–reward system. Many social processes are designed to ensure that this is the case. Furthermore, while many discussions do indeed focus primarily on the incongruous subordinate conceptions of desirable behaviour, there is obviously no idealised specification of the behaviours which are necessary for achieving the purposes of the human grouping seen in organisational terms. Not only do purposes evolve rather than being given, but in the evaluative situation, as in others, they also have to be interpreted by superior managers, and although flattering, the view that senior managers are somehow interested in the overall success of the organisation in a wider, altruistic sense is unsatisfactory. Conflicts of interests occur at all levels of management and the measurement–reward system is designed to encourage all levels of management, superior and subordinate alike, to be concerned with those behaviours which are reflected in the measurement system.

By now you must also be asking whether it is reasonable to assume that people's motivational structures are so simple that an alignment of interests can be achieved so readily and so easily. From the discussions in Chapter 2, we already know that they cannot. And what about the difficulties of measuring performance? What is to be included and excluded? How do we deal with interdependent tasks and different time horizons? What happens if our measures of performance just have to be imperfect and imprecise? And are these approaches so generally applicable? If the ability to measure and to control and influence varies, should not the approach to structuring organisational rewards also vary?

These seem the obvious questions to ask but while some people have given them detailed thought, many of these more careful analyses have not as yet had the impact on practice which they deserve. Certainly they are not reflected in many of the recommendations for change and guides to action. The search for the general and the simple has been a pervasive and powerful force to overcome.

5.2 *Some Empirical Findings*

However, while it is easy to criticise the partiality of many measurement–reward approaches to motivation from a social science point of view, it must be remembered that there is considerable evidence of a relationship between rewards and performance. A number of recent social science writers may have chosen not to emphasise this in their search for alternative philosophies for managing complex organisations, but I feel that the view must be investigated with an open mind.

In a study of over six hundred workers in an American domestic appliance factory, Georgopopulus, Mahoney and Jones found that production workers who reported on a questionnaire that there was a positive relationship between their performance and their wage tended to be better performers than those reporting no such connection.[2] In addition, those workers who believed that low productivity would worsen their chances of promotion tended to be more efficient than those believing that productivity was irrelevant for promotion. While the finding is not direct evidence of a causal relationship between reward and performance, the causal interpretation is certainly strengthened by the fact that the difference in productivity between those believing that promotions were based on performance and those believing that performance was irrelevant, was greatest for workers who reported that promotion was important to them and who saw themselves as having control over their speed of work.

A more direct relationship between performance and the structure of rewards on the shop floor was found in a series of field experiments conducted in another factory manufacturing domestic appliances.[3] Miller studied a group of workers who were responsible for classifying an important piece of equipment according to size. The company faced a problem in that a substantial number of items were being misclassified. Several different approaches were tried in an attempt to reduce the number of incorrectly classified items. In the first approach, the foreman in charge of the group attempted to solve the problem by using communication and persuasion – a typical human relations approach. He talked to each worker, individually informed him of the nature of the problem and the need for improvement, showed him examples of misclassified items and reviewed his work methods with him. There was no significant or lasting improvement, each worker disclaiming responsibility and blaming others for the problem. Subsequently, a second approach was tried in which each worker was provided with very rapid feedback on the number of items which he had misclassified. This time there was an actual improvement in performance, but by the end of seven weeks, the percentage of items misclassified had almost increased to the previous level: so a third approach was tried. This involved backing up the feedback information with warnings and reprimands – not a direct monetary reward but nevertheless an important part of the overall system of rewards and punishments in most organisations. As a result, the number of misclassified items abruptly dropped to zero and remained there for the rest of the period of observation. A number of similar experiments were conducted in other departments of the same company, using slightly different methods of reward, longer periods of observation and some instances where only group performance could be measured. The findings were very similar.

The evidence from this study is certainly in agreement with the surveys of experiences with wage incentive schemes which have found substantial increases in productivity following their introduction.[4] However, great care is needed in interpreting such evidence, particularly in generalising it to all circumstances. For although there have been reports of greater output, lower unit costs and higher wages in comparison with the results of straight payment schemes, the introduction of incentive schemes rarely occurs in isolation and the productivity increases are often difficult to measure. In addition, the careful reader may already have guessed that the task described in the series of organisational experiments conducted by Miller was simple, speedy and precise, and the requisite dimension of performance could be easily and accurately measured and related to the individual worker. Similarly, in the study conducted by Georgopoulus, Mahoney and Jones, we know that the perceived relationship between rewards and performance was greater for those having control over their speed of work: but what if such conditions do not apply? Increasingly in large organisations, tasks are getting more interdependent, time cycles longer and the work of one person is highly dependent upon that of his colleagues. So much so, that the problems of management increasingly relate to the management of this interdependence rather than the management of tasks in isolation. It is becoming much more difficult to say precisely what is involved in the concept of a controllable task or cost, and individual performance related rewards are becoming more difficult to apply at the shop floor level. They may even be counterproductive.[5]

However, research indicates that even if it is meaningful and possible to base organisational rewards solely or mainly on the basis of measureable aspects of individual performance, it is not clear that it is always advantageous to do so. For a successful scheme, the rewards must also be seen as sufficiently attractive to overcome all the effects of the individual effort required to attain them, the jobs must have a relatively short time cycle so that the reward follows fairly quickly after the performance and individuals must see themselves as having some control over the dimensions of performance on which the rewards are based. What is more, in recent years, people in industry have been increasingly aware of the erosion of the effectiveness of incentive schemes. Very often, over time, they fail to motivate in the way which was expected of them when they were installed. Workers attempt to gain some measure of personal control and security. They fiddle the schemes in many ingenious ways, and when important tasks are not explicitly rewarded they are often neglected in favour of tasks which directly contribute to financial reward. In also seeking to satisfy their need to affiliate with colleagues and to gain social approval from their friends and acquaintances, work groups develop norms or informal rules and expectations concerning appropriate levels of performance that are below the maximum achievable.[6] After looking at the operation of two hundred and fifty payment by result schemes, one commentator was forced to conclude that 'financial incentive schemes rest to a considerable extent on faith in their effectiveness rather than on proof of their effectiveness.'[7]

In order to reconcile these seemingly discrepant findings we must stop arguing for the merits of any approach in isolation, but look for the individual, social, procedural and structural factors which influence the relative success of various approaches. The idea of a fit between the method of payment for shop floor workers and such features as the job time cycle, work flow arrangements, labour market conditions, and individual and social factors has been the subject of a systematic body of research at the Manchester Business School. After studying the experiences of many organisations, Lupton and Gowler have outlined a classification of payment schemes and a means for producing profiles of situations. On these bases, they provide a procedure for choosing from amongst the available payment schemes, the one which is suitable for a particular purpose in a given situation. While the method is neither simple nor non-problematic, it does start to deal with the complexities of the problem in practice and it is a refreshing exception to the previous claims for seemingly general solutions. Even if not able to give precise answers, the procedure certainly provides a way of thinking about the problem.

Perhaps even more difficult problems are operative at the managerial level where tasks are highly interdependent and time horizons longer. Unfortunately, the evidence on the effects of performance related rewards on those doing such complex cognitive tasks is less clear than at the shop floor level. There is surprisingly little research to refer to, although there is no shortage of impassioned pleas, recommended methods and fashionable procedures. Some of the most systematic evidence on the influence of rewards on managerial behaviour and performance comes from a large scale field study conducted in the United States by Porter and Lawler.[9] On the basis of data collected from questionnaires filled in by managers in both private industry and government, they found a definite tendency for managers who believed that their performance on the job would have an important effect on their pay, to be assessed by their superiors as more effective than managers who believed that their performance was a relatively unimportant influence on their pay. The difference was found to be most significant, however, for managers who rated pay as being important to them. Furthermore, the managers' reports of the effect of performance on pay were much more closely related to their superiors' ratings of the amount of effort put into the job than to ratings of the final effectiveness of their performance.

However, the type of reward systems and the way in which they were used were not specified. As soon as we turn to more detailed studies there is a wealth of more distrubing evidence. Even where performance measures are instituted solely for the purpose of information, they are often interpreted as definitions of important dimensions of the job and have important implications for motivating behaviour. Many investigations have noted the tendency of managers to pad their budgets either in anticipation of cuts by superiors or to make the subsequent variances more favourable.[10] Perhaps of even more concern are the numerous examples of managers making decisions in response to performance indices, even though the decisions are contrary to the wider purposes of the organisation.[11] Dearden has reported many such anecdotes in a series of publications.[12] For instance, he tells of managers who were reluctant to replace equipment and make new investments even when these actions were in the company's economic interest, because of the heavy book losses which would be unfavourably reflected in current performance reports with the first action, or the detrimental effect on the short-term return on investment with the second action. Similarly, in a study of the response of government administrators to evaluation on the basis of statistical performance indices, Blau found that the administrators behaved so as to increase their performance on the basis of the indices even if this resulted in dysfunctional consequences for the organisation.[13] While the indices were originally developed to increase the efficiency of the organisation, their very presence and use lead to a transference of interest from the wider purposes of the organisation to the detailed behaviours which were necessary to improve them.

These studies provide considerable insight into the operation of procedures for the evaluation of managerial performance and their individual and organisational consequences. They raise fundamental questions about the accounting measurements, how they were used and their wider organisational context. However, while an enormous amount of attention has been devoted to describing the dysfunctional consequences, surprisingly little consideration has been given to studying their precise determinants. The approach has been pathological rather than diagnostic. Yet a deeper understanding of the reasons and underlying processes is essential for anyone who is concerned with the intelligent management of change and improvement.

5.3 *Technical Approaches to the Problem*

The solution to many of these evaluation problems, both at the employee and managerial level, is very often seen in terms of further accounting and behavioural techniques, which although at times are distinguished for their sophistication and rigor of analysis, basically call for more and more of the same. This is true, for instance, of such accounting suggestions as the use of a measure of residual income rather than return on investment in order to eliminate at least some of the possibilities for dysfunctional responses. It is true of some of the arguments in favour of controllable costing and it is also true of McGregor's version of 'management by objectives', an approach which is widely known in British industry after its development and propogation by Humble, a management consultant.[14] Like so many of the other proposals, it appears to be a plausible, palatable and universally applicable answer to important organisational problems. Yet already it is known that management by objectives can suffer from precisely the same problems as the more narrowly conceived traditional control systems.[15]

Although no equivalent investigations have been made of the suggestions for including human variables in formal accounting systems which are currently in vogue, one would expect the same problems to apply. The proposals arose from Likert's discussion of the more problematic long-term impact of cost control programmes, despite their apparent short-term success.[16] He found that as people strived to obtain the necessary cost reductions, the heightened pressure and tension could eventually result in increased absenteeism and labour turnover, the cost implications of which were either not reflected in the accounting reports of the responsible manager or else reflected with a delay. His own solution to the problem included the reporting of employee attitudes as an additional evaluation and monitoring device,[17] but his comments have resulted in a considerable amount of thought and experimentation which has attempted to reflect these more widespread human implications of pressure in current accounting performance reports.

The experiments and suggestions have taken three principal forms:

(1)   *Human Asset Accounting.*[18] Human members of the organisation are valued on the basis of traditional accounting concepts. The asset values are derived from the original acquisition cost of recruitment,

Figure 5.2 *Human Asset Accounting in Practice – the Accounts of R. G. Barry Corporation*

BALANCE SHEET	1972	1972
	Conventional and	Conventional
Assets	Human Resource	Only
Total Current Assets.........................	$16,408,620	$16,408,620
Net Property, Plant and Equipment.............	3,371,943	3,371,943
Excess of Purchase Price over Net Assets Acquired .	1,288,454	1,288,454
Deferred Financing Costs......................	183,152	183,152
Net Investments in Human Resources	1,779,950	—
Other Assets	232,264	232,264
	$23,264,383	$21,484,433

Liabilities and Stockholders' Equity		
Total Current Liabilities	3,218,204	3,218,204
Long Term Debt, Excluding Current Installments.	7,285,000	7,285,000
Deferred Compensation.......................	116,533	116,533
Deferred Federal Income Tax Based Upon Full Tax		
Deduction for Human Resource Costs	889,975	—
Stockholders' Equity:		
Capital Stock...............................	1,818,780	1,818,780
Additional Capital in Excess of Par Value	5,047,480	5,047,480
Retained Earnings:		
Financial	3,998,436	3,998,436
Human Resources........................	889,975	—
	$23,264,383	$21,484,433

STATEMENT OF INCOME		
Net Sales	$39,162,301	$39,162,301
Cost of Sales...............................	25,667,737	25,667,737
Gross Profit	13,494,564	13,494,564
Selling, General and Administrative Expenses.....	10,190,773	10,190,773
Operating Income	3,303,791	3,303,791
Interest Expense	549,225	549,225
Income Before Federal Income Taxes..	2,754,566	2,754,566
Net Increase in Human Resource Investment	218,686	—
Adjusted Income Before Federal Income Taxes....	2,973,252	2,754,566
Federal Income Taxes	1,414,343	1,305,000
Net Income	$1,558,909	$1,449,566

hiring, training and development, and depreciation is recognised over the estimated years of service or upon departure. As an example, the pioneering accounts of the R G Barry Corporation are shown in Figure 5.2.

(2)   *Human Capital Accounting.*[19] The monetary values of managers and employees are determined by capitalising their expected future wages and salaries.

(3)   *Human Goodwill Accounting.*[20] Perhaps this is the most arbitrary of all the approaches. The capital value of senior and middle management and supervisory, clerical and operative employees is determined by multiplying their respective salaries and expenses by a series of factors such that the total is about 90 per cent of the accountant's estimates of the company's goodwill. Goodwill, in this sense, is defined as the difference between an estimate of the stock market value of the company as a going concern and net assets shown in the traditional financial accounts.

In addition, a number of other suggestions have been made, some more seriously than others, including the valuation of the service of scarce employees and managers by competitive bidding amongst organisational components.[21]

Obviously a great deal of further theoretical development and practical experimentation is required before the relative advantages of the various approaches, let alone the ethics and merits of the overall concept can be evaluated. There is also a need to consider additional measurement indices including the assessment of the productivity, transferability and promotability of human members of the organisation.[22] However, despite the present attempts and the potential for further work, one must add an element of caution. Measures of managerial performance will never be perfect and precise, a difficulty in fact which faces the design of most, if not all, accounting techniques and procedures.

There are many reasons for this pessimistic comment. First, not all relevant dimensions of managerial or employee performance can be included in accounting reports since neither accountants nor other specialists have developed comprehensive measures and standards.[23] Second, even considering the economic aspects of performance, an organisation's economic cost function is rarely known and an accounting system can only attempt to approximately represent its complexity, particularly for highly interdependent patterns of activity. Third, accounting data are primarily concerned with representing objective outcomes, while managerial and employee activity is concerned with the detailed processes and efforts giving rise to the final outcomes. If there are factors which constrain the reported efficiency of the processes, despite the quality of the managerial or employee performance, the accounting data will be an inadequate reflection of the human performance. For a fair evaluation, the controllable component of the reports should be isolated, yet this is a difficult task. Indeed, in a basic sense, the problem is insoluble because the determination of whether a budget variance, for instance, is due to a manager's efforts or uncontrollable environmental factors would, in the last resort, require a model of the organisation and its relationship to the environment. In this way, we would certainly be able to measure the influences of the manager, but if such a model existed might not the manager be redundant? Fourth, the main emphasis of accounting reports is on short-term performance indices while the evaluation of managerial and employee performance is often concerned with more long-term considerations, or at least with balancing the short-term and the long-term. Fifth, accounting systems are also trying to serve many purposes. Each purpose may ideally necessitate the preparation of a unique set of data, although accountants frequently try to produce general purpose reports which are of some value for at least some of the many purposes. The reports may, however, in trying to satisfy a series of purposes, fail to perfectly satisfy the requirements for any single purpose – the appraisal of performance, for instance. Ultimately, the very cost of providing the information is an important constraining factor.

Certainly, it is frequently, if not usually, possible to improve an accounting performance measurement system and work should be devoted to that end. It should also be remembered, however, that beyond some point the search for technical perfection is doomed to failure and can easily result in a diversion of effort from the identification of other central problems. The necessary limits on the task need to be recognised, and viewed not as frustrating yet enticing constraints but as a challenge pointing to the need for a fundamental reconsideration of the problem and a complementary programme of action. We should stop compiling lists of the perfect measures of performance, and some of us should, for the

Figure 5.3 The measurement-reward process with imperfect measurements

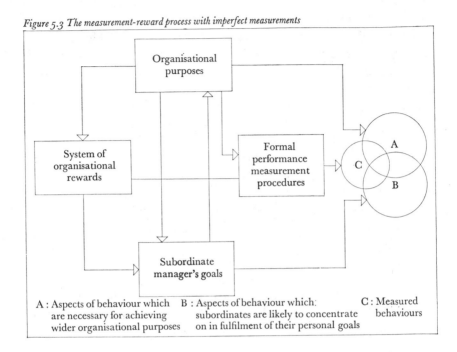

A : Aspects of behaviour which   B : Aspects of behaviour which: C : Measured
    are necessary for achieving   subordinates are likely to concentrate   behaviours
    wider organisational purposes   on in fulfilment of their personal goals

time being at least, stop tinkering with performance measures. For the human and organisational problems with performance measurement and reward systems often reflect not the inadequacies of present procedures, but the way in which these procedures are used. What is required is an appreciation of the appropriate use of imperfect but nevertheless valuable reports and indices and then, on this firmer basis, we can return to consider what procedural and technical changes may be necessary.

It should be apparent by now that the more usual state of affairs is represented by the ambiguous situation in Figure 5.3 rather than the idealised representation of the performance measurement system's exclusive concern with organisationally significant behaviour which was shown in Figure 5.1. The measurement system is not perfect and while some measured behaviours have organisational significance, others do not; in which case, the relationship between the performance measurement process and the reward system can conceivably encourage a concern with what is measured, regardless of organisational relevance. We know that this can happen, but at the same time, despite their imperfections, the measurement procedures are recognised as valuable and are used. Indeed one interpretation of studies which point to the popularity of particularly imperfect measures – the return on investment, for instance – is that managers use them in ways which are much more complex than the recommendations embodied in many conventional accounting texts. Therefore, why not try to enrich our understandings of the effective use of imperfect procedures by observing the contexts in which such measures are in fact used? To such a study, we now turn.

5.4 *The Use of Budget Reports in Managerial Performance Evaluation*[24]

The final impact which any accounting system has on managerial and employee behaviour is dependent not only upon its design and technical characteristics but also upon the precise manner in which the resulting information is used. Even standard accounting reports which show, for instance, a cost centre's budgeted and actual costs, can be used in various ways in performance evaluation. In the extreme, of course, even the most sophisticated system can contribute little to the efficiency of a company's operations if the information is ignored.[25] More generally, however, despite the amount of care and consideration which may have gone into its design, its value may be questionable if managers and employees use the information in an inappropriate manner attributing either too much, or too little validity to it or being unaware of its intended purposes. An appreciation of the different ways of using accounting information must, however, be based upon an understanding of the human context in which it is used. The information is given but its interpretation is, as we will consider in more detail in Chapter 7, the outcome of a personal and social process which is sustained by the meanings, beliefs, pressures and purposes that are brought to bear by the people using the information. In providing it with a personal significance and placing it in their own wider context, managers and employees are able to use the information, perhaps without reflection, in a variety of ways – appropriate and inappropriate.

From a review of previous research findings and extensive interviews in the manufacturing division of one large American company, three distinct ways of using budgetary information in the evaluation of managerial performance have been distinguished and operationally defined.*

(1)   *Budget Constrained Style of Evaluation.* Despite the many problems of using budgetary information as a comprehensive measure of managerial performance, the manager's performance is primarily evaluated upon the basis of his ability to continually meet the budget on a short-term basis. This criterion of performance is stressed at the expense of other valued and important criteria and the manager will receive unfavourable feedback from his superior if, for instance, his actual costs exceed the budgeted costs, regardless of other considerations.

(2)   *Profit Conscious Style of Evaluation.* The manager's performance is evaluated on the basis of his ability to increase the general effectiveness of his unit's operations in relation to the long-term purposes of the organisation. For instance, at the cost centre level one important aspect of this ability concerns the attention which he devotes to reducing long-run costs. For this purpose, however, the budgetary information has to be used with great care in a rather flexible manner.

(3)   *Nonaccounting Style of Evaluation.* The budgetary information plays a relatively unimportant part in the superior's evaluation of the manager's performance.

While budgetary information obviously indicates whether or not a manager has succeeded in meeting his current budget, it does not necessarily indicate whether he is behaving in a manner which is consistent with achieving the organisation's longer-term effectiveness. Current cost savings can, for instance, be made at longer term expense and some current cost overruns can also ensure lower cost operations in the future.

* It is easier to distinguish styles of evaluation in a general sense than move towards defining them in an operational manner. In this study, the problem of operationally defining the styles was approached by probing into the meanings developed by the managers in the company. They certainly did not use the terms used in describing the styles in a general sense, but they did distinguish between their colleagues and superiors on the basis of evaluative behaviours which were in basic agreement, and the language which they used to make such distinctions provided the operational definitions.

There are many such problems and the budgetary reports have not only to be used with care but also supplemented by information drawn from other sources in order to assess the manager's impact on future as well as current operations. Unlike a 'budget constrained' evaluation, a 'profit conscious' evaluation is therefore concerned with the wider information content, or lack of it, of the budget reports and not just with a rigid analysis of the direction and magnitude of the reported variances. The budget is, in other words, seen as a means to an end rather than an end in itself.

Empirical evidence indicated that both the 'budget constrained' and 'profit conscious' styles of evaluation resulted in a higher degree of involvement with costs than the 'nonaccounting' style. Only the 'profit conscious' style, however, succeeded in attaining this involvement without incurring either emotional costs for the managers in charge of the cost centres or defensive behaviour which was undesirable from the company's point of view.

The 'budget constrained' style resulted in a belief that the evaluation was unjust, and widespread tension and worry on the job. In the words of one manager:

> 'I don't think [the 'budget constrained' supervisor] properly evaluates my performance. He looks at the figures but he doesn't know what they are doing. He's real good at seeing that you are over your budget. He is as straight and narrow as the book is written. He doesn't give common judgment a say: none'.

Another manager commented on the effects of this in the following way:

> 'You have to get yourself out of the woods. It's a process of staying out of the red. You have to. It's true and it makes a job so much more difficult. They'd be times when I could do a good job and save some money by spending a bit now. But no, the only thing I concentrate on is what I've got forthcoming that's going to put me in the red. I've got to concentrate to see . . . there's no more money to spend. God, it causes me some problems'.

Such frantic and, at times, unsuccessful attempts only resulted in more problems, more tension and more worry.

It was hardly surprising that such a simple minded concern with the budget was met with manipulation of the accounting reports and even decisions which were less innovative and which, at times, increased the total processing costs for the company as a whole. Costs were charged to incorrect accounts and repairs delayed until the money was available in the budget, in spite of this resulting in higher costs, and, in the words of one manager:

> 'Simply no one will take the decision to spend. Most people in this position try to make themselves look good. They don't want to see negative signs on their reports. They're aiming for promotion without worrying about the future. It's let's look good today, tomorrow I'll get promoted. It's someone else's problem then'.

Manipulation and undesirable decision behaviour were not, however, the only means of relieving the tensions created by the 'budget constrained' style. The manager's relationships with the 'budget constrained' supervisors were allowed to deteriorate and the rigid emphasis on the short-term budget results also highlighted the interdependent nature of their tasks, with the result that the immediate instrumental concerns permeated the patterns of social relationships amongst colleagues. When the managers were continually asked about budget variances over which they had no control they each went out to improve their own reports regardless of the detrimental effects for the organisation of such a narrow parochialism, and if this failed, they tried to pass on the responsibility by blaming their colleagues. The ensuing rivalry and conflict often impeded the cooperation which was so essential for controlling their interdependent activities.

In contrast, the 'profit conscious' style resulted in similar levels of tension, supervisor satisfaction and cooperation with colleagues as prevailed under a 'nonaccounting' style, and there was little or no fiddling of the reports. While the style was accepted, even respected, it was also seen as very demanding. A profit conscious supervisor, according to one of his subordinate managers . . .

> '. . . is always asking about costs – all the time. This is basically the heart of it, I guess, costs. Anytime we get together or whenever he gets you, it's costs, costs, costs. "See if we can cut down". "It's going pretty fast, we'd

better talk about it." He's a little bit too strict really. I'm used to discipline, but he runs a tight ship. He does not like us to get sloppy; he gets hot under the collar. He tries to save whatever he can. He just likes to operate that way. He is just that type of person, but to be fair, he applies pressure where it is appropriate'.

The 'profit conscious' style was far from being an easy style to satisfy, but the pressure was seen as being applied fairly rather than along the rigid lines of a 'budget constrained' style. The latter's approach was 'just don't do it', rather than asking for explanations.

A summary of the effects of the three styles of evaluation is given in Table 5.1. Unfortunately, the study did not directly investigate the

Table 5.1 *A summary of the effects of the three styles of evaluation*

| | Style of evaluation | | |
	Budget constrained	Profit conscious	Nonaccounting
Involvement with costs	High	High	Low
Job related tension	High	Medium	Medium
Manipulation of the accounting reports	Extensive	Little	Little
Relations with the supervisor	Poor	Good	Good
Relations with colleagues	Poor	Good	Good

overall impact of the different styles on the effectiveness of operations. The presence of extensive manipulation in some of the reports made the accounting information unreliable for this purpose and given the subject of the research, it was difficult to revert to subjective assessments. The fiddling, short time horizons, distrust, rivalry and parochial attitudes engendered by the 'budget constrained' style are nevertheless vital considerations in all companies and the 'profit conscious' style avoided these problems while at the same time ensuring an active involvement with the financial aspects of operations. The costs associated with unreliable accounting records, short time horizons and the difficulties of controlling interdependent operations will, however, vary from situation to situation. Therefore the precise balance of costs and benefits associated with the three styles might well be very different for the control of a stable, technologically simple situation, for instance, than for that of an uncertain and highly complex situation.[26]

5.5 *But What Influences How Budgetary Information is Used?*

The contrast between the 'budget constrained' and 'profit conscious' styles of evaluation suggests that accounting information need not of itself pose a threat to the managers and employees of a company when it is used in performance evaluation. Therefore a manager is not faced with a simple choice between using or not using the information in evaluation. Instead, it would appear, that he can reap many of the benefits of an accounting system by stressing factors which it attempts to measure, albeit imperfectly, without this resulting in undesirable defensive behaviour. To do so, however, consideration must be given to the precise manner in which the information is used: but what influences how it is used? Certainly it is not sufficient to merely acknowledge their presence. It is also necessary to consider the factors determining the styles because a systematic understanding of their nature is an essential prerequisite for the intelligent management of change.

Due no doubt to the arithmetical nature of accounting reports, the study found that it was difficult to resist passing down the 'budget constrained' style once it had been established at one level in the organisational hierarchy. If a manager was called upon to meet his budget, he could only ensure doing so by making his subordinates do likewise. All but one of the managers who were themselves subject to a 'budget constrained' evaluation assessed the performance of a significant proportion of their own subordinates on a similar basis. In contrast, neither of the other two styles of evaluation were passed down from one level to the next. For instance, while many of the managers maintained the concern with the budget reports expressed in their own 'profit conscious' evaluation, whether this concern was interpreted in a flexible or rigid manner depended upon the second factor influencing the styles, namely the manager's own capabilities.

The ways in which the accounting information was used were very clearly associated with much more widespread differences in managerial style. Using the well accepted distinction between task and employee oriented approaches which is reflected in the dimensions of management style developed at Ohio State University, namely 'Initiation of Structure' and 'Consideration',[27] it was found that both the 'budget constrained' and 'profit conscious' managers, unlike those using a 'nonaccounting' style, were seen as trying to create a structured, task oriented job environment. The 'profit conscious' managers, however, were also seen as maintaining a warm and friendly atmosphere which was supportive and conducive for mutual trust and respect. In this regard, they were similar to the 'non-accounting' managers, but very different from the 'budget constrained' ones. Without the moderating effect of the considerate, employee oriented attitudes, the concern for the budget reports was seen as threatening and stressful.

Hence, the accounting information was one vehicle through which the managers were able to express their more general approaches to the job. The way in which it was used was often, in fact, a reasonable indicator of the managerial philosophy and ethos which pervaded any section of the company. The 'profit conscious' style, for instance, appeared to be only one aspect of the problem solving approach to management, as distinct from an approach which attempted to impose a false measure of simplicity onto a complex and highly interdependent series of activities. The evaluation of performance was itself of primary importance with the 'budget constrained' style, influencing all aspects of the managers' behaviours. Evaluation was not viewed as an ongoing part of the managerial process, interrelated with other important aspects of the job and itself a problematic activity. Rather, it was seen as a distinct and dominant activity, and the primary source of influence and control, overshadowing other vital elements of the process. The budget became not an aid to management, but a constraint upon it.

5.6 *Implications for the Operation of Accounting System;*

The effectiveness with which an accounting system satisfies both its own immediate objectives as well as an organisation's wider purposes depends on both the relevance and accuracy of the information which it provides and the way in which the information is used by members of the organisation. Therefore, at the very least, accountants have an important educational function to serve – one which has not perhaps so far been used to the fullest extent. With the increasing complexity of accounting procedures, it is unrealistic to expect managers and employees at any level in an organisation to use the information appropriately without adequate preparation and training. They need to be informed of more than the mere objectives of accounting systems and their alleged advantages, however real. They also need to be informed of the assumptions and approximations which are of necessity incorporated into accounting systems, of the inadequacies of the information and of the consequences of attaching too much importance to it. This is often a far more difficult task.*

The different ways of using accounting information in performance evaluation are not, however, based simply on ignorance. They are, as we have seen, associated with much more widespread differences in managerial behaviour and attitudes and, for the 'budget constrained' style of evaluation, with the evaluative styles of superiors. An educational programme is not, therefore, an easy solution to the problem. It would certainly have to be directed at senior managers in addition to employees and middle managers since we know that training programmes conducted at lower levels in an organisation can be of doubtful value if attitudes and behaviours remain unchanged at higher levels. Even so, it is still not certain whether the ways in which accounting information is used in performance evaluation can be changed without trying to substantially modify general approaches to management, a difficult task at best, and one which requires the skills of specialists in organisational development as well as accounting.

In view of such difficulties, consideration needs to be given to changing some aspects of accounting systems and in doing this, there is a real need for a view of accounting which sees it as a part of a much more complex process for influencing behaviour in organisations. Accounting systems for performance measurement represent only one means of control and their final effectiveness is dependent upon how they interact with the other approaches to the control problem. For instance, the behaviours so

---

* Understandably, it is easy for accountants to be defensive about any suggestion that their procedures are imprecise. Many would say that there are already enough problems in gaining the acceptance of accounting systems without adding any more. My comment is not, however, meant to be critical. While the imprecision and partiality may really reflect inadequate efforts in some situations, in many other cases, they simply reflect, as we have discussed above, the current state of the art. Sophisticated though many procedures have become, they still have a long way to go. Therefore, there is no need to be defensive if the full implications of the problem are recognised.

inadequately reflected within the dimensions of management style are also trying to influence behaviour. It is all too easy to concentrate on separate mechanisms for influencing behaviour, and perhaps even achieve some satisfaction in the individual situation, but by not taking an integrated view, still fail to achieve their full potential.

At the technical level, however, there is a need to move towards designing accounting systems which are less evaluative in approach. At the present time, so much of the ethos which is reflected in the design of accounting systems stresses personal responsibility, accountability and past achievement, often at the expense of providing the information which is necessary for learning and improvement. Where this is the case, the procedures themselves do little to encourage problem solving rather than evaluative uses of the information. As a first step, it would be helpful if the different purposes served by performance appraisals were clearly distinguished, for many of the difficulties arise when the same techniques and information are used to achieve incompatible ends.[28] Overall personal assessment may be necessary for maintaining inventories of personnel resources and abilities, and deciding on salaries and promotions. Even in this area the need is for more wide ranging and more forward looking information than many of the traditional financial reports provide. It is unlikely, however, that the information which is necessary for satisfying these organisational purposes will also be useful for revealing to individual managers and employees where they stand, helping them to learn from their previous experiences and stimulating them to improve their performance in the future. To be fair, the outlines of the information which is required to satisfy these purposes are already incorporated in the design of many management accounting systems but their development and refinement will present an important challenge to accountants in the years ahead.

5.7 *References*

1. BEHREND, H, 'Financial Incentives as The Expression of a System of Beliefs', *British Journal of Sociology*, vol 10, no 2, 1959, pp 137–47
2. GEORPOPOULUS, B S, MAHONEY, G M and JONES, N W, 'A Path Goal Approach to Productivity', *Journal of Applied Psychology*, vol 41, no 6, 1967, pp 345–53
   In interpreting these findings, the impact of national culture should not be ignored. For in a business exercise, managers from two industralised countries (USA and Sweden) perceived pay as being more closely linked to performance

than those from two developing countries (India and Colombia), and acted accordingly. See:

RYTERBAND, E C, and THIAGERAJAN, K M, 'Managerial Attitudes Toward Salaries as a Function of Social and Economic Development', Technical Report No 24, Mangement Research Centre, University of Rochester, 1968

3. MILLER, L, *The Use of Knowledge of Results in Improving the Performance of Hourly Operators*, Behavioural Research Service, General Electric, 1965

4. VITELES, M S, *Motivation and Morale in Industry*, Norton Bailey and Co, 1953

5. See:

OPAHL, R L and DUNNETTE, M D, 'The Role of Financial Compensation in Industrial Motivation', *Psychological Bulletin*, vol 66, no 2, 1966, pp 94–118

MARRIOTT, R, *Incentive Payment Systems: A Review of Research and Opinion*, Staples Press, 1957

6. See, for instance:

LUPTON, T, *On The Shop Floor*, Pergamon Press, 1963

ROETHLISBERGER, F J and DIXON, W J, *Management and the Worker*, John Wiley and Sons, 1964

WHYTE, W F, *Money and Motivation*, Harper and Row, 1955

7. BEHREND, H, 'Effort-control Through Bargaining', *Nature*, vol 179, no 4570, June 1957, pp 1,106–7

8. LUPTON, T and GOWLER, D, *Selecting a Wage Payment System*, Kogan Page, 1968

Details of the implementation of their methods are reported in:

GILLESPIE, A, *The Management of Wage Payment Systems*, Kogen Page, 1973

Also see:

BOWEY, A M and LUPTON, T, 'Productivity Drift and the Structure of the Pay Packet', *Journal of Management Studies*, vol 7, nos 2 and 3, May and October 1970, pp 156–71, and 310–34

9. PORTER, L W and LAWLER, E E, *Attitudes of Effective Managers*, Richard D Irwin, 1968

10. LOWE, E A and SHAW, R W, 'An Analysis of Managerial Biasing: Some Evidence From a Company's Budgeting Process', *Journal of Management Studies*, vol 5, no 3, October 1968, pp 304–315

SCHIFF, M and LEWIN, A Y, 'The Impact of People on Budgets', *The Accounting Review*, vol 45, no 2, April 1970, pp 259–68

11. See, for instance:

JASINSKI, F J, 'Use and Misuse of Efficiency Controls', *Harvard Business Review*, July–August, 1956, pp 105–112

RIDGWAY, V F, 'Dysfunctional Consequences of Performance Measurements', *Administrative Science Quarterly*, vol 1, 1956, pp 240–7

ETZIONI, A and LEHMANN, E W, 'Some Dangers in "Valid" Social Measurement', *Annals of the American Academy of Political and Social Science*, vol 323, 1967, pp 1–15

12. DEARDEN, J, 'Problem of Decentralized Profit Responsibility', *Harvard Business Review*, May–June, 1960, pp 79–86

DEARDEN, J, 'Problem in Decentralized Financial Control', *Harvard Business Review*, May–June, 1961, pp 72–80

13. BLAU, P M, *The Dynamics of Bureaucracy*, University of Chicago Press, 1955
14. MCGREGOR, D, *The Professional Manager*, McGraw-Hill, 1967
    HUMBLE, J, *Management By Objectives*, Industrial Educational Research Foundation, 1969
15. CARROLL, S J and TOSI, H L, *Management By Objectives: Applications and Research*, Macmillan, 1973
16. LIKERT, R, *The Human Organization*, McGraw-Hill, 1967
    Also see:
    LIKERT, R and SEASHORE, S E, 'Making Cost Control Work', *Harvard Business Review*, vol 41, no 6, November–December 1963, pp 96–108
17. On this topic, see:
    HOFSTEDE, G H, 'Employee Surveys – A Tool for Participation', *European Business*, Autumn 1973, pp 62–9
18. See:
    BRUMMET, R L, PYLE, W C and FLAMHOLTZ, E G, *Human Resource Accounting: Development and Implementation in Industry*, Foundation for Research on Human Behaviour, 1969
    Details of the application of these methods are given in:
    STONE, F, 'Investment in Human Resources at AT & T', *Management Review*, vol 61, no 10, October 1972, pp 23–7
    WOODRUFF, R L and WHITMAN, R G, 'The Behavioural Aspects of Accounting Data for Performance Evaluation at R G Barry Corporation (with special reference to human resource accounting)', *The Behavioural Aspects of Accounting Data for Performance Evaluation*, College of Administrative Science, Ohio State University, 1970, pp 1–33
19. LEV, B and SCHWARTZ, A, 'On the Use of the Economic Concept of Human Capital in Financial Statements', *The Accounting Review*, vol 46, no 1, January 1971, pp 103–12
20. GILES, W J and ROBINSON, D F, *Human Asset Accounting*, Institute of Personnel Management and Institute of Cost and Management Accountants, 1972
21. HEKIMIAN, J S and JONES, C H, 'Put *People* on Your Balance Sheet', *Harvard Business Review*, January–February, 1967, pp 105–13
    A bibliography of the human asset literature is given in:
    'The Report of the Committee on Human Resource Accounting', *The Accounting Review*, supplement to vol 48, 1973, pp 169–85
22. FLAMHOLTZ, E G, 'Toward a Theory of Human Resource Value', *The Accounting Review*, vol 47, no 4, October 1972, pp 666–78
23. AMERICAN ACCOUNTING ASSOCIATION, 'Report of the Committee on Non-Financial Measures of Effectiveness', *The Accounting Review*, supplement to vol 46, 1971, pp 165–212
24. A more detailed report of the methods, statistical analysis and findings on which this summary is based is given in:

HOPWOOD, A G, *An Accounting System and Managerial Behaviour*, Saxon House, 1973

25. See, for instance:
BERESFORD DEW, R and GEE, K P, *Management Control and Information*, Macmillan, 1973

26. Some recent research has addressed itself to closely related problems. See:
BAUMLER, J V, 'Defined Criteria of Performance in Organizational Control', *Administrative Science Quarterly*, vol 16, no 3, September 1971, pp 340–50
MURRAY, W, *Management Controls in Action*, Irish National Productivity Committee, Development Division, 1970

27. FLEISHMAN, E A, 'The Description of Supervisory Behaviour', *Journal of Applied Psychology*, vol 37, 1953, pp 153–8
STOGDILL, R M and COONS, A E, *Leader Behaviour: Its Description and Measurement*, Bureau of Business Research, Ohio State University, 1957, pp 120–33

28. On this topic, see the interesting discussion in:
MEYER, H H, KAY, E and FRENCH, J R P, 'Split Roles in Performance Appraisal', *Harvard Business Review*, January–February 1965, pp 123–9

CHAPTER SIX

Accounting Information and the Decision Process

Decision making can be viewed as the very fabric of which organised activity is made. The high level strategic decisions which help to determine the future policy and direction of the organisation are, of course, infrequent and often rest in the hands of only a few members of the top management team. Decisions of a more mundane variety are, however, being made all the time – hiring a new employee; deciding when to repair an essential piece of equipment; increasing purchases of an essential raw material, the price of which is expected to rise; purchasing a new piece of equipment, and so on. Such decisions have their equivalents at all levels of an organisation, at all periods of time.

An understanding of how decisions are made is essential for anyone concerned with the design and operation of accounting systems. The very justification of any accounting system rests on at least the assumption that the data and reports improve the quality of decision making. This is true whether the decision makers be the managers and employees of the organisation, in the case of internal accounting systems, or the shareholders, officials of various government agencies and investment analysts, with external reporting systems. Yet although so simple and general a statement of purpose might appear immediately obvious and devoid of any real significance, one has to ask whether the underlying rationale is sufficiently understood and acted upon by accountants. I doubt it. Of course we consider decision models and various facilitating techniques and procedures. We also talk of the utility, relevance and value of our systems but this is not enough. If the basic purpose is to be taken seriously and accounting systems are to be seen as essential parts of a wider information and decision process within organisations, it is necessary to considerably expand our perspectives for viewing and appraising their design and operation. It is necessary to have a detailed appreciation of the whole decision process. Attention must be given to the way in which people communicate, interpret and use information, and how it is translated, through people, into decisions and actions. We consider some important aspects of the process of managerial decision making in the present chapter. We take a more detailed look at some aspects of the interpretation of information in Chapter 7, and finally, in Chapter 8, we examine the way accounting information is used to aid investor transactions on the stock exchange.

6.1 *Approaches to the Study of Decision Making*

The literature on decision making can be thought of as falling into three broad categories, each representing rather different approaches to the study of the subject. First of all, a number of people who have established a reputation for their own decision making capacities have taken time to articulate their personal impressions and philosophies. I call this the intuitive approach. It is, not too surprisingly, the pursuit of the elderly statesman, the successful industrialist, the retired military officer and the prestigious management consultant. Quite naturally, they have tended to see decision making as an age old art calling on personal resources and organising skills, rather than a new science. Some of their contributions have unfortunately been no more than crude exhortations for imposing a rather superficial order onto a somewhat threatening underlying chaos, but others have certainly provided us with penetrating and highly provocative insights.[1] The problem in all cases is, however, that while the intuitive guide may be valid in some circumstances, in others it has a great probability of being wrong. In the absence of a more general understanding of the problem there is no way of telling which is most likely.

A second group of writers on decision making have been primarily concerned with the decisions which people should make as against those which they do make.[2] I call this the normative approach. They have developed a wide variety of techniques which seek to improve the quality and effectiveness of decisions by aiding the selection of a preferable course of action. There are many examples of these in the fields of operational research and industrial engineering as well as in accounting and finance. Capital budgeting models are of this type as are a number of the more recent approaches to corporate planning. The primary objective in all cases has not been to predict or explain the behaviour of decision makers, but to determine an optimal choice in situations where the alternatives are fairly well specified.[3] They have, in other words, tried to establish decision making as a rational and orderly activity based on reasoned and articulated premises. This is an admirable rationale, but we should, nevertheless, be aware of its limitations.

The complexity of factors influencing decision making in many situations has severely limited the application of many of these normative procedures. In a number of cases it is difficult to appreciate the role which they play unless it is realised that their presence reflects an attempt to shift the balance of power in the organisation rather than any direct impact on the quality of decision making. Their single minded preoccupation with the evaluation of alternative courses of action also raises a number of problems. For one thing, they rarely consider the means by which the alternatives are to be generated and their concern with evaluation presumes values. Yet it is possible that the value premises inherent in the decision procedures differ radically from those of the decision makers for whom they are intended. In addition, the decision process includes much more than the comparison of several alternative courses of action and the selection of what is, in some senses, a preferable one. With less than perfect knowledge of either the alternatives or their consequences, such factors as how the problem arose, the means by which the alternatives were determined, who supplied the information, and with what aims in mind, can all have a strong influence on the final selection.

A comprehensive understanding of the process by which people actually make decisions, and of what influences them in these endeavours, is therefore essential for a more effective utilisation of normative decision models. This has been the concern of the descriptive approach to decision making. Sometimes writers following this approach have done no more

Figure 6.1 The decision process

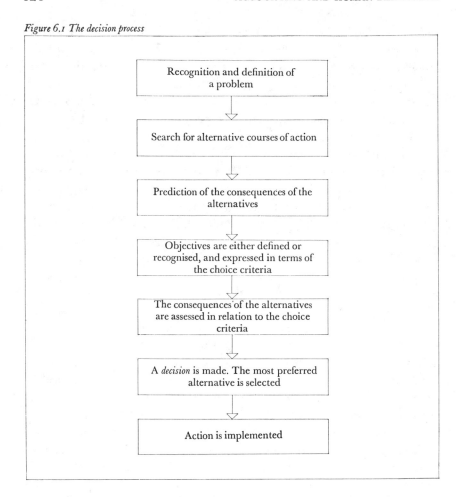

than suggest ways of categorising the various stages of the decision process. There have also been some reports of studies of decision makers in action, but increasingly, there has been a concern with providing intensive, systematic and empirically based studies of the decision process and to this approach we now turn.

6.2 *The Decision Process*

Like many other social activities, the process of decision making has been viewed as a sequential series of activities. A simple representation of the process seen in those terms is illustrated in Figure 6.1. The decision maker's behaviour is followed from the initial recognition and definition of the problem, through the search for alternative courses of action and the selection of a preferred alternative, to the implementation of action.

In reality, of course, the process is rarely so simple or so well specified. There are usually conflicting objectives to be reconciled, there are constraints, both technical and social, on action, and rather than each stage being separately identifiable, they may, in practice, be highly interrelated. The whole process can also be iterative in nature, moving from one alternative to its consideration and rejection, and then to the search for another, and so on. Not all decisions even go through all stages in any systematic sense. Immediate pressures may result in a quick solution with little analysis of the problem, no search for alternative solutions and few attempts to weigh the consequences.

However, in providing us with a framework for looking at the various influences on the decision process, the relative simplicity of the sequential view has its advantages for the moment. In our discussion, we emphasise three main stages:

(1)   finding occasions for making a decision or recognising a problem;
(2)   searching for, and analysing alternative courses of action; and
(3)   choosing among the alternatives.

6.3. *Problem Recognition*
Surprisingly, the crucial early stages of the decision making process are the least understood.[4] At a rather general level the process is usually characterised as a response to an event, either within the organisation or in its external environment, which is seen as problematic. This is thought to occur when a discrepancy is seen between the existing situation and some desired situation. There may, for instance, be a difference between current performance and managerial expectations or aspirations or the problem may involve a major new opportunity or some external threat. Over time, even some relatively minor disturbances may be seen as recurring and in need of further consideration. Threats and opportunities often have to be discovered, and discrepancies are not given but perceived. So, in fact, such conventional generalities tend to beg the issue rather than providing us with any real insights into either the personal or

organisational factors which influence whether any event is seen as problematic.

Paradoxically it is easier to comment on the events which are not seen as problematic. Not only are they in the majority but managers are quite effective in ensuring that this is the case. There are very good reasons why this should be so. In complex and changing environments, many potential problem situations are occurring all the time. The very viability of the organisation requires that only a limited number be identified as significant and important. If the manager were to even attempt to see all situations as problematic, which conceivably he could, his time would be completely absorbed in monitoring his environment and trying to proceed on too many fronts at the same time. Consequently, managers learn to react to situations in a selective manner. Experience is often the main guide.[5] They learn to sense what constitutes a satisfactory level of performance, whose ideas are worth listening to and what events are significant predictors of future opportunities and calamities. At the organisational level, plans and budgets, standard operating procedures, selected information flows and specialist departments do much to shield the manager from many unpredictabilities which could be problematic.

Yet although some controls on problem recognition are necessary for organised activity, serving to limit uncertainty and focus attention, they are also capable of explaining inactivity and a more passive style of management. There is certainly no guarantee that they always lead to longer term success. Indeed both personal impressions and research evidence suggest that successful decision making may be even more dependent upon the ability to continually recognise and define important problems, and a wide range of alternative course of action, than on carefully choosing between them.[6]

Whether any event initiates a decision process by being seen as problematic partly depends upon the individual decision maker. Managers, for instance, allocate different amounts of time to the active search for problems and opportunities as against the management of existing operations. They differ in background, education and experience and they also have different temperaments and personalities. Some are inquiring in nature, easily aroused and revel in conflicts and inconsistencies. Others are contemplative, stable and more passively react to unanticipated events.[7]

Such personal factors are important, but the only way in which they can be influenced by senior management is through the selection of people to fill critical organisational roles. Moreover, the problem oriented organisation requires much more than active managers and employees. They are important prerequisites, but we all know of the bright, eager and enthusiastic entrepreneur who was numbed into relative conformity by a highly structured and disciplined organisation.* However creative and aware a manager may be, he needs a conducive organisational environment.

The organisational conditions associated with the problem oriented organisation have recently been the subject of intensive study.[8] While many doubts certainly remain, the findings quite clearly point to the importance of the following social and structural prerequisites for active problem recognition and innovative decision making:

(1) The problem oriented organisation requires a diversity of attitudes, activities and purposes to stimulate the generation of problems and ideas. The diversity also provides the variety and richness of experiences which are necessary conditions for meeting and adapting to a changing environment.

(2) Power and influence are more broadly based in the problem oriented organisation. Rather than omniscience lying with a select few, the essential technical and commercial knowledge is recognised as being widely dispersed and often fragmented throughout the organisation. This results in a wider diffusion of uncertainty and more members of the organisation are stimulated to search for, recognise and define potential problem areas. The decentralisation of authority and influence can also result in a greater amount of communication, up, down and across the hierarchy, which in turn encourages the conflicts and arguments within the organisation which are necessary for change and progress.

(3) While the hierarchical design of problem oriented organisations may be different, this does not mean that there is no superior authority: there is, although it tends to be an authority of expertise and knowledge. Indeed, the superior's role can be all the more

---

* Equally, we know of the community of scholars, all well qualified and respected, who contentedly nod in consent at each other's rather tied and stereotyped ideas.

important in the problem oriented organisation because diversity and conflict can also lead to chaos and strife. The focus of the role is different, however. He becomes more concerned with providing coordination and integration, the means for constant feedback, and stimulation and support.

(4)   Managers in the problem oriented organisation are also aware of the need to anticipate likely opportunities and constraints on the organisation. While many external events cannot be controlled, they can often lose their disorienting effect if they are anticipated.

(5)   The problem oriented organisation is characterised by some degree of structural looseness with over lapping and duplicated responsibilities, and a good deal of communication running laterally as well as vertically. Managers have to continually define and redefine their responsibilities. They have to probe, to question and to seek help, and tasks have to be discharged much more in the light of knowledge of the organisation as a whole. In contrast, the strict departmentalisation of the organisation with a low problem recognition capability can easily promote parochial views and a greater resistance to new ideas from outside.

(6)   There are fewer enforced rules and procedures in the problem oriented organisation, for a highly formalised organisation provides little freedom for considering alternative procedures and practices. Little initiative is called for, and the rules can encourage conformity and discourage new ideas.

(7)   Closely related to this is the fact that rewards in the problem oriented organisation are not so immediately dependent on extrinsic payments and formal status. The satisfactions of searching and discovering and the esteem of colleagues become much more important.

At first glance, these conditions might appear to be of little relevance to the decision process. Certainly, they are at variance with the usual precise and mechanistic recommendations on decision making. There is an increasing amount of empirical support for the notion that these patterns of organisational and interpersonal relationships at least start to deal with the uncertain nature of the task by focusing on the crucial early stages of the decision making process. The fact that they focus on the forms of organisational structure and the systems used to measure and reward managerial performance is important because those are precisely the factors which are subject to top management influence.

Indeed many of the principles underlying these conditions are already being accepted and acted upon. An increasing number of organisations are establishing 'development activities' to mediate between the people with ideas and the formal organisational procedures for appraisal and authorisation. Interfunctional project teams are also being used to capitalise on some of the requirements for problem recognition. Specialists from very different backgrounds are being brought together to deal with a limited range of problems and are then reassigned when the task is completed. The teams are purposeful but temporary, representing irregular additions to the organisational structure. Similarly, the more permanent cross-hatching and interlocking responsibilities which are characteristic of matrix designs for organisations attempt to ensure increased interdependence and communication. While some of the experiments undoubtedly reflect no more than current fashions and fads, many others do reflect a genuine dissatisfaction with the relevance of the more traditional approaches in times of rapid technological change.[9]

There are many ways of interpreting both the conditions and the practical responses. The different organisational structures can themselves be emphasised; so can the changing patterns of power and influence. It is also productive to view the organisational conditions associated with the problem oriented organisation in terms of their implications for information processing. The active concern for innovation and discovery itself places a premium on new information and the uncertainty created by the lack of rigid controls on managerial activities and the dispersion of power and influence tend to increase the need for information in decision making. In turn, the overlapping responsibilities and the emphasis on expert authority make it easier to transfer information across departmental boundaries. Together with appropriate forms of planning, the resultant diversity of attitudes, experiences and purposes serve to increase the amount of information which is available.

The relevance of such an information processing view was illustrated by a study of innovation in hospitals which was conducted by Martin Rosner.[10] In line with the conditions which have been described above, Rosner found that the presence of detailed controls on the activities of medical staff was associated with a low propensity to try new drugs.

Organisational procedures which were aimed at increasing the amount of information which was available on organisational performance had the opposite effect. Hospitals which had detailed and regular reviews of performance were much more willing to try new drugs.

The problem oriented organisation is, in other words, one that is rich in flows of information, both formal and informal. Such a requirement is, of course, reflected in the design of most management accounting systems. The means for providing detailed appraisals of deviations from expected levels of performance are part of the accountant's collection of techniques, but their focus is usually retrospective and narrowly financial. Moreover, many of these formal flows of accounting information are associated with particular forms of organisation structure – forms which tend to emphasise individual accountability, the performance of separate components of the enterprise and vertical as against horizontal relationships. Not only do most accounting systems pay little attention to evolving relationships between components, but as we have already discussed in Chapter 5, if used inappropriately, their underlying organisational assumptions can also result in the parochial attitudes and interdepartmental conflict which stifle some of the essential informal flows of information.[11]

6.4 *The Search for Alternative Courses of Action*

The search for the alternative ways of dealing with a problem is rarely detached from the specification of the problem itself. The training and work experiences which managers receive is very often designed to provide a particular orientation to problems. As a consequence, they are very often defined in a partial manner which is suggestive of the means for their solution.

The nature of the process was illustrated by Tinker's study of the way in which different persons formulated interdepartmental problems.[12] For instance, in one case, the initial difficulty resulted from the fact that purchase of drums had exceeded the budgeted level because customers were not returning the drums which were used to deliver their goods. In response to a request to give a more precise definition of the problem, however, the following explanations were provided:

Marketing Manager: 'We can't increase the deposits for drums because this would give our competitors an advantage. I believe we would do best by seeking to educate customers. . . . I think we should attempt a long campaign at trying to foster the customer's cooperation. It's a long and difficult process, I know.'

Finance Manager: 'Perhaps by locating the difficult customers we could either surcharge them or offer them a financial incentive. An incentive would be difficult to devise and I don't think they would accept a surcharge here.'

Distribution Manager: 'I'm sure we could save a lot of money repairing or remaking a lot of drums that are currently classified as scrap. I argued for this at the original enquiry but nobody would listen.'

Production Manager: 'Personally I think you've got a very difficult problem; I'm not sure there is a solution. Of course, when plastic or some other substitute becomes cheap enough we should be able to avoid deterioration costs.'

The managers were, in other words, perceiving the problem, and the alternative courses of action, in terms of their experiences and objectives. The marketing manager looked to his customers and the production manager to the raw materials and costs. The finance manager not surprisingly emphasised the monetary considerations, while the distribution manager stressed the efficient recycling of the drums. Already there was the basis for conflict and disagreement which could have been very productive if all the varying perceptions had been brought together but if only a single department had been involved, the very definition of the problem contained within it the seeds for its own solution.

Because of such tendencies, a number of writers have characterised the search for solutions to problems as a simple-minded and biased activity.[13] The generation of alternative courses of action and their consequences is, in their view, focused in the area of the perceived symptom. Until proved otherwise, the implication is that the cause is generally near to its effect, and the complex patterns of interrelationships in the organisation are initially ignored and nearly always simplified. The search is practical in nature, directed at finding a satisfactory but speedy solution to the problem. 'Will it work' is often the first question, and this does not mean 'is it the perfect solution' or even 'is it a desirable solution', but 'can we easily put it into operation'.

Search often begins by looking at past precedents and the characteristics of the existing situation. If a satisfactory solution is found, it may even stop at this stage. If not, the search may be directed to other areas with which the manager is familiar. Very often, only if this does not provide promising alternatives will the search be expanded to include the experiences of similar organisations and more radical proposals for change.

Similar considerations are thought to influence the specification of the consequences of the various alternatives. These may initially be very limited. Not only are side effects and long-term consequences difficult and costly to assess, but immediate pressures may necessitate a curtailed consideration and the experiences and values of the participating managers again impose further bounds on the scope of the analysis. Even a single project can be justified in a multiplicity of ways dependent upon its purpose, its sponsorship and the people who have analysed and commented upon it. The costs and benefits of a proposal to change the methods of wage payment, for instance, could be very different if formulated by the production manager rather than a personnel executive.

However, the characteristics of the search process can be influenced in very much the same way as those of the earlier process of problem recognition. Indeed the germs of this potential were evident in the drum example which we discussed briefly above. For if the different functional managers had been placed in a project team or had operated in an organisation with looser departmental and functional boundaries, it is possible that their different perceptions and shared sources of information could have resulted in that degree of conflict and disagreement which is associated with creative search and exploration.* In a wider context, through their effect on both the flows of information and managerial aspirations, the forms of organisational structure, information and reward structures, and anticipatory planning can have a pronounced influence on the locus and extent of search. By carefully changing these factors, senior management has some potential to engineer a more positive opportunity oriented search rather than the more passive process which is described above.

6.5 Evaluation and the Choice of Alternatives
Evaluation and choice rarely occur at a single point in time as the end

* In .fact, the Operational Research Department was asked to investigate the problem. Yet their perceptions may have been equally partial and not infrequently, such specialists experience problems in gaining the acceptance, and thereby opinions and information of other managers.

product of a grand, comprehensive and rational decision process. They are not climatic actions which can be effectively isolated for analytical purposes. Rather, the alternatives generated by the search process are analysed and evaluated in relation to various criteria of feasibility at a whole series of stages. Some preliminary evaluations take place shortly after an alternative is recognised and formulated. Does it offer any potential? Is it worth further consideration? Some possible courses of action are dropped at this early stage and, for whatever reasons or no matter how interesting, may never seep through for more detailed investigation. Others may even be similarly dropped at a later stage when more detrimental information is available or they are shown to be obviously outweighed by other courses of action. Evaluation consists, in other words, of a stream of successive and often temporary commitments, each of which is heavily conditioned by the network of prior decisions and is subject to later alterations on the basis of additional information, adjusted goals and newly emerging pressures and alternatives. In this process, the appraisals made by people at many levels in the hierarchy can have a significant impact on the final choice.

At each stage, before a possible course of action is pushed along the road towards what may be called 'the final decision', each participant in the process is concerned with providing an assessment of its technical quality. Are the cost estimates satisfactory? Is the presumed market potential realistic? Is it likely to meet its stated objectives? These appraisals, although technical in nature, are often made in a highly subjective manner with each participant applying his own specialist skills, experiences and personal values. They are, therefore, subject to the personal and social influences which we have already described and a project may well be set aside by one manager even though it may be appealing to others.

In many cases, however, the factors which determine these technical evaluations are not supreme.

'In the process of moving a project towards funding, there is a critical movement when an idea that has been viewed solely in technical and economic terms is first introduced to general management as a proposal for funding. It is at that moment when a project first begins to move from a study to a facility. Someone says, "I've got a *great* idea", and means it. He puts his judgment behind a proposal. Whereas previously an idea *might* have had to compete with others for engineering study manpower, now it *must* compete with others for the attention and sponsorship of division general management'.[14]

The willingness of a manager to take this next step of committing himself to sponsor a project as *his* project depends upon his evaluation of the personal costs and benefits associated with the project. Is this the type of project with which he should be associated? Does it conflict with other projects which he is sponsoring? Is the project consistent with the criteria which he sees more senior managers applying to his judgment and management skills? A manager, in other words, sponsors projects which he thinks are in his interest to sponsor, given his understandings of the political and organisational rules of the game.

To some extent, the factors influencing this personal appraisal are within the control of senior management. Yet again the organisational structure and patterns of managerial relationships are important. The expectations and associations which they create help to define what the organisation is looking for and hence play a role in shaping the evaluative criteria and decision rules used by individual managers. So do the formal flows of information and the means for measuring and rewarding performance. In this latter area in particular, problems can arise when the measures used in the evaluation of managerial performance conflict with the factors which senior management would like to be considered in on-going decision making. As we noted in Chapter 5, the short-term concerns of nearly all financial performance measures ensure that the potential for such conflicts is not uncommon. When return on investment is used as a measure of performance, for instance, the comissioning of major new facilities can easily be penalised despite their long-term economic value.[15]

However, in addition to the detailed and personal appraisals which all courses of action are submitted to as they move upwards through the organisation, at some stage, there is usually a final and systematic evaluation of the information on the remaining courses of action. An attempt is made to compare them with a choice criterion or criteria. Characteristically, accountants and financial managers, and increasingly, senior general managers, insist that the criteria are expressed in such financial terms as payback period, internal rate of return, net present value and the accounting rate of return. A recent study of the investments made by a sample of British companies found, for example, that 70 per cent of the total were appraised in some systematic financial manner.[16] With the use of these financial procedures, the final evaluation stage often has the appearance of formality, if not rationality, with extensive documentation, formal meetings, and ponderous consideration and debate. We should not allow these procedures, important though they may be at times, to prevent us from considering the equally important social, political and psychological processes which accompany them.

For one thing, the specifications of the projects being considered are themselves the outcome of a social process. In the words of Bower:

> 'Although the project definition may not have changed at all from the conception of the originator "down in the organization", the request justifying the project has been screened, revised, and politically disinfected so that it now tells an attractive story in professional tones.'[17]

People's aspirations and reputations are associated with the proposal and the financial forecasts cannot be considered in isolation from the motives and interests of the managers who provided them. The forecasts of likely outcomes and consequences are often, in fact, moves in a game which has important personal and organisational, as well as economic, implications. The reaction of one manager to hearing that the minimum acceptable rate for new investment had been increased from 12 per cent to 16 per cent, to cite only one example, was not to set aside the marginal projects which would have previously been approved. No, he was so convinced of their worthiness, that he ordered a recheck of their profitability. Not surprisingly, the previous estimates were found to be in error! Sales had unfortunately been underestimated and costs equally overestimated. With the 'errors' corrected, the projects could go ahead to satisfy the financial criterion.

Of course, senior managers and financial analysts often develop some skills in noticing and eliminating such biases but the task is often difficult because the decision process involves many levels of the management hierarchy. Information has already been selectively sifted and reported, and reflects many people's commitments, interests and aspirations, as well as facts. The persons making the final evaluation are rarely completely ignorant of such factors, but they often have a comparative ignorance especially if the alternatives are technically sophisticated and complex or their environment uncertain.

Such biasing is only one manifestation of the commitment which is often associated with projects. By the time of the final evaluation, a project has a history and it is already only one part of a mutually reinforcing set of policies and actions. These interrelationships, and the expectations and commitments which they engender, can often ensure the ultimate acceptance of a project despite the aura of apparent choice which surrounds the final decision stage. In the words of one manager:

> 'Division people become committed to large investments pretty easily and we tend to get committed to the idea ourselves in many cases. Somehow we have to find ways of remaining flexible during the time it takes to put proposals together. . . .'[18]

The problem is a real one. In this company, the final authorisation was often an anticlimax. Indeed, the manager went on to say that he 'would be very surprised if the request had been refused'. In Chapter 1 we discussed the similar experiences of one large British company. Once a proposal had reached the stage of formal application, it will be remembered, it was assured of ultimate acceptance.[19] After studying the investment process in four American companies, Bower also found that the formal capital budgeting procedures had a minimum degree of influence:

> '. . . once a project emerges from the initial stages of definition it is not only hard to change it, but in many cases hard to reject it. Too much time has been invested, too many organizational stakes get committed, and at very high levels of management too little substantive expertise exists to justify second guessing the proposers.'[20]

Yet even Bower's comments introduce an important element of contingency into the process. Despite the reduced role of formal financial appraisal procedures, their impact is seen as depending on the degree of managerial commitment and the expertise of senior management, and these do vary. What is more, senior managers are often called upon to allocate scarce funds between competing projects and to change organisational priorities by encouraging some projects and rejecting others. On such occasions, the manner in which the final choice is exercised is important.

Thompson and Tuden have suggested a useful scheme for considering the manner in which these final organisational decisions are made.[21] They see the approach to decision making as being dependent upon the nature of the uncertainties involved in the situation. To gain some insights into the difficult question of uncertainty, they distinguish between (1) uncertainty over the cause and effect relationships assumed within a proposed project and (2) uncertainty over the preferences regarding alternative outcomes. Uncertainty over cause and effect

Figure 6.2 Styles of decision making

| | | Preferences about possible outcomes | |
		Certain	Uncertain
Beliefs about causation	Certain	Decision by computation	Decision by compromise
	Uncertain	Decision by judgment	Decision by inspiration

relationships is seen as occurring when the decision makers are not sure of the outcomes associated with different projects. Or alternatively, even if the decision makers are confident about the likely outcomes, they may be uncertain about the costs or undesirable effects associated with the projects. Uncertainty over preferences, on the other hand, is seen as occurring when the decision makers are uncertain as to which projects are desirable or undesirable. Obviously, both types of uncertainty are a matter of degree. By dichotomising them to achieve some simplicity, Thompson and Tuden define four general types of decision situations and suggest an approach to decision making for each case. Their schema is summarised in Figure 6.2.

Where the preference ordering is clear and understandings about the likely costs and benefits of projects are believed to be available, decision making is a technical matter. In the extreme, this situation offers little room for genuine choice but in many situations, despite the certainty, the solution may be far from obvious. The data may be complex and voluminous, and the appropriate techniques for integrating the under- standings about the projects may be sufficiently complicated as to lie within the province of skilled specialists. The approach to decision making in such situations remains, however, analytical. This is what Simon has termed a 'programmed decision'.[22] Thompson and Tuden, however, describe this approach as 'decision by computation'.

Where the decision situation is novel, complex or unpredictable, the underlying patterns of cause and effect may be seen as uncertain – or at least subject to dispute – even though preferences are clear. Decisions in these circumstances must be based on 'judgments' of likely outcomes. If, however, the expected consequences of alternative projects are reason- ably clear, but the projects satisfy conflicting objectives, the decision makers' preferences may be subject to a great deal of ambiguity and debate. In these circumstances, the final choice is often the outcome of a bargaining process. Thompson and Tuden have termed it 'decision by compromise'.

Commentators have used such terms as 'wicked' and 'fuzzy' to characterise the lack of structure in situations where there is uncertainty over both causation and preferences.[23] Such terms do indeed reflect the many dilemmas which decision makers undoubtedly face in these situations. Yet such circumstances are not uncommon and managers do attempt to cope with them.

> 'Although this situation seems far removed from usual discussions of organised decision making, it may have empirical as well as theoretical relevance. The most likely action, perhaps, is [a] decision not to face the issue, and organizations which are paralyzed on certain issues may, in fact, be preserving their integrity. On occasions, however, someone in the organization attains and articulates enough imagination to create a new vision or image or belief, and thereby pull together a disintegrating or paralyzed organization.'[24]

If it is forthcoming at all, the resolution of such ambiguities (for solution is hardly the appropriate term), requires what Thompson and Tuden have termed 'decision by inspiration'.

The Thompson and Tuden classification of approaches to decision making provides a useful way of considering the role of financial decision procedures. Obviously, if the objectives of the organisation are seen in financial terms, the analytical approach inherent in net present value techniques, for instance, can quite legitimately have a powerful and direct influence on the final choice in situations where there is little or no uncertainty. This is repeatedly demonstrated in all accounting and financial management textbooks. Uncertainty is, however, a fact of organisational life and many significant decisions are not therefore of the computational variety. Yet we know that analytical financial tools are still used. Just what role do they serve?

When judgment is required to deal with uncertain patterns of cause and effect, financial procedures are often used to structure the decision situation. At one level, this is undoubtedly achieved by using them to absorb some of the threatening uncertainty and substitute in its place a set of seemingly precise calculations. If, however, the decision makers are willing to face the uncertainty inherent in the situation, the procedures can serve as a learning device, helping to demonstrate the consequences of assumptions. The use of sensitivity analysis and risk analysis[25] can help decision makers to understand the implications of their assumptions and even suggest those areas of uncertainty which are the most important. While in this way influencing the final choice, their role always remains partial because they do not show which assumptions are capable of eliciting the greatest confidence or commitment.

In the bargaining process, where preferences are uncertain, the financial decision procedures can play a very similar role. They can often help managers to discover what their preferences or value premises are, and in the process, expose the inconsistencies which need to be resolved.[26] In addition, when the final preference orderings have to be moulded rather than served, the financial procedures can themselves be used as powerful bargaining strategies by managers who value financial objectives. At such times, their ability to persuasively express a mass of complex and voluminous data in terms of precise indices is at a premium, for in doing this, well specified financial procedures can increase the visibility and thereby the salience of the financial aspects of performance. Indeed in many organisations where there is now an apparent consensus over the supremacy of financial values, one might, albeit cautiously, go on to surmise that the use of such procedures is only a residue of the past conflicts and bargaining among different functional groups over the appropriate criteria for choice.[27]

Decision by inspiration and net present value hardly appear to be a happy pair. It has to be admitted that the role of such procedures in these circumstances is less certain, but casual observations suggest that they can play a role in the after-the-fact attempts to legitimise the inspired choice or the decision not to face the issue. In the words of March:

> 'It seems to me perfectly obvious that a description that assumes goals come first and action comes later is frequently radically wrong. Human choice behaviour is at least as much a process for discovering goals as for acting on them. Although it is true enough that goals and decisions are "conceptually" distinct, that is simply a statement of the theory. It is not a defence of it. They are conceptually distinct if we choose to make them so'.[28]

On such occasions, the important element of ritual which is associated with the use of many other financial procedures, has a special significance in helping to sanctify the highly uncertain and often controversial actions.

Rather than speculating further, we can be content with emphasising yet again the fact that the role played by financial procedures in the decision process is determined by both social and economic considerations. The economic factors are easily isolated and receive much attention but although the social and psychological factors are often less obvious, they are usually far more important for understanding the inherently uncertain context within which decisions are made.[29]

6.6 *The Function of Accounting in Decision Making*

As we have seen, accounting systems serve two principle purposes in the decision process. First, they provide some of the stimuli by which problems are both recognised and defined, and the alternative courses of action are isolated and their consequences elaborated. Second, accounting plays a role in the analysis and appraisal of the alternatives.

As problem stimuli, accounting systems are only a part of the whole complex of information in any organisation, both formal and informal, which is relevant for recognising, defining and moulding alternative courses of action, and it is rarely possible to put bounds on the sources of ideas. It is possible, however, to design information systems which specifically attempt to focus managerial attention.[30] Performance measures, financial and otherwise, are designed to do just this and the ideas of variance analysis and management by exception which are so influential in accounting are founded on such a rationale.

In practice, however, the emphasis on ideas of individual managerial performance and personal accountability which influences the design and operation of so many financial reporting systems easily results in the reinforcement of individual perspectives and prejudices rather than the stimulation of inquiry and debate. If genuine consideration is to be given to the creation of decision oriented accounting systems, accounting may well require a new vision and ideology, one based on an organisational rather than an individual view of decision making. The focus for analysis could well become the decision or activity centre rather than the individual responsibility centre, with decision centres including one or many managers. Much more attention would have to be given to the relationship between the decision centres and both the other parts of the organisation and the wider organisational environment. Explicitly recognising the need to coordinate and guide group decisions, information systems in these settings would aim to link people, upwards, downwards and sideways, according to the demands of the task. Much more consideration would have to be given to the regular and formal surveillance of the decision units' environments.

The value of design principles which explicitly aim to stimulate the wider decision process is already recognised in the common belief that the process of establishing financial standards, budgets and plans may be just as important a means of recognising and responding to problems as the comparative reporting of actual events. The questioning and the analysis which can take place at this time are thought to be capable, if organised in an appropriate manner, of making a much more positive contribution to the expansion of opportunities than the more cautious reaction to the subsequent exceptions. If there is any truth in such beliefs, and it must be emphasised that there is an urgent need for both fundamental research and practical experimentation in these vital areas, then much greater consideration needs to be given to the design of information systems which actively incorporate the future oriented perspectives which are elicited at these times.

Much lip service is paid to such ideas in the accounting literature but practice remains entrenched in retrospective reporting. There is a need to experiment with reporting systems based on cost to complete, and current contributions to future performance, rather than on historical performance. Consideration needs to be given to planning and reporting on the creation of the whole range of resources and capabilities, human, organisational, physical and financial, in addition to costs incurred and revenues generated.

Turning to the role of accounting in the evaluation of alternative courses of action, it should be stated that whilst earlier in the chapter I have emphasised the social processes inherent in evaluation and choice, this does not imply that financial appraisals have no role to play. They do. Indeed as the technological and economic environment becomes increasingly more complex and rules of thumb, intuition or reliance on past experience become less adequate for dealing with it, there is a need for rigorous analysis of alternative courses of action and their implications. At the same time, the normative models of decision making which underlie the financial procedures, have most validity in situations where there is a single well-specified objective, usually profit maximisation, and a great deal of understanding about the factors involved. Therefore, unless care is taken to recognise the limits on their potential and scope, the procedures may be at their most practical in those situations where there is the least need for them.

One response to this dilemma has been to develop decision criteria which more effectively allow for risk, uncertainty and complexity in the choice of alternative courses of action.[31] A complemetary approach emerges, however, if the highly interdependent nature of the various stages of the decision process is explicitly recognised. By doing this, it is possible to see that the usefulness of analytical choice criteria may often rest less on the logic of the computational procedures for aggregating, discounting and comparing assumed outlays and incomes, than on how they influence the behavioural processes which give rise to the alternatives to be evaluated.

Different methods of review and appraisal can result in different search procedures, the comparison of different alternatives, and the provision of different types of information to justify their selection. Unlike textbook examples which compare two or more alternative approaches to appraisal by showing how differently they rank a series of specified alternatives, in practice, the information on the alternatives is not given. The particular criterion in use will partly determine the specification of the alternatives. One may call for more detailed data than another or for more explicit consideration of project interdependencies or for data over a longer period of time. These differences are capable of affecting the perceptions and attitudes of the managers, the alternatives submitted for final review, and thereby, be it indirectly rather than directly, the final choice.

Such considerations were discussed by Wildavsky and Hammond in their study of the impact of 'planning, programming, budgeting systems' in the United States Department of Agriculture.[32] They noted how the justification for the new system shifted from the specific advantages of comprehensive calculation and comparative analysis to such psychological effects as breaking managers' habitual patterns of thought. One official commented:

> 'We were interested in [PPBS] as a therapeutic device for agency and budget people. It's easy to get into the habit of doing things the same way. Starting out with the idea that nothing is sacred is therapeutic in itself. Any device which will encourage people to give a deeper and broader consideration of operations will lead to better understandings of where improvements might be made'.

Recognition is now being given to the type of stimulus which appraisal and review procedures can give to the whole decision process, although as yet, our understanding of how to achieve such effects are only in their early stages. However, as accountants and other information specialists begin to pay increasing attention to the social and political, as well as economic components of the decision process, we can expect many of the existing highly generalised and often simplistic outcomes to be replaced by more realistic perspectives. As a broader range of questions are considered, accountants can start to supply more relevant answers. Progress will come not only from the development of more sophisticated aids to decision making, but also from the achievement of some degree of synthesis between these and the processes by which managers do in fact cope with the uncertainties of organisational life. In this way, accounting as I have sought to demonstrate, has the potential of being a richer and broader discipline than tradition would recognise.

6.7 *References*

1. See, for instance:
   DEVONS, E, *Planning in Pràctice*, Cambridge University Press, 1950
   DRUCKER, P F, *The Practice of Management*, Heineman, 1955
   VICKERS, G, *The Art of Judgment*, Chapman and Hall, 1965
   and possibly:
   PARKINSON, C N, *Parkinson's Law or the Pursuit of Progress*, John Murray, 1958
   TOWNSEND, R, *Up the Organization*, Michael Joseph, 1970

2. See, for instance:
   RAIFFA, H, *Decision Analysis: Introductory Lectures on Choices Under Uncertainty*, Addison–Wesley, 1970
   SCHLAIFER, R, *Probability and Statistics for Business Decisions*, McGraw-Hill, 1959

3. The relationships between human behaviour and the assumptions inherent in normative models of decision making are reviewed in:
   PETERSON, C R and BEACH, L R, 'Man as an Intuitive Statistician', *Psychological Bulletin*, vol 68, no 1, 1967, pp 29–46

4. One of the few articles on the subject is:
   POUNDS, W F, 'The Process of Problem Finding', *Industrial Management Review*, Fall 1969, pp 1–19

5. For a discussion of the role of experience in decision making is see:
   ECCLES, A J and WOOD, D, 'How Do Managers Decide?', *The Journal of Management Studies*, vol 9, no 3, October 1972, pp 291–303

6. See, for instance:
   NEWELL, A, SHAW, J C and SIMON, H A, 'Chess-Playing Programs and the Problem of Complexity', *IBM Journal of Research and Development*, October 1958, pp 320–35
   SIMON, H A, *The New Science of Management Decision*, Harper and Brothers, 1960

7. The related findings on individual creativity are summarised in:
   STEIN, M I and HEINZE, S J, *Creativity and the Individual*, Free Press, 1960
   BARRON, F, 'The Psychology of Creativity', in: NEWCOMBE, T M, *et al*, *New Directions in Psychology, II*, Holt Rinehart and Winston, 1965

8. For a more comprehensive discussion of the topic see, for instance:
   BURNS, T and STALKER, G M, *The Management of Innovation*, Tavistock, 1961
   HAGE, J and AIKEN, M, *Social Change in Complex Organizations*, Random House, 1970
   PELZ, D C and ANDREWS, F M, *Scientists in Organizations*, John Wiley and Sons, 1966

9. It is of some interest to note that most of these approaches received their initial impetus in attempts to deal with the vast technological complexities of the aerospace industry. For further details see:
   GALBRAITH, J R, 'Matrix Organization Designs: How to Combine Functional and Project Forms', *Business Horizons*, February 1971, pp 29–40
   GALBRAITH, J R, (ed), *Matrix Organizations: Organization Design for High Technology*, MIT Press, 1971

GALBRAITH, J R, *Designing Complex Organizations*, Addison-Wesley, 1973
A discussion of applications at the individual and group level is given in:
GORDON, W J J, *Synetics: The Development of Creative Capacity*, Harper and Row, 1961

10. ROSNER, M M, 'Administrative Controls and Innovation', *Behavioral Science* vol 13, 1968, pp 36–43

11. After studying the influence of organisational structure and information flows on the early stages of the capital investment process, Joseph Bower, commented as follows:

> '. . . the definition of jobs, the hierarchical relationships, the management information, and the reward systems often diverted or confused the managers involved in the [problem recognition] process. In the instance of Specialty Plastics, these factors cut a project off from wisdom and judgment that might have improved it, as well as its sources of support. *The reason [organizational] content is sometimes dysfunctional may be that the set of problems that require specialization are more evident to the designers [of information systems] . . . than the problems of planning that require synthesis*'. (Emphasis added).

BOWER, J, *Managing The Resource Allocation Process*, Division of Research, Graduate School of Business Administration, Harvard University, 1970, p 262

12. TINKER, A M, *Organizational Change and Change Agents at Work*, unpublished MSc dissertation, University of Bradford, 1970

13. See, for instance:
BRAYBROOKE, D and LINDBLOM, C E, *A Strategy of Decision*, The Free Press, 1963
CYERT, R M and MARCH, J G, *A Behavioural Theory of the Firm*, Prentice-Hall, 1963, especially pp 83–127
Some extensions of the Cyert and March framework are discussed in:
CARTER, E E, 'The Behavioural Theory of the Firm and Top Level Corporate Decisions', *Administrative Science Quarterly*, vol 16, no 4, December 1971, pp 413–29

14. BOWER, J L, *Managing The Resource Allocation Process*, Division of Research, Graduate School of Business Administration, Harvard University, 1970, p 77

15. Such problems are discussed and illustrated in numerous articles and monographs. See, for instance:
BOWER, J L, *Managing The Resource Allocation Process*, Division of Research, Graduate School of Business Administration, Harvard University, 1970
DEARDEN, J, 'Limits on Decentralized Profit Responsibility', *Harvard Business Review*, July–August 1962, pp 81–9
DEARDEN, J, 'Mirage of Profit Decentralization', *Harvard Business Review*, November–December 1962, pp 140–54
DEARDEN J, 'The Case Against ROI Control', *Harvard Business Review*, May–June 1969, pp 124–135
Yet despite such discussions which have appeared in the academic,

professional and management literatures, numerous firms continue to maintain
the conflict. Reports on current practice in this area are given in:
MAURIEL, J J and ANTHONY, R N, 'Misevaluation of Investment Centre Per-
formance', *Harvard Business Review*, March–April 1966, pp 98–105
MCINNES, J M, HOPWOOD, A G and LOWE, E A, *Measuring Performance Within the
Enterprise*, Working Paper No 2(a), Manchester Business School, 1971

16. The study was undertaken for the Ministry of Technology. Summary findings
are reported in:
Hansard, December 14, 1970
Other surveys of actual practice in the United Kingdom appear in:
BARNA, T, *Investment and Growth Policies in British Industrial Firms*, Cambridge
University Press, 1962
CANNON, C H, 'The Limited Application of Minimum Profitability Require-
ments to Capital Expenditure Proposals', and 'Private Capital Investment:
A Case Study Approach Towards Testing Alternative Theories', *Journal of
Industrial Economics*, vol XV, no 1, November 1966, pp 54–64 and vol XVI,
no 3, July 1968, pp 186–95
ROCKLEY, L E, *Investment for Profitability*, Business Books, 1973
WILLIAMS, B R and SCOTT, W P, *Investment Proposals and Decisions*, Allen and
Unwin, 1965
American practice is discussed in:
CHRISTY, G A, *Capital Budgeting – Current Practices and Their Efficiency*, Bureau of
Business and Economic Research, University of Oregon, 1966
ISTVAN, D F, *Capital Expenditure Decisions: How They are Made in Large Corpor-
ations*, Bureau of Business Research, Indiana University, 1961
KLANIMER, T, 'Empirical Evidence on the Adoption of Sophisticated Capital
Budgeting Techniques', *Journal of Business*, vol 45, no 3, July 1972, pp 387–97

17. BOWER, J, *Managing the Resource Allocation Process*, Division of Research,
Graduate School of Business Administration, Harvard University, 1970

18. ACKERMAN, R W, 'Influence on Integration and Diversity on the Investment
Process', *Administrative Science Quarterly*, vol 15, no 3, September 1970, p 348
The idea of commitment is also discussed and illustrated in:
AHARONI, Y, *The Foreign Investment Decision Process*, Division of Research,
Graduate School of Business Administration, Harvard University, 1966

19. MORGAN, J R and LUCK, M, *The Investment System in the Firm*, Institute for
Operational Resarch, 1968

20. BOWER, J L, *Managing The Resource Allocation Process*, Division of Research,
Graduate School of Business Administration, Harvard University, 1970, p 54

21. THOMPSON, J D and TUDEN, A, 'Strategies, Structures and Processes of Organiza-
tional Decision', in: THOMPSON, J D, et al, (eds) *Comparative Studies in
Administration*, University of Pittsburgh Press, 1959
Some supporting findings are presented in:
CONRATH, D W, 'Organizational Decision Making Behaviour Under Varying
Conditions of Uncertainty', *Management Science*, vol 13, no 3, April, 1967,
pp B487–B500

22. SIMON, H A, *The New Science of Management Decision*, Harper and Row, 1960.
23. See, for instance:
BELLMAN, Z, 'Decision Making in a Fuzzy Environment' *a published paper*
RITTEL, H W J and WEBBER, M M, 'Dilemmas in a General Theory of Planning',
Policy Sciences, vol 4, no 2, June, 1973, pp 155–69
24. THOMPSON, J D, 'Decision Making, The Firm and the Market', in: COOPER,
W W, LEAVITT, H J and SHELLY, M W, *New Perspectives in Organization Research*,
John Wiley and Sons, 1964, p 337
25. See, for instance:
HERTZ, D B, 'Risk Analysis in Capital Investment', *Harvard Business Review*,
January–February, 1964, pp 95–106
HOUSE, W C, *Sensitivity Analysis in Making Capital Investment Decisions*, National
Association of Accountants, 1968
26. MARCH, J G, 'The Technology of Foolishness', *Civilokonomen*, May 1971
27. On the role of bargaining in capital budgeting, see the brief article by:
PONDY, L R, 'Budgeting and Intergroup Conflict in Organizations', *Pittsburgh
Business Review*, vol 34, no 3, April 1964, pp 1–3
28. MARCH, J G, 'The Technology of Foolishness', *Civilokonomen*, May 1971
29. The discussion has tried to cover some of these factors, albeit in a rather cur-
tained manner. If the reader would like to gain a greater insight into the
realities of organisational decision making I can do no better than recommend
you to read some more detailed descriptions of the process in action. There
are, as yet, none of a specifically accounting nature, although the following
are very revealing:
DALTON, M, *Men Who Manage*, John Wiley and Sons, 1959
PETTIGREW, A M, *The Politics of Organizational Decision Making*, Tavistock, 1973
WILDAVSKY, A, *The Politics of the Budgetary Process*, Little, Brown, 1964
30. See, for instance:
DOPUCH, N, BIRNBERG, J G and DEMSKI, J, 'An Extension of Standard Cost
Variance Analysis', *The Accounting Review*, vol 42, no 3, July 1967, pp 526–36
ZANETOS, Z S, 'Standard Costs as a First Step to Probabilistic Control: A
Theoretical Justification, an Extension and Implications', *The Accounting
Review*, vol 39, no 2, April 1964, pp 296–304
31. See, for instance:
HERTZ, D B, 'Risk Analysis in Capital Investment', *Harvard Business Review*,
January–February 1964, pp 95–106
HESPOS, R F and STRASSMAN, P A, 'Stochastic Decision Trees for the Analysis of
Investment Decisions', *Management Science*, vol 11, no 10, August 1965, pp
244–59
WEINGARTNER, H M, 'Capital Budgeting of Interrelated Projects: Survey and
Synthesis', *Management Science*, vol 12, no 7, March 1966, pp 485–516
32. WILDAVSKY, A and HAMMOND, A, 'Comprehensive Versus Incremental Budget-
ing in the Department of Agriculture', *Administrative Science Quarterly*, vol 10,
no 3, December 1965, pp 321–46

CHAPTER SEVEN

The Interpretation of Information

A manager acts on the basis of the social meanings that he ascribes to the world around him. Rather than just passively absorbing the information which he is either given or directly observes, he attaches meanings to it in accordance with his attitudes and values, and his previous social experiences. All situations are interpreted, they are never merely seen as physical stimuli, but are inevitably shaped by the manager's personality and the social nature of his environment.

In order to illustrate the importance of our subjective conceptions of reality, let us briefly examine an example of an organisation during a period of crisis.[1] The senior executives of a large car company were attempting to isolate the cause of some problems in one of their plants. Against the best advice of their own managers, they had decided to hurriedly convert the plant to the production of a new type of engine. Perhaps because of this initial disagreement, they became so strongly committed to the decision that they rejected information which suggested that the problems were due to the confusion caused by the rapid change, the inadequately prepared automation programme and the splintering of loyal work groups. Instead, another explanation was found. They diagnosed the problem as being due to an inefficient work force and poor plant management.

149

A new plant manager was found to deal with the situation. Under considerable pressure from his superiors to increase efficiency, he further misinterpreted the discontent which followed the managerial coup. Not without some justification, he was sure that the managers and employees resented the demotion of their previous boss, who they had respected. But knowledgeable managers who attempted to explain their understanding of the situation to him were accused of being too sympathetic to the employees and unwilling to accept the need for change. They were transferred to jobs in other plants, and new subordinates who shared his viewpoint were brought in.

The basic problem persisted, however, reinforcing his suspicions that the employees were actively resisting his own tactics for improvement. He did make some efforts to isolate the cause of the difficulties by talking to a whole series of people at all levels in the plant. Unfortunately, he only used the information to learn who was 'for' him and who was 'against' him. On this basis, he transferred the employees whom he thought were the ringleaders of the resistance, but this worsened the situation as employees now began to fear for their very jobs.

The example is extreme, although it is suggestive of problems encountered in many organisations. One only has to think of the fate of the Edsel, a huge, dazzling car designed by the Ford Motor Company in 1955, introduced in 1957, and discontinued in 1959 after a loss exceeding a third of a billion dollars, or even the continued allied faith in strategic area bombing during World War II. In both these cases, as in our example, alternative information and diagnoses were available. In fact, they were almost begging for recognition and attention, but the personal and organisational barriers to their utilisation were so great that they were rejected and ignored. In the example, right the way through the crisis, the senior managers failed to set aside their strong preconceptions. They failed to understand why such a promising young manager had failed, and remained convinced, despite all indications to the contrary, that the managers and employees of the plant were responsible for its misfortunes.

As far back as the seventeenth century, the great English philosopher and statesman, Francis Bacon, could note that 'the mind, darkened by it's covering the body, is far from being a flat, equal and clear mirror that receives and reflects the rays without mixture, but is rather . . . an uneven mirror which imports its own properties to different objects . . . and distorts and disfigures them'.

7.1 *Some Influences on Individual Perceptions*
The interpretation of information involves not only abbreviation and simplification to bring it within the scope of our limited memories, but also reconstruction and elaboration. The human mind is not disposed to stop at the facts with which it is presented. In seeing a situation, we transform the facts and often proceed to go far beyond their limited associations and implications.

The mind of man is an elusive matter and the logic inherent in this reconstruction knows no precise philosophy and method. It cannot be directly observed and inferences about it are notoriously difficult. Individuals vary greatly in the way in which they react to situations. Some react by suppressing events, having learnt to avoid seeing certain threatening aspects of the environment; other people react quite differently, being sensitive and vigilant. It is known however, that in general, people suppose a greater degree of order in things than really exists. We make some effort to produce a coherent picture, often suppressing detail which does not appear to fit in and inventing details to fill troublesome gaps.

Particularly in ambiguous situations there is a tendency to distort the original material so as to make it more regular and symmetrical. An extreme, but nevertheless revealing example of this was provided by a famous experiment conducted by Skinner.[2] He found that when hungry birds (of the feathered variety) were given food at brief random intervals, they developed very idiosyncratic, repetitive actions. The precise behaviour varied from bird to bird, however, because the arrival of food increased the probability of whatever form of behaviour immediately preceeded it occurring again. This form of behaviour was seen as being reinforced. But given the increasing incidence of this one type of behaviour, it was all the more likely to be reinforced further as the food continued to arrive at random intervals. Then as this further reinforcement occurred, the behaviour was all the more likely to occur again, which yet again improved its chances of being reinforced, and so on. After a short time the birds were found to be turning rapidly round the cage, hopping from side to side and making strange head movements. And because these behaviours were reinforced less than 100 per cent of the time, they tended to persist even when reinforcement stopped altogether. Skinner referred to these actions as superstitions. There are, of course, problems in generalising from the behaviour of birds to that of humans. Many detailed sociological and anthropological studies of magic, superstition, ritual and myth in human societies provide, however, some basis for thinking that humans develop equally complex forms of belief in such unpredictable circumstances.

We tend to emphasise the principal aspects of situations, ignoring, absorbing or contrasting other properties. Often the content is divided into clear cut categories, with graduations of viewpoint reduced both by exaggerating some differences and losing others. This may take the form of distorting a situation in line with a simple two-value logic. Indeed, it has been consistently found in studies of human perception that one of the major influences is evaluation and this obtains even in cases where great care has been taken not to suggest in any way that the perceptions should or should not be evaluatory. The most natural of such evaluations seems to be the general nature of like against dislike, although there are many other bases. In the introductory example to this chapter, the manager interpreted the views of his colleagues, and subordinates, complex as they may have been, in terms of whether they were for or against him. Similarly, standard cost variances are often summarised as either good or bad, favourable or unfavourable. In all cases, there is a consequent loss of detail and content, and a confounding of facts with values and aspirations.

At times, the slightest clue can be highlighted and emphasised, just one aspect of an event being given inordinate weight, its 'halo' overshadowing the rest of the situation. Unfortunately, we have few specifically accounting examples of such phenomena to refer to; the necessary research has yet to be done. We can, however, illustrate their significance by referring to one of the early studies of the process by which we form impressions of other people's personalities.

Asch read the following list of personality traits to a group of experimental subjects, implying as he did so that the traits described some real person:[3]

> 'intelligent, skilfull, industrious, warm, determined, practical, cautious'

On being asked to give a brief description of the person brought to mind by the traits, all of the subjects proved willing to do so, even on this, the meagrest of evidence. One example will suffice: 'A scientist performing experiments and persevering after many setbacks. He is driven by the desire to accomplish something that would be of benefit'.

However, Asch varied the fourth trait in the list. For some subjects, the trait was 'warm', as in the listing above, but other subjects were told that the person was 'cold'. Otherwise the lists were identical. The change from 'warm' to 'cold' made a profound difference in the persons imagined. With the set of traits including 'warm', most subjects thought that the person described would also be generous, humane, humorous, sociable and popular, but when the list included 'cold', most of them thought that the person was less likely to have any of these rather agreeable character-istics. He was, in the words of one subject, seen as 'a rather snobbish person who feels that his success and intelligence set him apart from the run-of-the-mill individual; calculating and unsympathetic'.

Such perceptions, despite being based on little evidence, are quite capable of affecting behaviour. In another study of the warm–cold vari-able, a group of university students were informed that their usual teacher could not take the class and that another person would substitute for him.[4] Before the new teacher arrived, the students were given a brief biographical statement about him. All were the same, except that one half of the class were told that he was a 'warm' person and the other half that he was a 'cold' person. After only a brief discussion in the class, the students were asked for a short written evaluation of their new teacher. On first impressions at least, despite the fact that all of the students had experienced exactly the same situation, he was consistently seen in more favourable terms by the students who had been told that he was 'warm'. Not only did they see him as being more informal and humane, but a significantly larger number of these students actually participated in the class discussion.

People also tend to interpret information in the light of clues as to the possible decisions for which it is to be used and are quite capable of incorporating their own views of the decision situation into their per-ceptions and the information which they send to other people. Such factors as their feelings about the possible reactions of other managers to different types of information can influence the biases and distortions by which perceptions and interpretations are systematically, if subjectively adjusted.

In a novel experiment, Cyert and March asked a group of thirty-two graduate students to specify a summary statistic for a series of numbers which represented different estimates presumably submitted by two assistants.[5] In one case, the set of numbers was presented as a group of cost estimates, while in another case the identical set was presented as a group of sales estimates. All the students worked on both sets of numbers, with a ten week interval between the two versions, one half receiving the cost version first and the other half, the sales version.

Table 7.1 Comparison of values submitted by individual students

	Summary statistic greater in sales version	Equal	Summary statistic greater in cost version
Sales version first	2	3	11
Cost version first	3	1	12
Total	5	4	23

As can be seen in Table 7.1, despite the identical nature of the basic data, the students tended to give different values of the summary statistic in the two contrived situations. As cost analysts, they tended to over-estimate costs, whilst as sales analysts, they underestimated sales. The values were obviously modified in the light of the different contexts, although the precise reasons and subjective logic underlying the process were less clear. Might it be that the students were trying to appreciate some of the wider organisational consequences which could result from the use of their summaries? In responding differently to what was presented as cost information than to what was presented as sales information, could they, for instance, have intuitively felt that the possible losses associated with underestimated costs exceed those of overestimated sales? Such an interpretation, whilst admittedly speculative in this instance, is consistent with psychological evidence which suggests that man is often a rather conservative processor of information.[6]

In experimental conditions, people are known to respond to

information by revising their prior expectations in the same direction as would occur by the straight application of statistical methods, but the revision is less than that which such methods would regard as optimal. In some studies, for instance, people have required as many as nine related presentations of information to revise their expectations as much as the theory would prescribe after just one presentation. These results, or at least the generalisations from them, are still controversial, but Edwards, one of the pioneering researchers in the area, thinks that while men may often be aware of the meaning of individual pieces of inform-ation, they are unable to combine the meanings contained in a stream of information with either each other or their prior opinions.[7]

These reactions to minimal information are fairly general and often rather important in their consequences.[8] We all know how readily we stereotype whole nationalities and minority groups. On a smaller scale, as is testified by the so called 'go-go' syndrome on the stock market, large companies are characterised on the basis of the age of their managing director, the growth of just one product or the number of recent acquis-itions, whether or not the subsequent rationalisation has been successful. The impression gained of a person seen as a manager is very different from when the same individual is thought to be a trade union official.[9] People are even apparently willing to characterise the owners of different makes of cars not only on the basis of their socio-economic status, which might bear some relationship to the price of the car, but also in terms of their virility and sensibility.[10]

The ordinary, the typical and the popular exert a profound effect on our interpretation of any situation. The process of perceiving is less dependent upon an absolute judgment of the current situation than upon the relationship of even the slightest hint in the present to our previous understanding. Events are seen as part of a continual stream, whose consistency of flow and movement can seemingly persuade us into seeing a greater similarity between the new and the old.

A person's education, training and background are all factors, which in influencing the extent and variety of his previous understanding and experiences, can affect how he sees any situation or event. The division of labour and the consequent work specialisation in modern organisations create different conceptions of interest and reality, with members of each department often seeing only those aspects of a situation which specifically relate to the activities and purposes of their own jobs. As we discussed in the last chapter, such factors are vitally important for understanding the nature of the decision process because the very identification of a problem and the possible courses of action involves attaching intuitive meanings and prominence to situations.

Another illustration of the significance of these factors was provided in an experiment which Dearborn and Simon conducted with a group of managers from a large manufacturing company who were enrolled in an executive training course.[11] The managers, who represented different functional areas including sales, production and accounting, were asked to read an industrial case study and then identify the most important problem facing the concern. The majority of the managers identified the principal problem as being one related to their own departmental affiliation. For instance, 83 per cent of the sales managers mentioned sales as the most important problem, while this aspect was only seen as significant by 29 per cent of the other managers. Similarly, 80 per cent of the production managers identified the importance of organisational problems as against 22 per cent of the other members of the course. The managers' interpretations of the situation were clearly being influenced by their own previous experiences and personal identities.

Our needs and aspirations, and our values and beliefs, are often closely related to our socialisation and background, and are therefore also important forces influencing how we see the world around us. Perceptions can be distorted when aspirations are attached to events. People with a strong need for money, for example, consistently overestimate the size of coins[12] and persons in search of success or acceptance can see events through a filter which reflects their hopes rather than the reality of the situation. Frequently, we see what we expect to see and engage in wishful thinking whereby events of unpleasant association are either suppressed or distorted. If, however, there are some obvious and disturbing signs to the contrary, our views of the entire situation can potentially be clouded with distress.

A manager faced with a choice between several possible courses of action, for instance, will go through a process of evaluating each alternative, considering the desirable and undesirable features of each, before choosing that course of action which seems more desirable to him. After he has made a choice and committed himself to a course of action, all the information and knowledge which he has on the desirable features of the chosen action are consistent with the action. However, in the process of making his choice, the manager has also acquired information concerning the attractive aspects of the courses of action which he rejected. In the words of Festinger, an eminent social psychologist who has studied man's reactions to such situations, these perceptions are 'dissonant' with the chosen action.[13]

Festinger has argued that 'dissonance is an almost inevitable consequence of having made a decision'. He maintains, however, that the existence of dissonance between prior understandings and an individual's actions produces pressure to reduce or eliminate it. These reductive pressures can sometimes act to change the subsequent behaviour although in many situations they may alter some of the perceptions. The rejected courses of action come, for example, to be seen as less desirable than was originally anticipated.

The processing of information is not, therefore, a mechanical, routine procedure. To come to life and to influence events, information has to be perceived and interpreted. Information systems, whether accounting or otherwise, involve human beings and for any comprehensive viewpoint, the human characteristics are just as relevant as the more technical devices with which the accountant is so concerned. Personalities, and individual needs and experiences are intimately woven into how people see the world around them.

7.2 Social Influences On Perception

The social nature of organisations makes it essential that we also consider perception in the context of groups of individuals, informal and organised. Through group identifications and expectations, and a rather basic need for the validation of our views by other people, social factors can radically alter the way in which information is interpreted. In addition, groups of individuals have their own defences against the seeming pathologies of individual perception. They are adaptive and learning, and in this manner, many biases have their own counterbiases.

While we use our senses to obtain a great deal of information about our environment, we also lean heavily on the opinions of other people. The relative importance of these two sources of information varies from situation to situation, although in general, when a situation is clear and precise, the individual tends to rely less on other people. If the situation is difficult and ambiguous, however, with perceptions merging with judgments, the individual is more likely to rely on the opinions of others. He seeks a basis for the subjective validity of his views, attitudes and observations in whether they are shared by his colleagues and acquaintances.

A classically simple case of a highly ambiguous situation, known as the autokinetic effect, was discovered by the astronomers of old staring at a single star in the night sky and it has been used by psychologists to study the effects of group pressure on perception and judgment. A single point of light in a completely dark room cannot be precisely localised because there is no external referent to compare it with. Though it is perfectly stationary, the light will seem to move in an erratic manner.

In a famous experiment, Sherif[14] asked his subjects to estimate the extent to which the light moved. It didn't really move even the slightest fraction of an inch, but the subjects all reported movement. At first, a person's estimates ranged widely, although in the course of a hundred attempts, each person settled down to his own rather narrow range. When two or three people were put into the room and asked to report their judgments aloud, initially as one would expect, their judgments differed, but over time, they tended to converge. Despite the fact that there were no requests for unanimity, no arguments, no efforts to persuade and most individuals insisted that they had not been influenced by the opinions of others, a group interpretation nevertheless emerged.

Over many experiments and using other stimuli, there does appear to be a tendency for members of a group to move towards agreement in such totally ambiguous situations. Indeed, a group consensus may be the only form of reality in such a context because problems of this nature have no direct stable evidence. But what if there is some objectively verifiable correct solution? How do social pressures influence individual interpretations then?

Psychologists have been hard at work on this problem too and they have found that at least some people are willing to report in line with a group majority even when this is clearly incorrect.[15] Of course, the reasons are complex and this is one of the many areas where there are dangers in relying too heavily on psychological experiments because the frequent lack of discussion and detailed search can only increase the conformist tendencies compared with more realistic situations. In addition, the precise interpretation of the findings is further complicated because it is often difficult to distinguish between people who are really not aware of their error, those who acknowledge the difference between their own and the majority view but feel that the latter must be correct, and those who merely report in line with the majority because they do not want to appear different or in any sense inferior. Over time the differences can become confounded as people perhaps change their basic attitudes to restore some element of consistency.

Nevertheless, the large body of work which has been done in this area has emerged with interesting and generalisable conclusions. Certainly, they are consistent with the results of many field studies as well as anecdotal tales. The factors which influence the impact of group pressures can be separated into three categories: situational, the nature of the social group and individual characteristics.

The situation being viewed is an important factor. Conformity with the prevailing group interpretation is greater in ambiguous situations and where a person has minimal prior knowledge and understanding. In these cases, a person is less certain of his own judgments and will tend to seek validation from other people. The number of people in the group is crucial at this stage, there being an increased tendency to yield as more people express contrary views. Extreme minority views can perhaps be rejected by most, although even this depends on whether the other people are seen as experts, peers or members of some racial or ethnic minority group.

If individual interpretations are difficult to identify and monitor, there is a reduced tendency to yield one's own interpretation, although this is influenced by the social and power structures of the group. Persons of medium status, perhaps having most to lose by being rejected, tend to yield more than either the leaders or people of lower status. In our introductory example, the new manager could reject the interpretations of his subordinates, identifying, as he did, with those of his immediate superiors.

At the individual level, there are extremely large differences between people. The conformists tend to be less intelligent, more rigid in style, less tolerant of uncertainty and lacking in self confidence. They have an intense preoccupation with other people, being rather dependent upon them for acceptance, and they hold rather conventional political and social attitudes and values. Perhaps the most heartening piece of evidence, however, is that even in many of these distressing experimental conditions, and there is evidence that they are sufficiently distressing to result in physiological changes, a vast majority of people do resist the pressure to conform. Group pressures are important but by no means all pervasive.

7.3 Counter-biasing Behaviour

However, while we are familiar with the impact of both individual and group influence on how information is interpreted, the final effect of the various biases on the behaviour of the organisation as a larger social grouping is still not clear. In novel and uncertain situations, the influences may take their toll, although often not without debate and conflict, as one group argues with another. In the case of repetitive biases, decision makers tend to compensate for the biases and make decisions which are more or less consistent with unbiased information. Comments like the following are not unfamiliar: 'Harry is always optimistic; you have to take his budgets with a pinch of salt'. Or 'Fred is a conservative, you know; he tends to see the world through tinted lenses'.

Cyert and March attempted to empirically investigate the phenomenon of counter-biasing.[16] They established an experimental situation under which groups of three persons worked on an interdependent task. Some of the groups had members with conflicting objectives; the individuals therefore being encouraged to separately bias their communications to one another even though their overall task was interrelated. Other groups had internally consistent objectives. Initially the different arrangements influenced group performance, although over time there was a convergence as the members of the groups with internal conflict adapted to the biased information. Eventually, the information communicated by one person was not taken at its face value by another. Counter-biasing was in operation.

Of course, some caution is necessary in too readily generalising the results of a relatively simple experiment. It does suggest, however, that counter-biasing behaviour is more likely to occur in situations which provide an opportunity for learning. The potential for such learning is greater in stable, repetitive situations. Whether or not it occurs depends upon whether the organisation and the individuals within it provide the means for continually confronting independent sources of knowledge and for gaining feedback on the validity of previous understanding and expectations.

An organisation has many defences against interpretative pathologies ranging from the subtle counter interpretations of other people to the use of reliable and easily verifiable feedback information. Accounting information itself, as we have already seen, is not beyond being distorted. It has to be interpreted, but in line with the many other intriguing paradoxes of accounting, it is itself part of an organisation's strategy for counter interpretation. By helping people to detect the unusual and the questionable, to compare their expectations with the actual data which is reported, it can encourage people to learn through experience and behave in an adaptive manner. If it is used in an appropriate problem solving context, accounting information is one part of a delicate system of checks and balances, designed to guide the adjustment of consistent biases.

7.4 Conclusion

The perspectives discussed in this chapter serve to emphasise that reality is not an external view imposed on an individual's mind. 'Challenging' budgets or 'realistic' standards, for instance, are not merely 5 or 10 per cent less than last year's figures. The accountant may well see a numerical cut in such terms, but a manager sees it in his own terms, based on his own experiences, expectations and needs. The cut, small though it may be, may endanger his chances of promotion, increase the uncertainties inherent in the task, or be seen as an indicator of the prevailing management style. Is it then likely to be seen as challenging or realistic? Similarly, it is easy for an accountant to give a precise definition of allocated costs as including certain things, excluding others and derived on the basis of a predetermined formula. But a manager may see the accountant's precise efforts in very different terms, and respond to them accordingly.

Reality is, in other words, the outcome of a process of personal perception and social interchange. Accordingly, social scientists have been concerned with a concept of man who questions and interprets the world – a world which he in part creates by his interactions and a world which he is in part influenced by and in part free from. That man is creative and critical in this sense means, however, that we should not only emphasise the seeming pathologies of perception and interpretation. In many situations, knowing more than one is told, adding to or subtracting from the underlying sources of information is a powerful characteristic of intelligent human behaviour.

We are beginning to understand much more about how man organises his perceptions of the world around him. As one would perhaps expect, the greatest advances have been made in individual psychology. Research is now being directed at understanding the organising principles inherent in human cognitions and the systematic differences in cognitive style which can be observed between individuals.[17] However, as yet, comparatively little research has been conducted into the wider organisational, let alone the societal and cultural influences on these aspects of the human mind. In these vital areas, many of our insights are of a philosophical rather than empirical nature.[18]

This is a pity because an understanding of the organisational role of accounting systems requires not only an appreciation of the manner in which they provide additional information, but also of the way in which they help managers to understand, process and organise the mass of information which is available to them. In reporting on costs, to provide just one example, it is often expensive, if not impossible, to follow the theoretical framework inherent in the economist's classification of costs. Yet the benefits which can be derived from so doing extend well beyond the confines of the immediate information. Accountants already recognise that the benefits come from the way in which the information supplies a framework for analysing, influencing and predicting costs. If it is true that in the absence of such cognitive aids, managers often employ rather primitive conceptual frameworks for dealing with information, accounting may be able to gain real benefits by attending to the ways in which it can so improve the information processing ability of managers. In this way, it would help them to deal more effectively with the information they already have, rather than merely adding to, or directly improving the mass of data which already surrounds them.

7.5 *References*

1. ROSENTHAL, R A and WEISS, R S, 'Problems of Organizational Feedback Processes', in: BAUER, R A, *Social Indicators*, MIT Press, 1966

2. SKINNER, B F, 'Superstition in the Pigeon', *Journal of Experimental Psychology*, vol 38, no 2, 1948, pp 168–72

3. ASCH, S E, 'Forming Impressions of Personality', *Journal of Abnormal and Social Psychology*, vol 41, no 3, July 1946, pp 258–90

4. KELLEY, H H, 'The Warm–Cold Variable in First Impressions of Persons', *Journal of Personality*, vol 18, April 1950, pp 431–39

5. CYERT, R M and MARCH, J G, *A Behavioural Theory of the Firm*, Prentice-Hall, 1963, pp 67–71

6. The literature is reviewed in:

   EDWARDS, W, LINDMAN, H and PHILLIPS, L D, 'Emerging Technologies for Making Decisions', in: *New Directions in Psychology: II*, Holt, Rinehart and Winston, 1965, pp 261–325

   PETERSON, C R and BEACH, L R, 'Man As An Intuitive Statistician', *Psychological Bulletin*, vol 68, no 1, 1967, pp 29–46

   Some discussion of the relevance of the findings for the design of management information systems is contained in:

   MASON, R O and MOSKOWITZ, H, 'Conservatism in Information Processing: Implications for Management Information Systems', *Decision Sciences*, vol 3, no 4, October 1972, pp 35–54

7. EDWARDS, W, 'Conservatism in Human Information Processing', in: KLEINMINTZ, B, (ed), *Formal Representation of Human Judgment*, John Wiley and Sons, 1968, pp 17–52

8. SLOVIC, P and LICHTENSTEIN, S, 'Comparison of Bayesian and Regression Approaches to the Study of Information Processing in Judgment', *Organizational Behaviour and Human Performance*, vol 6, no 6, 1971, pp 649–744

9. HAIRE, M, 'Role-Perception in Labour-Management Relations: An Experimental Approach', *Industrial and Labour Relations Review*, vol 8, 1955, pp 204–16

10. WELL, W D, GOI, F J and SEADER, S, 'A Change in Product Image', *Journal of Applied Psychology*, vol 42, 1958, pp 120–1

    Much of the literature on the factors influencing interpersonal perceptions is concisely reviewed in:

    COOK, M, *Interperpersonal Perception*, Penguin Books, 1971

11. DEARBORN, D C and SIMON, H A, 'Selective Perception: A Note On the Departmental Identification of Executives', *Sociometry*, vol 21, no 2, June 1958, pp 140–4

    Also see the interesting observations reported in:

    RITTI, R R, and GOLDNER, F H, 'Professional Pluralism in an Industrial Organization', *Management Science*, vol 16, no 4, December 1969, pp B233–B246

12. SECORD, P F, and BACKMAN, E W, *Social Psychology*, McGraw-Hill, 1964, pp 38–46

13. FESTINGER, L, *A Theory of Cognitive Dissonance*, Row, Peterson and Company, 1957

14. SHERIF, M, *The Psychology of Social Norms*, Harper and Row, 1936

15. See:
ASCH, S E, 'Studies of Independence and Conformity: A Minority of One Against a Unanimous Majority', *Psychological Monograph*, vol 70, no 9, 1956
FESTINGER, L, 'A Theory of Social Comparison Processes', *Human Relations*, vol 7, no 2, May 1954, pp 117–40
KRECH, D and CRUTCHFIELD, R S, *Individual in Society*, McGraw-Hill, 1962

16. CYERT, R M and MARCH, J G, *A Behavioural Theory of the Firm*, Prentice-Hall, 1963, pp 71–7

17. The influential early contributions to the area are discussed in:
HUMPHREY, G, *Thinking: An Introduction to Its Experimental Psychology*, Methuen, 1951
KOHLER, W, *Gestalt Psychology: An Introduction to New Concepts in Modern Psychology*, Liveright Publishing Corporation, 1947
The recent literature includes the following:
BANNISTER, D and FRANSELLA, F, *Inquiring Man: The Theory of Personal Constructs*, Penguin Books, 1971
SCHRODER, H, DRIVER, M and STREUFERT, S, *Human Information Processing*, Holt, Rinehart and Winston, 1967
SCOTT, W A, 'Structure of Natural Cognitions', *Journal of Personality and Social Psychology*, vol 12, no 4, 1969, pp 261–78
Student readers, in particular, may be interested in the related discussions in:
HUDSON, L, *Contrary Imaginations: A Psychological Study of the English Schoolboy*, Methuen, 1966

18. BERGER, P L and LUCKMAN, T, *The Social Construction of Reality*, Allen Lane: The Penguin Press, 1967

CHAPTER EIGHT

The Use of External Accounting Reports

Despite the crucial relationship between accounting information and users' decision processes, the debates on alternative reporting procedures are all too often directed towards the purely technical considerations of how the resulting information differs depending upon the accounting methods used. Many articles, speeches and research studies have described how companies increase their reported profits by changing their accounting procedures.[1] This is only a part of a larger and much more significant debate, within the accountancy profession and the wider financial community, on the multiplicity of accounting principles and procedures which a company can use. There have been numerous requests for the range of acceptable accounting practices to be greatly reduced so that the reader of a set of accounts can be sure that the reported information is due to real economic factors, rather than mere accounting variations and managerial motives.[2]

Most of these writers and commentators assumed that the recipients of accounting reports – investors, investment analysts and the like, are not only inconvenienced by the present diversity, but also that they can be successfully fooled. I would agree that senior managers and corporate accountants must believe that this is so, or why would they bother to engage in such practices? The assumption suggests, however, a uniformly unintelligent and naïve concept of investors – a dubious starting point for any argument. One wonders whether this is really the case.

The rather superficial acknowledgment given to accounting information's relationship to a wider decision process can also be observed in many of the important approaches to searching for more desirable standards of accounting practice. Probably the most common approaches are well grounded on the observation of past and present procedures. Attempts are frequently made to compile an inventory of the practices and conventions which appear to be generally accepted by accountants – Grady's report for the American Institute of Certified Public Accountants probably being the most famous.[3] While such approaches allow us to say what accountants generally do in particular situations, they do not provide a satisfactory basis for formulating a series of standards indicative of desirable practice. It is just not true that current or past practice necessarily reflects desirable practice. These approaches provide no basis for considering either the desirability or direction of major changes. More germane to the present argument, however is the fact that such approaches do not directly consider the behaviour of people who are receiving accounting information and possibly basing their decisions on an interpretation of it. This aspect of the problem is generally relegated to a minor role on the presumption that the continued existence of a procedure is indicative of its use and value. Such a view is, of course, inadequate.

Other approaches compare either current or conceivable accounting practice with a normative economic theory. Perhaps not too surprisingly, accounting practice usually falls far short of the ideal in such a comparison. For instance, the accounting concept of value is clearly different from the usual economic interpretation but while these are useful, perhaps even essential, approaches to what accountants ought to do in particular situations, they are still partial. Again they are framed outside of any realistic concept of an organisation reporting the results of its activities to a concerned group of investors and other outsiders..No explicit consideration is given to the difficulties of communicating, interpreting and using the accounting information.

Some researchers have fallen into similar difficulties. As an example, we can consider Bonini's computer simulation of a firm's information and decision processes.[4] He found that compared with the use of an average cost method of stock valuation the last-in-first-out method, in certain circumstances, greatly increased real business profits.

A whole organisation was found to be capable of being radically influenced by a change in an apparently simple accounting procedure. On further examination, however, we find that the organisation and its simulated managers were equally simple: the very essence of the problem was assumed away. The managers uncompromisingly took the accounting information at its face value, and the results, intriguing and ingenious as they may be, reflect no more than one possible extension of the assumption. In other words, very little was added to our understanding.

It is easier to see the difficulties in the artificial context of a computer simulation, but on reflection is it so very different from many of the more generally conceived arguments and debates on the need for accounting standards for external reporting which frequently appear in the professional and academic literature? Do not these make similar assumptions? The more basic questions of whether and how accounting information is used by investors, whether the accounting practices are capable of affecting their final decisions and if they are, under what conditions, are rarely considered.

8.1 *Towards a Conditional View*

While accountants have recently devoted more time and effort to learning about the effects of alternative accounting procedures on decision making, much of the work has unfortunately been characterised by both elementary conceptual bases and unreliable research methods.[5] It has also been directed towards finding a universal answer to whether or not different accounting methods affect decisions, rather than probing into the more meaningful problem of the conditions under which this is or is not likely to occur.

One refreshing exception is Livingstone's empirical investigation of the reaction of American government agencies to the diversity of accounting methods.[6] Electricity generating companies in the United States, like other regulated industries, are under the jurisdiction of state agencies which can prescribe both the accounting methods to be used and the maximum rate of return on investment that the companies are permitted to earn. The selection of the accounting method is capable of influencing the decision on the return on investment, and this provided Livingstone with an ideal opportunity to study the responses of decision makers to different accounting methods.

Livingstone focused on a period in which companies were faced with the possibility of using a variety of accounting procedures for recording the inter-period allocation of tax and thereby influencing their reported after-tax profits. He found that the government agencies which were already accustomed to adjusting for the effects of different accounting methods used by the companies under their jurisdiction did not take the after-tax profit figures at their face value. Instead, the permitted rates of return were based on adjusted figures. In contrast, agencies accustomed to dealing with relatively uniform accounting practices did indeed take the new after-tax profits at their face value: they appeared to be fooled by the diversity of practices.

Although one study can only be suggestive, the findings add a vital element of realism to the debate. They suggest that once users of accounting information have learned to recognise and adjust for the effects of some alternative accounting methods, they are more likely to appraise and evaluate future information, adjusting it quite rapidly whenever appropriate. They develop a critical attitude towards the information, drawing on wider sources of intelligence and a greater understanding.

8.2 *Investor Behaviour*

Let us, for the moment, *assume* that all investors on the stock market behave in a similarly informed and intelligent manner. Furthermore, in so doing, let us examine the consequences of publically making available a *new* piece of information which is capable of favourably affecting investors' expectations of a company's future performance. The new information may relate to such things as a change in management, a profit leak, the success of a current research project, a major new export order, or any other actual or anticipated change which is capable of influencing the company's prospects.

The information will be examined by a large number of our investors. They will analyse its consequences, and at least some of them will decide to increase their shareholdings. As long as the information is known to a sufficient number of people, and we presume that this is the case, they will tend to outbid each other in competition for the shares until the price reaches some new equilibrium level where supply equals demand. At this new level, because of the size and competitive nature of the stock market, the price will unbiasedly reflect the stock market's expectation of the share's worth.

Of course, in an uncertain world there is always room for disagreement among investors, which will give rise to differences between actual share prices and what might be thought of as the share's intrinsic worth. Given our initial assumptions, however, the actions of at least some of our highly intelligent and calculating investors should cause the share price to fluctuate randomly around its intrinsic worth. For if there is a systematic rather than a random difference, some investors will attempt to take advantage of this knowledge, and in doing so, neutralise the systematic component of price behaviour and in this way profits may be made.

The share price will be maintained until a new piece of information causes it to change, but information is only new when it has not been deduced from earlier information. In other words, old news is no news. Therefore, in order to have any effect on share prices a piece of information must be independent of previous information, and if this is so, the effect of the information on the share price will be independent of anything that may have happened before. In other words, the implication of our initial assumptions is that the company's share price will exhibit a *random* pattern of behaviour. The change in the share price one day will be unrelated to the change the following day.

By now, I am sure, you are beginning to question the naïvety of the analysis. Surely, you must be saying, in a book which is concerned with analysing the human aspects of accounting you cannot presume to swallow such a simple, rational economic interpretation of investor behaviour. Regardless of the logical extension of the argument, you must feel that the process is contrary to any realistic understanding of human behaviour. But while I have deliberately chosen to state the argument in over simple terms,[7] the stock market is, in practice, an extremely competitive market place with quite efficient methods of collecting and processing information and it should be emphasised that I have only considered the outcome of the behaviour of many investors rather than any single one. What is more, there is a substantial body of evidence which supports the general outline of the process which I have described.[8] While it is unlikely that the random characteristic provides an exact description of share price behaviour, for most practical purposes the resemblance is very close indeed. The amount of dependence between successive price changes is very small.

Furthermore, if share prices behave in a random manner, a series of price changes will have no memory. Therefore their past history cannot be used to predict the future. By merely relying on either an analysis of the past history or publically available information, which is already reflected in the price, it should be impossible to devise mechanical trading rules which would make an investor's expected profits higher than they would be with a simple random selection of shares. On appealing to the available evidence, we certainly find that it has proved impossible to devise such rules, if trading costs are taken into account. Although the possibility remains that successful rules are much more complex and subtle than the ones tested so far, the large amount of evidence which has been accumulated to date is nevertheless persuasive. Perhaps even stronger evidence of our presumption of informed investor behaviour is provided by the studies of portfolio selections made by expert unit trust managers. As the theory would predict, these selections have not, on average, exhibited any pronounced and persistent superiority over a randomly selected portfolio.[9]

Hence, a large amount of evidence is consistent with the view that, in general, investors are efficient processors of information. If this is so, do they really take accounting information at its face value? The conclusion should, by now, seem more doubtful. Unfortunately, while there are many reports of companies manipulating their profits, many studies of the possible reasons for doing so, and a great deal of uneasiness about the presumed consequences, there are only a few studies of how investors, as a group, interpret and use such information. To these we now turn.

8.3 *Investor Responses to Accounting Manipulations*

Let us consider one instance where manipulation was possible. The opportunity which we examine was provided by the confusion in the accounting profession as a result of the United States Internal Revenue Act of 1962. The Act provided for an investment credit whereby tax payments to the federal government were reduced in years in which a company aquired specific kinds of assets. The credit was equal to seven per cent of current expenditures on the specified assets, subject to certain maximum limitations prescribed in the Act.

The government's attempt to stimulate the economy in this manner resulted in a major debate in the accountancy profession over the appropriate method of reporting the credit. Three major methods emerged:

(1)   *The flow-through method.* The entire reduction in taxes is reflected as increased profits in the current year.
(2)   *The 48–52 method.* 48 per cent of the credit is reflected in current earnings and 52 per cent is considered to be a deferred tax which will be paid over future years.
(3)   *The productive life method.* The full credit is deferred to the years benefitted by the use of the asset.

This is certainly not the place to argue the relative advantages of the various alternatives.[10] I only wish to point out that they are obviously capable of significantly influencing the reported net profits in any one year and the trend over a series of years.

In a highly controversial opinion issued in December 1962, the Accounting Principles Board of the American Institute of Certified Public Accountants argued that the investment credit was not a valid component of current profit. The Board stated that the amount of the credit ought to be spread over the life of the assets acquired. However, in 1964, in response to much criticism, the Board also allowed the immediate recognition of profit as an acceptable reporting alternative. Companies could then choose which method to use and accordingly influence the level of reported profits. Some companies changed to the flow-through method; others did not.[11] The interesting question is whether investors were fooled by these accounting gymnastics.

Kaplan and Roll have investigated this very question.[12] They identified 275 companies that changed to the flow-through method and 57 companies that maintained the more conservative productive life method and thereby voluntarily reported current profits lower than what was possible within accepted practice. The reaction of investors to the change was analysed by observing the trend of the company's share prices – the outcome of aggregate investor behaviour. A multitude of factors can, however, influence share prices. Statistical means were therefore used to eliminate the effects attributable to two other major factors – general economic conditions and interest rates, and then the

Figure 8.1 Investor reactions to profit announcements

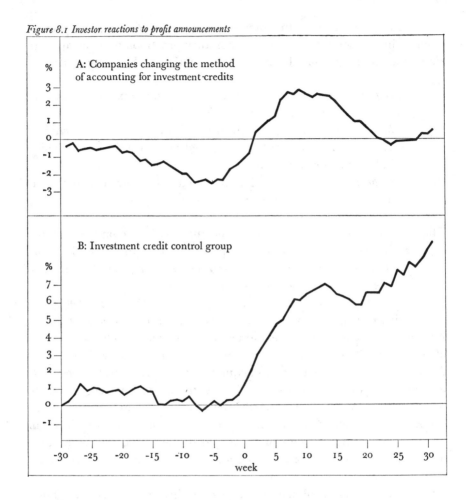

residual results for the companies were averaged in an attempt to eliminate the effects of other extraneous effects.

The cumulative average residual returns accruing to the shareholders after eliminating general economic and interest rate effects are
shown in Figure 8.1. The diagram shows the returns for thirty weeks on
either side of the day on which profits were announced. The shares of the
companies which reported higher current profits by adopting the flow-
through method of accounting for the investment credit experienced
abnormally good times in the ten weeks surrounding the profit announce-

ment (Part A). The good period started before the actual announcement date, suggesting either a preliminary announcement or a leakage of information by insiders. However, after a few weeks, on average, the stock-market reacted negatively to these same shares. The effect of the abnormally high reported profits was only temporary, information on the underlying situation leaking through over time.

Moreover, a comparison with the returns of the companies who did not change their method of reporting (Part B) reveals a perhaps even more interesting result. Although these companies reported profits below the level permitted by accounting practices, their share prices not only increased in value around the date of the profit announcement, but stayed at this high level. The contrast is suggestive that companies who knew that their earnings were going to be high without the help of any manipulation, did not manipulate, while the firms who did change, were already poor performers.

While there are only a few similar studies, the results are not inconsistent with the hypothesis that, in some situations at least, investors react to accounting information in an informed manner, not simply taking it at its face value. The same authors found that companies which tried to increase reported profits by changing from accelerated to straight-line depreciation between 1962 and 1968 were, on average, already poor performers. Again, there was a temporary positive effect resulting from the change, starting before the announcement date, but its effect was very short lived. A similar manipulation initiated by a number of American steel companies in 1968 in response to a fear of takeover bids resulted in a relative devaluation of the inflated earnings by the stock market.[13] Similarly, some findings by Beaver and Dukes suggest that investors adjust for differences in both depreciation methods and interperiod tax allocations.[14] Investors in electricity generating companies have been found to make their own estimates of profit, rather than accept the reported earnings which reflect different methods of interperiod tax allocation.[15] One final piece of evidence is perhaps the most intriguing. There is some suggestion that investors are quite capable of making some allowance for the impact of inflation on a company's operations, even though this is not explicitly recognised by present reporting practices.[16]

8.4 *The Investor as a Processor of Information*

Why is it that these studies all produce results so much at variance with the frenzied outcrys from so many members of the financial community? Many factors are involved, including a tendency by accountants to inflate the importance of their own reports even if this involves regarding the typical investor as relatively simplistic. However solid experience does suggest that on numerous occasions investors are misled by the reported accounting information. Pergamon Press, GEC, Vehicle and General, Rolls-Royce are recent examples which come to mind and in the light of these cases, the relevant question becomes under what conditions do such deceptions occur.

The problem can be tackled at two levels, either by trying to understand the behaviour of individual investors or alternatively, by probing further into the aggregate behaviour of a large group of investors as it is reflected in share prices. Since behaviour in the stock market is known to be highly interactive and interdependent, with one investor trying to anticipate the behaviour of other investors, we will continue to examine the behaviour of investors as a group – as we have done above.

Some important clues to the problem are provided by Ball and Brown's investigation of how the stock market reacted to reported profits.[17] For each of the years 1957 to 1965, 261 companies were classified according to whether their actual reported profits were better or worse than the average level of company profits. They then investigated the behaviour of the companies' stock market prices during the period preceding and immediately following the profit announcement, again using an index which estimated the change in price above and beyond that which resulted from general economic factors. The results are shown in the diagrams in Figure 8.2. Both the diagrams cover the period from twelve months before the publication of the profit report to six months after. It is immediately obvious that price behaviour is in line with the final profit report. For companies which produced above average profits there was a rise in the share price over the period. Where profits were below average, the price fell over the period. In fact, one-half or more of all the information about a firm which is used by the stock market during a year to determine the share prices, is reflected in the year's profits. However, on average, only 10 per cent of the adjustment took place at the time of the profit announcement, the remainder of the adjustment occurring in

Figure 8.2 *Average share price movements around the date of profit announcements*

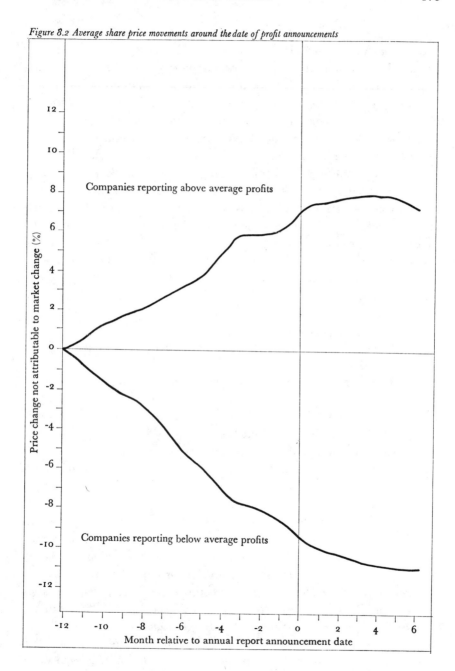

the preceding twelve months. The annual profit report is obviously far
from being a timely medium.

That investors anticipated the announcement of the accounting
profit suggests that there is a regular flow of information on the factors
determining the future prospects of most companies and that the annual
accounting report contains, on average, little surprising information.
Other researchers have provided evidence which is consistent with this
explanation. For instance, Fama and his colleagues found that the stock
market's judgments of the information implications of stock splits or bonus
issues are reflected in the price of shares by the time of the announcement.[18]

Accounting information must be seen as only a part of a competitive market in information which is both available to and used by
investors as a group. One way of considering the wider market in information on any company's operations is to distinguish between the following
three factors which can influence a company's scope of operations and
efficiency:

- general economic factors
- factors affecting the industry within which the company
  operates
- factors which are specific to the particular company

The behaviour of a company's share price can be explained in terms of
these three factors, the latter factor usually being regarded as a residual
component. More germane to the present argument, however, is the fact
that some of the vital information which is necessary for the evaluation of
a particular company can be obtained from general economic and
industry wide sources of intelligence.

Publically available information comes from many sources.
Government reports on the economy, reports on prices and incomes, and
new government taxation and investment policies are all highly relevant.
Similarly, trade association reports and reports on new products and
technological innovations all represent competitive sources of information
for investors. This information is not just for the specialist and institutional
analyst, but also for the smaller and more average investor. In this area
the role of the press as a selector, filter and reporter of such details is
crucial: one shareholder recently pointed out in the *Financial Times* that he

had learnt more about his company from the press than from a decade of company accounts! Articles on such matters as strikes, changes in senior management and investment plans, together with stock broker reports and the recommendations of share tipsters must all be acknowledged when considering the informational context of a firm within which investors operate.[19] Their potential impact is sufficiently illustrated by the reaction to share tipsters' recommendations. The share price can reflect the information contained in the recommendation and its anticipated effects, even before trading starts on the very same day – such is the speed of adjustment. *The Guardian*, for instance, found that readers had to pay, on average, twenty per cent more than the price at which the shares were originally recommended.[20]

The nature of the market in information is further illustrated by a study in which Brealey attempted to quantify the relative importance of general economic, industry and specific company factors on the profits of 217 American companies.[21] The annual percentage change in profits for each of the companies between 1948 and 1966 were correlated with first, the corresponding change in a representative sample of all companies in order to ascertain the estimate of the proportion of the change in each company's profits that was related to the general economic situation impinging on the industrial sector. Second, the change was related to the changes in industrial indices of profitability for an estimate of the impact of specific industry factors.

The results, grouped by industry, as shown in Table 8.1. First, it should be noted that on average, 21 per cent of the profit changes could be attributable to wider economic factors and a further 21 per cent to industry factors. Although this leaves 58 per cent of the variation unexplained, it is necessary to point out that it is very doubtful whether all of this is due to specific company factors. Industry definitions are notoriously imprecise, and some companies may be related in a non-industry sense – as government contractors, sharing the same union, large exporters and so on. Second, not all companies are dependent on general economic and industry factors to the same extent. Automobile manufacturers, steel producers and departmental stores are quite closely related to the general economy, as one would expect, but companies in the cosmetics, tobacco and food supermarket industries much less so. Similarly, there are wide differences in the importance of industry factors. The oil companies share

Table 8.1 Proportion of profit changes attributable to
general economic and industry influences

Industry	General economic influence (%)	Industry influence (%)
Automobiles	48	11
Cement	6	32
Chemicals	41	8
Cosmetics	5	6
Department stores	30	37
Drugs	14	7
Electricals	24	8
Food	10	10
Machinery	19	16
Nonferrous metals	26	25
Oil	13	49
Paper	27	28
Rubber	26	48
Steel	32	21
Supermarkets	6	33
Textiles	25	29
Tobacco	8	19
All Companies included in the study	21%	21%

Based on: Brealey, R A, 'Some Implications of the Comovement of American Company Earnings', *Applied Economics*, 1971, p. 187.

a similar production technology, similar raw material markets and serve similar customers, and their prices both at the raw material and final product ends are negotiated. Companies in the rubber industry may be similar.

Hence, in many cases, investors are not constrained to use only the information publically reported by accountants when evaluating the prospects of companies. They can, and do, use relevant economic, industry and company information from many sources. Therefore it is necessary to view investors as a group, as processors of information; comparing, shifting and being selective. There is no reason to expect them to always follow the accounting numbers. If a considered evaluation in the market place shows them to be unreliable, then, on average, the accounting numbers may be set aside, except in so far as the distortions have information value in themselves – as indicators of managerial motives and expectations.

There are differences between companies, however, as the above data have served to emphasise. Some companies may operate in a highly competitive information market, others in a very monopolistic one. These differences need to be stressed for they allow us to probe into some questions, if not doubts, which I am sure remain in your mind. Surely, you must be asking by now, investors have been, are presently and will no doubt remain fooled by manipulated accounting reports and the multiplicity of methods. I can only agree. The *Financial Times*, the *Times* and the *Guardian* abound with examples, although I would already caution you to exercise some care in pursuing your argument. Do not such press reports in themselves constitute part of the competitive information structure? Do not the press, who continually criticise the accounting profession for its standards of reporting and audit, in some almost paradoxical sense, constitute another, perhaps at times an even more important, part of the information and audit system?

Nevertheless, I would still accept your comments. Investors have been fooled, even in circumstances where criminal fraud may not have been attempted. The above analysis is still highly relevant, because such instances might point not only to the inadequacies of the accountancy profession and the foolishness of investors, but to the different competitive contexts for information surrounding different companies. Consider one noted instance: the Pergamon Press affair.[22] Here there were real questions of the adequacy of financial reporting and audit, and the stock market certainly appeared to have been fooled but without offering any excuses, it is worthwhile to consider some features of Pergamon Press. It is an international company, operating in highly individual and specific markets which are to some extent isolated from immediate general economic pressures. Institutional libraries and academics serve as useful buffers! It was also a closely held company with large family holdings and a relatively small top management team and Robert Maxwell, its Chairman, had at that time, a certain credence in some sections of the press. For a period of time he had a good record for getting his point of view prominently and sometimes almost exclusively, reported in some journals. All these factors point to either an absence of competing sources of information or difficulties in using sources other than the published accounting reports. From the investors' point of view, the information context of Pergamon Press may have been moving towards a monopolistic position and in consequence it was difficult to appraise and compare the accounting reports: they almost had to be accepted.

The argument is illustrated in Figure 8.3. With a monopolistic information context, the set of events reported by the accountant constitute a major part of the relevant information available to the investor and they are not subject to validation by alternative sources of information. As the market in information becomes more competitive, however, not only is validation possible, but the role of accounting data becomes relatively less important. With many competing and often more timely sources of information, the investor can more readily gauge the precision and biases of the accounting data, and set them aside whenever appropriate.

8.5 *Some Difficulties*

I would be the first to admit that the viewpoint which I have presented is controversial.[23] The studies on which it is based are still few in number and much research remains to be done, particularly on the organisation of the stock market and its processes of decision making. Caution needs to be exercised in developing its implications for the arguments can also be used as a basis for maintaining the *status quo* in accounting. If accounting reports are only a part of a whole, some might argue, why worry so much about them? Certainly, I have tried to place accounting information in a wider context and in so doing, I may have accorded it relatively less importance but this is no basis for satisfaction since it does not imply that the present situation cannot be improved. The arguments point to some areas where improvement may be possible. The timing of accounting reports,[24] for instance, the disclosure of accounting procedures,[25] and the disaggregation of corporate reports into industrial sectors to aid comparability.

In addition, in presenting the argument I have not been directly concerned with investigating the wider functions served by accounting reports. Yet it may well be that the identification of the possibility of a quasi-monopolistic control over the information of even a few companies may heighten the real ethical concerns and responsibilities of the accountancy profession. More generally, accounting reports provide investors

Figure 8.3 Alternative information contexts

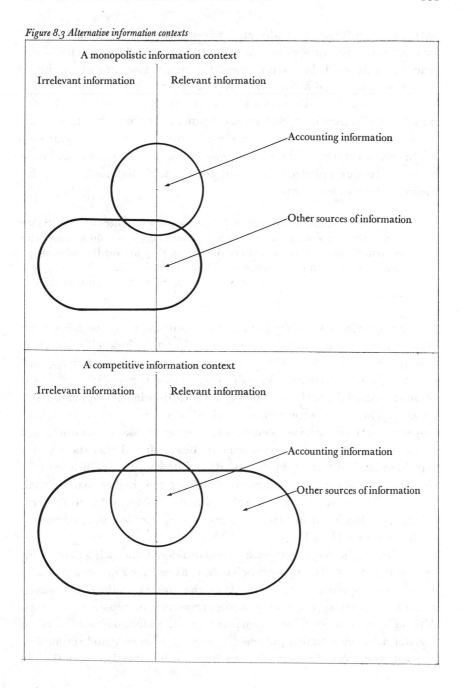

with an opportunity to audit and assess their own expectations. An investor may have anticipated the information included in a report long before it is released, but nevertheless, the report may provide a check, some reassurance and a vital element of feedback.

I have at least thrown some doubt on the argument that investors may be conditioned or misled by accounting procedures but there may be an element of conditioning in the reporting system itself. Marshall McLuhan, a controversial writer on modern communications, has introduced a famous aphorism into our vocabulary: 'the medium is the message'. In his own words:

> ' . . . "the medium is the message" because it is the medium that shapes
> and controls the scales and form of human association and action. The
> content or uses of such media are diverse as they are ineffectual in shap-
> ing the form of human communication. Indeed, it is only too typical
> that the "content" of any medium blinds us to the character of the
> medium.'[26]

Accounting reports are a medium of communication and we know that, at times, there are grounds on which to question how effective their contents may be. The possibility remains that the annual reports, and increasingly the quarterly and half yearly reports, may be a part of a complex financial ritual, encouraging and legitimising the appraisal and review of investors' expectations. Indeed despite the evidence which suggests that the information content of many reports has been anticipated by the time of the profit announcement, Beaver found that there was a very high level of trading in the few days following the publication of a company's profits.[27] Price changes were 67 per cent higher than normal, although the analysis could not isolate whether this was due to the new information (Ball and Brown's evidence would question this) or merely the high volume of trading.

So far, however, we have only considered the behaviour of investors as a group. Their group behaviour, as reflected in share prices, is an overall response, partly related to the interdependencies between individual investors and not just the responses of separate investors. Although the essence of our viewpoint at the individual level is of an investor as an information processor, scanning, searching and reconciling alternative sources of information, perhaps in this situation more than in most, we must be careful of assuming that the behaviour of the whole is necessarily the behaviour of the parts.

8.6 *The Use of Information by Individual Investors*
At the level of the individual investor we are dealing with a highly subjective process by which expectations are formulated, revised and acted upon. Even from a rational point of view, investors are not only trying to predict future dividends, profits and levels of risk. They are also trying to anticipate future share prices, because for many this is a far more crucial influence on their success as investors than dividends. In which case, investors must try to find out how they think the market works. They must predict what other people think other people think the price will be in the future!

From the gentle ebbs and flows of a rational model to the behavioural whirlpool is a big step which despite Clarkson's success in simulating the behaviour of a portfolio manager,[28] takes us into an area where comparatively little is known. Ijiri, Jaedicke and Knight have, however, attempted to construct a fairly simple model of the factors influencing the effect which accounting information can have on the decision process.[29]

First of all, if decision makers are inclined to take accounting information at its face value, attaching meaning to it as an object in itself rather than as an imperfect reflection of underlying events, the information is more likely to directly influence the decision outcomes. Ijiri and his colleagues call this functional fixation. We have already seen, however, that investors as a group, do not always behave in this manner and Livingstone's evidence suggests that the individual investor's degree of functional fixation is influenced by his range of experience. As he becomes familiar with alternative procedures and approaches, he is less likely to automatically accept any information at its face value. Second, the presence of feedback on the performance of the accounting system enables decision makers to determine whether the system is performing as they expect. If such information is available, decision makers can modify their interpretation and use of the information. Third, if the decision makers' environments are ill-structured and uncertain the value of feedback information is more questionable. Delays between action and outcomes also make monitoring difficult and the combination of different delay periods and simultaneous events makes interpretation almost impossible. Given the uncertainty over alternatives and preferences, decision makers will seek to add some element of structure to their situations. Many people, through the use of financial objectives and decision procedures, find this structure in the accounting system itself. At this stage, the accounting information can become a highly influential, but uncertain anchor on the stormy seas of the unknown.

In this chapter I have concentrated on a few questions which I deemed to be worthy of raising rather than trying to provide answers. Even so, despite the volume of comment and debate, the evidence is, as we have just seen, slight. I would be first to admit that there are many doubts, although the perspectives which I have presented are not only suggestive, but also based on a view of man as an intelligent, careful and considerate being. Many of the conventional arguments in this area take the opposite point of view as their starting point.

8.7 References

1. See, for instance:
   BRILOFF, A J, *Unaccountable Accounting: Games Accountants Play*, Harper and Row, 1972
   CUSHING, B E, 'An Empirical Study of Changes in Accounting Policy', *Journal of Accounting Research*, vol 7, no 2, Autumn 1969, pp 196–203
2. STAMP, E and MARLEY, C, *Accounting Principles and the City Code: The Case For Reform*, Butterworths, 1970
3. GRADY, P, *Inventory of Generally Accepted Accounting Principles for Business Enterprises*, American Institute of Certified Public Accountants, 1965
4. BONINI, C P, *Simulation of Information and Decision Systems of the Firm*, Prentice-Hall, 1963
5. For a critical evaluation of much of this literature see:
   BECKER, S, 'The Behaviour of Behavioural Accountants,' in: STERLING, R R and BENTZ, W F, (eds), *Accounting in Perspective: Contributions to Accounting Thought by Other Disciplines*, South-Western Publishing, 1971.
6. LIVINGSTONE, J L, 'A Behavioural Study of Tax Allocation in Electric Utility Regulation', *The Accounting Review*, vol 42, no 3, July 1967, pp 544–52
7. For a more formal argument see:
   FAMA, E F, 'Efficient Capital Markets: A Review of Theory and Empirical Work,' *The Journal of Finance*, vol 25, no 2, May 1970, pp 383–417
8. A fairly elementary review of this literature is given in:
   BREALEY, R A, *An Introduction to Risk and Return From Common Stocks*, MIT Press, 1969, and a collection of the important early articles is contained in:
   COOTNER, P H, (ed), *The Random Character of Stock Market Prices*, MIT Press, 1964

The European evidence is reported in:

SOLNIK, B H, *European Capital Markets*, Lexington, 1973

9. See:

JENSEN, M C, 'The Performance of Mutual Funds in the Period 1945–1964', *The Journal of Finance*, vol 23, no 2, May 1968, pp 389–416

For more impressionistic British evidence see *Money Which?*, September 1968. A theory of random price behaviour does not mean, however, that superior investment performance is impossible. It is certainly difficult if only publically available information is used since the prices tend, on average, to unbiasedly reflect all the information that is available to the market. But this process of adjustment does not rule out temporary over or under adjustments, although both are equally likely and the delay in obtaining a full adjustment is itself a random variable. If an investor can speedily identify situations where there are systematic differences between the price and intrinsic worth, he may be able to perform better than a randomly selected portfolio. The only clear means of purposely doing this at any level of risk, as against mere luck, is possibly through superior skill in information processing and more certainly through the possession of inside information which only a few persons have monopolistic access to.

10. See the articles collected in:

KELLER, T F and ZEFF, S A, *Financial Accounting Theory II: Issues and Controversies*, McGraw-Hill, 1969, pp 417–57

11. Studies of the factors influencing whether or not companies changed appear in:

ARCHIBALD, T R, 'The Return to Straight-Line Depreciation: An Analysis of a Change in Accounting Method', *Empirical Research in Accounting: Selected Studies* 1967, supplement to vol 5 of the *Journal of Accounting Research*, pp 164–80

GORDON, M J, HORWITZ, B and MEYERS, P,. 'Accounting Measurements and Normal Growth of the Firm', in: JAEDICKE, R K, *et al*, *Research in Accounting Measurement*, American Accounting Association, 1966, pp 221–31

SIMPSON, R H, 'An Empirical Study of Possible Income Manipulation', *The Accounting Review*, vol 44, no 4, October 1969, pp 806–17

SUMMERS, E L, 'Observation of Effects of Using Alternative Reporting Practices', *The Accounting Review*, vol 43, no 2, April 1968, pp 257–65.

12. KAPLAN, R A and ROLL, R, 'Investor Evaluation of Accounting Information: Some Empirical Evidence', *Journal of Business*, vol 45, April 1972, pp 225–57

13. COMISKEY, E E, 'Market Responses to Changes in Depreciation Accounting', *The Accounting Review*, vol 46, no 2, April 1971, pp 279–85

14. BEAVER, W H and DUKES, R E, 'Interperiod Tax Allocation and Depreciation Methods: Some Analytical and Empirical Results', unpublished working paper, Stanford University.

15. O'DONNELL, J L, 'Relationship Between Reported Earnings and Stock Prices in the Electric Utility Industry', *The Accounting Review*, vol 40, no 1, January 1965, pp 135–43

O'DONNELL, J L, 'Further Observations on Reported Earnings and Stock Prices', *The Accounting Review*, vol 42, no 3, July 1968, pp 549–53

MLYNARCZYK, F A, 'An Empirical Study of Accounting Methods and Stock Prices', *Empirical Research in Accounting: Selected Studies* 1969, supplement to vol 7 of the *Journal of Accounting Research*, pp 63–81

16. DE ALESSI, L, 'The Redistribution of Wealth by Inflation: An Empirical Test With United Kingdom Data', *Southern Economic Journal*, vol 30, October 1963, pp 113–27

    KESSEL, R A, 'Inflation – Caused Wealth Redistribution: A Test of a Hypothesis', *American Economic Review*, vol 46, no 1, March 1956, pp 128–41

17. BALL, R and BROWN, P, 'An Empirical Evaluation of Accounting Income Numbers', *Journal of Accounting Research*, vol 6, no 2, Autumn 1969, pp 159–78

    The study has been replicated using Australian data, for which see:

    BROWN, P, 'The Impact of the Annual Net Profit Report on the Stock Market', *The Australian Accountant*, July 1970, pp 277–83

18. FAMA, E F, FISHER, L, JENSEN, M C and ROLL, R, 'The Adjustment of Stock Prices to New Information', *International Economic Review*, vol 10, no 1, February 1969, pp 1–21

    SCHOLES, M S, 'The Market for Securities: Substitution Versus Price Pressure and the Effects of Information on Share Prices', *The Journal of Business*, vol 45, April 1972, pp 179–211

    Much of this literature is summarised in:

    BREALEY, R A, *Security Prices in a Competitive Market: More About Risk and Return from Common Stocks*, MIT Press, 1971

19. Surprisingly, there have been few studies of the financial press or its impact on share prices, although both topics would appear to be particularly rich fields for enquiry. Neiderhoffer has studied the impact of world events which gave rise to large headlines in the *New York Times*, and Reilly and Drzycimski considered share price behaviour after six particular events, including presidential speeches, the seizure of the Pueblo and the devaluation of the dollar. See:

    NEIDERHOFFER, V, 'The Analysis of World Events and Stock Prices', *Journal of Business*, vol 44, no 2, April 1971, pp 193–219

    REILLY, F K and DRZYCIMSKI, E, 'A Semi-Strong Test of Market Efficiency – Profit Opportunities After Major Announcements', working paper no 58, School of Business, University of Kansas, 1972

20. COYNE, J, 'Fresh Start With a Portfolio', *The Guardian*, 13th April 1971

    FIRTH, M A, 'Efficient Capital Markets', Unpublished MSc dissertation, University of Bradford, 1970

    More wide ranging research on this topic is currently being conducted at the Manchester Business School by M D Fitzgerald

21. BREALEY, R A, 'Some Implications of the Comovement of American Company Earnings', *Applied Economics*, vol 3, 1971, pp 183–96

The author notes that he found similar results when analysing data on a sample of British companies

22. DEPARTMENT OF TRADE AND INDUSTRY, 'Report on the Affairs of Maxwell Scientific International (Distribution Services) Limited, Robert Maxwell & Co Limited, and Final Report on the Affairs of Pergamon Press Limited', HMSO, 1973

23. A more detailed and systematic discussion of the arguments is given by Beaver, and Ball presents some more wide ranging but supportive evidence. Sterling, and Downes and Dyckman provide useful critical appraisals. A discussion of the type of institutional research which is required is given by Clarkson

BEAVER, W H, 'The Behaviour of Security Prices and its Implications for Accounting Research (Methods)' supplement to vol 47, *The Accounting Review*, 1972, pp 407–37

BALL, R, 'Changes in Accounting Techniques and Stock Prices', *Empirical Research in Accounting: Selected Studies* 1972, supplement to vol 10, *Journal of Accounting Research*, pp 1–38

STERLING, R, 'On Theory Construction and Vertification' *The Accounting Review*, vol 45, no 3, July 1970, pp 444–57

DOWNES, D and DYCKMAN, T R, 'A Critical Look at the Efficient Market Empirical Research Literature As It Relates to Accounting Information', *The Accounting Review*, vol 48, no 2, April 1973, pp 300–17

CLARKSON, G P E, 'A Theory of Stock Price Behaviour', *Industrial Management Review*, vol 6, Spring 1964, pp 93–103

24. BROWN, P and KENNELLY, J W, 'The Informational Content of Quarterly Earnings: An Extension and Some Further Evidence', *Journal of Business*, vol 45, July 1972, pp 403–15

25. The Kaplan and Roll findings, for instance, may in part reflect the extent to which changes from the productive life method to the flow-through method of accounting for the investment credit were disclosed in financial accounts See:

NEUMANN, F, 'The Auditing Standard of Consistency', *Empirical Research in Accounting: Selected Studies* 1968, supplement to vol 6, *Journal of Accounting Research*, pp 1–17

26. MCLUHAN, M, *Understanding Media: The Extensions of Man*, McGraw-Hill, 1964, p 24

27. BEAVER, W H, 'The Information Content of Annual Earnings Announcements', *Empirical Research in Accounting: Selected Studies* 1968, supplement to vol 6, *Journal of Accounting Research*, pp 67–92

However, different results were found on the Israeli stock exchange in 1968; see the discussion and evidence reported in:

LEV, B, and YAHALOMI, B , 'The Effect of Corporate Financial Statements on the Israeli Stock Exchange', *Management International Review*, vol 12, nos 2–3, 1972, pp 145–50

28. CLARKSON, G P E, *Portfolio Selection: A Simulation of Trust Investment*, Prentice-Hall, 1962

29. IJIRI, Y, JAEDICKE, R K and KNIGHT, K E, 'The Effects of Accounting Alternatives on Management Decisions' in: JAEDICKE, R K, *et al*, (eds), *Research in Accounting Measurement*, American Accounting Association, 1966, pp 186–99 Also see: SLOVIC, P, 'Psychological Study of Human Judgment: Implications for Investment Decision Making', *Journal of Finance*, vol 27, no 4, September 1972, pp 779–99

CHAPTER NINE

Designing
Accounting Systems

It is possible to discern three major trends in the way in which people have looked at management accounting systems, each of which complements rather than replaces the preceding viewpoint. Until recently, management accounting systems were primarily analysed in terms of their *techniques and procedures*. Accountants were concerned with identifying useful and efficient procedures for decision making and control, and the means for implementing and operating them. Different methods of costing were compared and contrasted. People debated the advantages of flexible budgeting and the different frequencies of budget revision. Consideration was given to the various ways of designing reporting systems and extensive attention was given to the relative merits of different methods of investment appraisal.

With the concern being very much on the impersonal procedural aspects of management accounting, there was a possibility of abstracting from rather than enriching the human fabric of the enterprise. Later, however, people saw the inadequacies and partialities of this view. As accountants became increasingly involved in the overall management of the enterprise, consideration started to be given to the *process* by which accounting systems influenced and in turn, themselves were influenced by managerial and employee attitudes and behaviours.

At one level, this second development was clearly represented in our language. We have, for instance, seen the stress shift from the more procedural 'cost accounting' to 'management accounting', just as there has been a tendency for 'budgeting' to become 'budgetary control'. The impact of this development was not confined to changes in language; it also affected peoples attitudes, and accounting practice. Accounting was increasingly seen as only one, albeit important, of the many means of communication and influence within the enterprise. Greater emphasis was placed on the events and interactions by which management accounting systems influenced managerial and employee behaviour, and people started to recognise the need for wider understanding, involvement and commitment.

The full impact of this second trend has still to be seen and in many enterprises it has highlighted the problems rather than providing any answers. but these problems are not new, only our realisation of their true significance. Once they have been recognised, it is all the more likely that we will start to consider their solutions.

However, even though the understanding of the human and social processes which accompany the operation of management accounting systems is important, on its own it rarely provides an adequate basis for the design of the systems themselves. Therefore, stimulated by the experiences of accountants and managers with insight, the comparative understanding gained by the increasing number of management consultants, and not least, the stimulating ideas of a growing number of researchers in organisational analysis and design, a third trend is in the process of emerging to remedy this gap. The third trend is based on the belief that in designing accounting systems for today's complex enterprises, better progress will be made if the previous technical and process understandings run in parallel with an awareness of the factors which both necessitate and constrain the control of the enterprises as a whole. Accordingly, it requires an analysis and assessment of these *organisational and environmental factors* which influence the design and effectiveness of accounting systems. Unlike the other two trends, however, this last one has hardly been conceptualised in accounting terms, although some of the people who talk of 'management information and control systems' are pointing in this direction.[1]

Of course, many accounting systems reflect an element of adaptiveness to organisational and environmental factors. For different enterprises use different accounting practices and procedures, and sometimes, although not always, since fashions and personal idiosyncrasies also have a role to play, these differences relate to the different technological, organisational and market environments in which the enterprise operates.[2] True, the practical consideration of these factors may often be implicit and it may even be based on trial and error but this partly reflects the fact that design factors of this type are a major ommission from the current literature on management accounting.

The relative neglect of the principles underlying the effective design and adaptation of accounting systems means that this is an area of considerable weakness in many enterprises. One only has to look at some of the procedural difficulties which companies faced during the recent wave of mergers and acquisitions when business and organisational environments radically changed. Of course, many factors were operative, but not least amongst them was the problem of fitting existing accounting systems to novel situations. All too often they just did not fit!

The three trends in the development of our understanding of the design and operation of management accounting systems can be seen in such detailed areas of application as budgeting, performance measurement and planning.[3] In planning, for instance, there is still a pronounced tendency for the early fascination with techniques, procedures and organisational arrangements to continue, although increasingly, people are beginning to be more concerned with the characteristics of the planning process. Attention is now being devoted to the way in which ideas are moved towards implementation and action, with the processes of personal commitment and with the development of what is rather ambiguously referred to as 'an attitude towards planning'. One can also detect a concern with the wider organisational and environmental influences on the planning process and procedures. It is now being recognised that, at least until recently, one form of planning may have been ideal for the oil industry, while other concepts may be much more relevant and useful for coping with the dynamics of high fashion, the uncertainties of the leisure industries, and the effects of the rapidly changing electronics industry.[4]

The idea of an adaptive accounting or planning system departs radically from the simple concept of one accounting system which is ideal for all circumstances. It also differs from the recommendations promulgated by some consultants and textbook prophets. Indeed, both the design and operation of management accounting systems can become more demanding, if not more difficult, as one moves from considering merely the techniques of accounting to considering their attendant social and human processes, and finally, to considering the environmental and technological factors which determine their wider organisational effectiveness. As this path is followed, the accountant's task as system designer and operator becomes more realistically related to organisational diagnosis and change, and in the process, more challenging at the personal level.

9.1 *Developing Perspectives on Organisational Design*

The significance of the last trend in the way people have looked at management accounting systems can best be illustrated by considering some of the related developments which have helped to shape our views of how to organise complex activities. Chronologically, it is possible to identify four major approaches to the study of organisational behaviour. Initially, practioners of scientific management emphasised the more technical aspects of the organisation of production activities, and in the process, tended to assume that human motivation primarily responds to economic incentives. The complementary management and administrative theorists focused on the bureaucratic aspects of organisations and sought to develop universal principles of good management. However, in trying to ascertain the optimal degree of such organisational characteristics as task specialisation, decentralisation of authority and span of control, their concerns can also be interpreted at a rather technical level. There was certainly a tendency for some writers to consider the organisation in isolation from its human members.

Later, partly as a reaction to the abstractions of the classical theories, members of the human relations movement started to take a more process view of organisational behaviour. They emphasised the actions and motives of people rather than the organisational arrangements, and despite some unease over the ideological commitments of the early writers, there is no doubt that they stimulated exciting developments in organisational psychology and sociology. Finally, and more recently, attempts have been made to integrate the previous ideas within a framework for the comparative analysis of organisations. Students of organisational behaviour are now trying to concern themselves with some of the complex problems which face managers in designing organisations.

Burns and Stalker, for instance, found that very different rates of technical innovation were associated with different kinds of organisational structure[5]. In a study of British companies, they discovered that innnovation was low in firms with 'mechanistic' systems of management which were characterised by functional specialisation and detailed definitions of duties and responsibilities. In contrast, rapid technical innovation was associated with firms which had 'organic' systems of management with more flexible organisational arrangements, more consultation and less rigorously specified tasks. Perhaps the most influential comparative study of organisations was conducted by Joan Woodward.[6] Contrary to many previous beliefs, her research into 100 manufacturing firms in South Essex disclosed that organisational differences were not accounted for by company size, the personality of senior executives or even the type of industry. Furthermore, she found that conformity to the classical principles of organisation had no relation to business success in the firms studied. In fact, some of the most successful firms were the most conspicuous deviates.

Woodward found, however, that the data concerning organisational structure fell into much clearer patterns when the firms were classified on the basis of the technology characterising their production processes. She used three main groupings:

(1)   firms that produced individual units or small batches of goods to satisfy customers' specific needs

(2)   large-batch or mass production firms

(3)   firms producing on a continuous process basis.

Moving from small batch to mass production and finally to continuous-flow, the technology tended to become better known and lent itself to increasing exercise of control over manufacturing operations. Targets could be set more readily and effectively in continuous-flow firms and factors likely to limit performance could be allowed for, whereas however sophisticated the control procedures might be in mass production operations, there would always be more uncertainty in predicting results. The difficulties of exercising effective control were greatest in unit production firms.

Not only were specific organisational structures associated with each technological grouping, but within each grouping, the companies that most nearly conformed to the median for each organisational characteristic were most successful—success being defined in terms of profits and growth. On the one hand, high performing firms with mass production technologies tended to have mechanistic management systems with clear-cut patterns of duties and responsibilities. High performing firms with unit or process production technologies tended, on the other hand, to have organic systems of management with a great deal of delegation of authority and decision making. The unit and process firms did not have identical organisational structures, however, and the firms in neither of these technological groupings displayed the variety of forms which were found among the mass production firms.*

Woodward concluded that there was no best way of organising manufacturing firms, although there seemed to be particular forms of organisation which were most appropriate to each technological situation. She also suggested that many of the classical writers on management apparently had mass production operations in mind when they formulated their principles of best management. In later studies, however, Woodward started to realise that such technological determinism provided far too sweeping a generalisation.[7] In particular, she started to wonder whether organisational structure might be less a function of technology than of the managerial control system. To investigate this possibility, she first had to develop a means of classifying control systems. Experience suggested a four-fold classification based on whether one or more control systems were used and whether the controls were of a personal or more mechanical nature.

An examination of the control systems of the companies helped in understanding some of the difficulties in the previous findings. For instance, the similarities in the organisational structures of unit and process production firms were due to the fact that single control systems tended to predominate in both groups. The differences between them were related to the fact that control processes in unit production firms were of a

* Woodward also found that technology was related to the power of different functional groups and the interrelationships between them. Each technological grouping appeared to have a critical function, and the more successful firms not only attached higher status to this function, but also tended to have a top executive who had been associated with it earlier in his career. Engineering development was critical in the unit firms, production in the mass production firms and marketing in the process firms.

personal nature while in continuous process firms they were of a more mechanical nature. In addition, it appeared that managers in mass production firms had considerably more choice in the selection of a control system. The weaker relationship between technology and organisational structure in this group was the result of the firms being spread across all control categories. Precisely why the managers adopted the control systems which they did was not considered.

Woodward and her colleagues thought that the various relationships between technology, control systems and organisational behaviour reflected the degree of uncertainty and unpredictability in the different technological situations.[8] In process firms, for instance, there was comparatively little uncertainty, and the control systems were designed to deal with that which existed by relatively simple mechanical means. In unit production firms the uncertainty was often so great that it could not be handled by either mechanical or administrative means. More flexible personal forms of control had to deal with the inherent unpredictability of the task. Finally, in the mass production firms, while product and process standardisation eliminated some of the potential uncertainty, what remained apparently had to be dealt with as the circumstances demanded.

Uncertainty does not result only from technological factors. Other factors such as the nature of the product and its market environment can also make a significant contribution to the overall degree of uncertainty with which managers have to cope. Later work has accordingly moved on to consider the relationship between organisational structure and environmental circumstances.

In their pioneering investigation of how organisations respond to the demands of their environments, Lawrence and Lorsch studied the structure and behaviour of companies operating in three industries which experienced very different rates of change in both products and processes.[9] In general, innovation and hence uncertainty were greatest for the firms in the plastics industry. By contrast, firms making standardised containers tended to have more stable and predictable environments which demanded consistent and reliable operations. The environments of the firms in the packaged food industry were intermediate in uncertainty. Although the firms' environments could be described in such general terms, in reality, each firm faced a series of different environments. The environmental contexts of their production departments could differ from those of their marketing departments, and both of these could be very different from those of the research and development departments. Lawrence and Lorsch were therefore concerned with discovering how firms succeeded in organising themselves to respond to the specific demands of a series of environments whilst at the same time maintaining the viability of the enterprise as a whole.

Companies that were successful in terms of sales, profits and return on investment were found to have organisational structures and personal orientations that were consistent with the demands of their environments. In the plastics industry, and to a slightly lesser extent in packaged foods, the production departments were highly structured, whilst structure was medium in the sales departments and low in research and development. Interpersonal relationships were also more formal and task oriented in the production departments than in either the sales or research and development departments. The individual managers' time horizons were short in production and sales but long in research. In contrast, the approaches to management in the different departments of the successful container firms tended to be similar. There was more structuring of work activities, interpersonal relations were more task oriented and the managers had shorter time horizons.

Although a matching of organisational structures and personal orientations to the demands of specific environments can contribute to successful performance, in order for this to be realised, managers must also achieve a high degree of overall integration. In practice, however, the greater the internal differentiation, the more difficult it is to achieve the requisite amount of integration.

Lawrence and Lorsch found that although there were differences in approach, the separate departments of the successful companies in all three industries were all highly integrated. In the container firms, where it was important to meet the demands of the customers, the activities of the production and sales departments were integrated through the management hierarchy and by the use of plans, budgets and schedules. However, with technical innovation being more important in the packaged foods and plastics firms, it was essential to link sales and research, and research and production. Administrative controls were also used for this purpose, but they were less important than other means. With the moderate differentiation in the successful food firms, managers assigned to integrating roles and temporary interdepartmental teams provided much of the necessary coordination. Firms in the plastics industry, however, used permanent interdepartmental teams and fully fledged integrating departments to pull their highly differentiated departments together.

We have only given an outline of some of the recent work on the technological and environmental factors which influence organisational structures and behavioural processes. An increasing number of studies are, however, not only providing further support for the underlying patterns of relationships but also doing much to extend our understanding to the point where it can help in diagnosing ongoing organisational problems.[10] Of course, in such a new area, many doubts and uncertainties remain[11] but more than ever before, students of organisational behaviour are now actively concerned with assisting managers to develop forms of organisational arrangements which are appropriate to their own particular circumstances. The ability to consciously design organisational structures is now emerging as an exciting possibility.

9.2 *Organisational Structures and Information Processing*

Very little comparable research has been conducted in order to ascertain the factors which influence the design of information systems, including accounting systems. However, the developments in organisation design do much more than illustrate the potential for such an approach. A number of writers have sought to explain why structural and behavioural attributes of organisations are related to technological and environmental factors in terms of the differing information processing requirements of enterprises.[12]

Jay Galbraith has given the most explicit view of organisations as information processing systems:

> 'The basic proposition is that the greater the uncertainty of the task, the greater the amount of information that has to be processed during the execution of the task. If the task is well understood prior to performing it, much of the activity can be preplanned. If it is not understood, then during the actual task execution more knowledge is learned which leads to changes in resource allocations, schedules, and priorities. All these changes require information processing during task performance. Therefore the greater the *task uncertainty*, the greater the *amount of information* that must be

processed in order to insure effective performance. From this proposition it follows that variations in organisational forms are variations in the ability to process varying amounts of information.'[13]

Organisational structures and relationships are viewed as means of processing information. Seen in this way, once much of the task has been defined by the use of rules and procedures, the more bureaucratic forms of organisation and their associated reporting systems are quite capable of processing the necessary amounts of information in comparatively certain situations. However, as the enterprise has to cope with greater amounts of uncertainty, be it technological or environmental in nature, the rules and procedures become increasingly less precise. More exceptions to the rule are bound to occur and as this happens, the ability of the hierarchical channels of communication to effectively process information must come under serious consideration. Managers then have to decide whether to reduce their need for information or to increase the organisation's capacity to process it.

The need for information is subject to management influence since it is dependent upon the desired level of performance and the interdependence of the tasks. If senior managers are willing to accept lower standards of performance, the more traditional forms of organisation may still be able to cope. Alternatively, it may be possible to reduce the degree of interdependence either by the use of inventory buffers[14] or by creating relatively self-contained tasks. In accounting terms, for instance, attempts may be made to establish autonomous profit and investment centres.

However, if none of these options are feasible, management must seek to improve the capacity of the organisation to process information. In part, this can be achieved by improving existing information systems, including accounting systems, by creating new ones and possibly by the use of more efficient data processing methods. But in addition, a movement towards forms of organisational structure which facilitate direct personal contacts between managers who share a problem can do much to improve the flow of information. As Lawrence and Lorsch noted in their study of the high performing firms in the uncertain plastics industry, organisational arrangements which emphasise the significance of horizontal rather than vertical relationships can do much in this respect.

A discussion of information processing in such broad terms may seem rather distant from the usual preoccupations of the accountant. Whilst organisational experts are often more concerned with the less formal and more organic means of transfering all types of information, the accountant is used to focusing on those formal and often routine flows of information which emphasise the financial aspects of an enterprise's activities. However, if the accountant's endeavours are to be seen in organisational terms, as they must, it is essential to adopt a wider viewpoint. For information is so vital to effective performance that it cannot be left to the specialists in particular forms of information processing to provide the overall framework.

The relevance of the wider perspective was demonstrated during the course of a survey which I made of the forecasting methods used by firms operating in highly uncertain market environments. I found that while some of the firms used quite complex statistical forecasting techniques during the course of their planning, budgeting and scheduling operations, such methods were completely rejected by other equally successful firms. Were the procedures of little use, I wondered, or was forecasting irrelevant in such rapidly changing circumstances? That forecasting was far from irrelevant was illustrated by the experiences of one company that retailed high fashion clothes to the teenage market. The managers had tried to use some of the most sophisticated statistical procedures, but had found that they consistently failed to forecast the peaks and the troughs in demand. Yet the financial consequences of this in terms of over-stocking and under-ordering were very important in such a volatile market.

In other areas of activity, the firm's management had learnt to appreciate the value of quantitative approaches, and accordingly, they were more willing to try new methods which were recommended to them. They remained dissatisfied, however, until one of their purchasing managers devised a new approach to forecasting. He proposed that the firm should employ a small group of teenage girls to scout the clubs, disco's and other meeting places used by the type of customers who frequented the firm's retail premises. They were to report on emerging trends and fashions, and to this end, were to be provided with generous expense accounts! With some measure of scepticism, the scheme was implemented and it appeared to work.

Having seen this approach to forecasting in operation, I returned to the other successful firms that did not use formal statistical methods.

Many of these not only used similar approaches, but also devised means of reducing the significance of incorrect forecasts. It became obvious that the behaviour of the firms could only be understood if the problem of forecasting was considered in its entirety rather than in terms of particular methods of coping with it, for the mechanistic approaches which were used by some firms were equivalent to the more organic approaches of others. Both were means of tackling the same underlying problem and their relative value depended upon the nature of the environment to be forecast.

In other firms in the fashion industry, for instance, managers visited the fashion houses and the art schools. In seeking to reduce their dependence on forecasting of an inherently uncertain future, time was always of the essence throughout the whole management process. They always had to pay attention to managing the flow from production to the holding of stocks of finished goods. The stocks were particularly important since if they were too low, profitable opportunities might be lost, but if they were too high, surpluses could be very costly. Ingenious ways were found of both reducing the overall dependence on stocks and shortening the lead time for production and restocking.

Other industries had their own approaches to coping with the uncertainty inherent in their tasks.[15] Many of these were not quite so novel but in all cases, the management of highly dynamic and interdependent sequences of activities could only be accomplished if the managers were provided with relevant flows of information. Amongst other things, stock levels had to be known, the production and order process clearly monitored, even forecasts of demand were still essential, and the financial consequences of all these had to be evaluated. Not surprisingly, a lot of this information was based on the accounting records but its relevance for management action was always determined by the nature of the firm's environment and its technological processes, and the particular strategies which the managers had selected to cope with them,[16] rather than by the internal logic of any particular information system.

9.3 *From Information Processing to Accounting Systems*
Accounting systems are just one means of processing information in organisations. Since they are concerned with the management of financial

resources and the representation of other aspects of the business in financial terms, they will always be important. But it must never be forgotten that an accounting system is always a means to a wider organisational end rather than an end in itself. Accordingly, the strategy for designing and operating any type of accounting system must reflect the wider purposes of the organisation which are to be served, the other strategies for control which management has adopted and their implications for information processing, and thereby, the internal distribution of power and influence.

It is perhaps easier to take a partial view when designing accounting systems for enterprises operating in relatively stable conditions. But with dynamic and rapidly changing conditions, when the information needed to make decisions is more fluid and complex, a wider organisational viewpoint is absolutely essential. In such circumstances, accounting systems and their organisational premises need to be consistent with the forms of organisational structure and patterns of responsibility which can cope with the inherent uncertainty and provide the necessary element of adaptiveness.[17] They must aim to reinforce the informal communication networks and the patterns of interpersonal relationships which constitute the more organic means of control. Finally, they must try to elicit the appropriate individual motivations. If, however, these objectives really cannot be achieved, then the current limitations on our ability to design accounting systems, real as they are, may need to be recognised as constraints on management's ability to adopt other means of control.

Such a view presents many challanges to members of the accounting profession, particularly those concerned with the design and operation of management accounting systems. Accountants need, for instance, to give a lot more consideration to the design of formal information systems that are consistent with organisational structures which emphasise horizontal rather than vertical forms of control. At present, many accounting techniques and procedures are more consistent with the organisational forms associated with mechanistic or bureaucratic approaches to management than they are with organic approaches. Progress has undoubtedly been made in this area in the last few years, but as yet, many difficult problems remain to be solved.[18]

More generally, however, the viewpoint suggests the need for a fundamental reconsideration of the management accountant's role.

Whilst he can never become responsible for the management of all information flows, as one of the few specialists on information in most enterprises, he has, I believe, the potential of broadening his concerns to cover as least the design of the formal sources of information if not a more general overview of the information processing capabilities of the enterprise. Of course, such a reorientation would necessitate major changes in outlook and training, and in reality, I remain pessimistic about whether the profession, as distinct from some of its more informed members, is likely to change in this way. But the need is real enough. Indeed, it may be so real that one wonders whether some other group will arise to move in this direction if accountants choose not to do so.

9.4 *Conclusion*

It is useful to end our discussion by briefly considering the resemblance which the accountant's task as designer of information systems might bear to that of the architect. Both professional groups are concerned with designing and constructing structures which are meant to serve human needs, and in doing this, they both tend to be more concerned with how things might be rather than how things necessarily are. The similarity might, however, go further. For accountants, like architects, can become involved with the technicalities and aesthetics of their edifaces to the detriment of the needs of the people who will be using them. We can all think of the equivalent in accounting of the architect whose ideas of civilised order have little relationship to what the citizens of actual cities really want. It does not require too much imagination to picture the equivalents of those idealistic planners whose efforts have yielded only vandalism and personal isolation.

Like architects, accountants must never regard human beings as unsolicited intrusions on their technical activities. It should not be forgotten that these technical activities have of themselves no meaning. Accounting systems must always be directed towards fulfilling the needs of the managers and employees who are striving to control complex but purposeful enterprises, and accordingly, their design and operation always needs a sensitivity to the attitudes, needs and even passions of the human members of the enterprise.

This need has provided the rationale for this monograph. Throughout our discussions, I have tried to provide some understanding of the way in which people behave in organisational settings and of the strategies by which the organisation as a purposeful whole is related to its wider environment. Wherever possible, consideration has been given to matters which are of particular relevance to the accountant. However, progress ultimately depends upon putting such understanding into practice. In this area, no amount of discussion on my behalf is comparable to the actions of people like *yourselves*. If my endeavours stimulate this, the monograph will have indeed served its purpose.

9.5 *References*

1. LOWE, E A and MCINNES, J M, 'Control in Socio-Economic Organizations: A Rationale for the Design of Management Control Systems, (Section I)', *Journal of Management Studies*, vol 8, no 2, May 1971, pp 213–27
2. See, for instance:
   KHANDWALLA, P N, 'The Effect of Different Types of Competition On the Use of Management Controls', *Journal of Accounting Research*, vol 10, no 2, Autumn 1972, pp 275–85
   LANGHOLM, O, 'Cost Structure and Costing Method: An Empirical Study', *Journal of Accounting Research*, vol 3, no 2, Autumn 1965, pp 218–27
3. The literature on technical developments is adequately described in many accounting textbooks and much of that on the human and social processes of accounting has been reviewed in earlier chapters. However, the emerging literature on the third trend in accounting is widely dispersed. The reader might like to consult:
   BAUMLER, J V, 'Defined Criteria of Performance in Organizational Control', *Administrative Science Quarterly*, vol 16, no 3, September 1971, pp 340–50
   MURRAY, W, *Management Controls in Action*, Human Science in Industry— Study Number 6, Irish National Productivity Committee, 1970
   SALTER, M. S, 'Management Appraisal and Reward Systems', *Journal of Business Policy*, vol 1, no 4, Summer 1971, pp 40–51
4. An excellent review of the planning literature is given in:
   FRIEDMAN, J and HUDSON, B, 'Knowledge and Action: A Guide to Planning Theory', *Journal of the American Institute of Planners*, vol 40, no 1, January 1974, pp 2–16
   Recent studies which have focused on the environmental and organisational influences on planning include:
   DENNING, B W and LEHR, M E, 'The Extent and Nature of Corporate Long-Range Planning in the United Kingdom—II'. *Journal of Management Studies*, vol 9, no 1, February 1972, pp 1–18
   JEFFERSON, R, 'Planning and the Innovation Process', *Progress in Planning*, vol 1, Part 3, Pergamon Press, 1973

LITSCHERT, R J, 'Some Characteristics of Long-Range Planning: An Industry Study', *Academy of Management Journal*, vol 11, no 3, September 1968, pp 315–28

LITSCHERT, R J, 'The Structure of Long-Range Planning Groups', *Academy of Management Journal*, vol 14, no 1, March 1971, pp 33–42

RHENMAN, E, *Organization Theory for Long-Range Planning*, John Wiley and Sons, 1973

5. BURNS, T and STALKER, G M, *The Management of Innovation*, Tavistock, 1961

6. WOODWARD, J, *Industrial Organization: Theory and Practice*, Oxford University Press, 1965

7. WOODWARD, J, ed, *Industrial Organization: Behaviour and Control*, Oxford University Press, 1970

8. There is a danger that Woodward and other similar writers are preoccupied with the differences between organisations to the neglect of differences within them. However, in a study of ten enterprises, Hall investigated whether the unpredictability of the task also accounted for variations in the organisation of different departments within the same organisation. In finding that the departments with more predictable tasks tended to have a more specialised division of labour, greater use of rules and a more structured hierarchy, Hall's findings increase our confidence in the generalisability of the underlying approach. See: HALL, R, 'Intra-Organisational Structure Variation', *Administrative Science Quarterly*, vol 7, no 3, December 1962, pp 295–308

9. LAWRENCE, P R and LORSCH, J W, *Organization and Environment: Managing Differentiation and Integration*, Division of Research, Harvard Business School, 1967.

10. The interested reader can consult:
    BLAUNER, R, *Alienation and Freedom*, University of Chicago Press, 1964
    CHANDLER, A, *Strategy and Structure*, MIT Press, 1962
    LAWRENCE, P R, and LORSCH, J W, *Studies in Organization Design*, Irwin-Dorsey, 1970
    THOMPSON, J, *Organizations in Action*, McGraw-Hill, 1967
    See also the numerous studies by members of the Aston school which have appeared in the *Administrative Science Quarterly*

11 See, for instance:
    MOHR, L B, 'Organizational Technology and Organizational Structure', *Administrative Science Quarterly*, vol 16, no 4, December 1971, pp 444–59
    TOSI, H, ALDAG, R, and STOREY, R, 'On the Measurement of the Environment: An Assessment of the Lawrence and Lorsch Environmental Uncertainty Questionnaire', *Administrative Science Quarterly*, vol 18, no 1, March 1973, pp 27–36

12. BECKER, S W and GORDON, G, 'An Entrepreneurial Theory of Formal Organizations. Part I: Patterns of Formal Organizations', *Administrative Science Quarterly*, vol 11, no 3, December 1966, pp 315–44
    GALBRAITH, J, *Designing Complex Organizations*, Addison-Wesley, 1973

13. GALBRAITH, J R, 'Organization Design: An Information Processing View', in:
LORSCH, J W and LAWRENCE, P R, eds, *Organization Planning: Cases and
Concepts*, Irwin-Dorsey, 1972, p 52

14. GALBRAITH, J R, 'Solving Production Smoothing Problems', *Management
Science*, vol 15, no 12, August 1969, pp B-665–74

15. The interested reader might consult such sources as:
THE COUNCIL FOR INDUSTRIAL DESIGN, *Design Management in Five Companies*,
1969
HIRSCH, P, *The Structure of the Popular Music Industry: The Filtering Process by
which Records are Preselected for Public Consumption*, Institute for Social Research,
University of Michigan, 1969
HIRSCH, P M, 'Processing Fads and Fashions: An Organization – Set Analysis
of Cultural Industry Systems', *American Journal of Sociology*, vol 77, no 4,
January 1972, pp 639–59
PETERSON, R A and BERGER, D G, 'Entrepreneurship in Organizations:
Evidence from the Popular Music Industry', *Administrative Science Quarterly*,
vol 16, no 1, March 1971, pp 97–107
SAYLES, L and CHANDLER, M K, *Managing Large Systems*, Harper and Row,
1971

16. It is important to emphasise the discretion which management can exercise
in selecting the means for processing information. They are certainly constrained by technological and environmental factors, but not determined by
them. For a discussion of this point within the context of organisational
structures see:
CHILD, J, 'Organization Structure, Environment and Performance: The
Role of Strategic Choice', *Sociology*, vol 6, no 1, January 1972, pp 1–22

17. VANCIL, R F, 'What Kind of Management Control Do You Need?', *Harvard
Business Review*, March–April 1973, pp 75–86

18. See the discussion in Chapter 1.

Index